Enriching Curriculum

FOR ALL STUDENTS

SECOND EDITION

JOSEPH S. RENZULLI ▪ SALLY M. REIS

Enriching Curriculum
FOR ALL STUDENTS

SECOND EDITION

CORWIN PRESS
A SAGE Company
Thousand Oaks, CA 91320

For information:

Corwin Press
A SAGE Company
2455 Teller Road
Thousand Oaks, California 91320
www.corwinpress.com

SAGE Ltd.
1 Oliver's Yard
55 City Road
London EC1Y 1SP
United Kingdom

SAGE India Pvt. Ltd.
B 1/I 1 Mohan Cooperative Industrial Area
Mathura Road, New Delhi 110 044
India

SAGE Asia-Pacific Pte. Ltd.
33 Pekin Street #02-01
Far East Square
Singapore 048763

Printed in the United States of America

Library of Congress Cataloging-in-Publication Data

Renzulli, Joseph S.
Enriching curriculum for all students/Joseph S. Renzulli, Sally M. Reis.—2nd ed.
        p. cm.
Includes bibliographical references and index.
ISBN 978-1-4129-5379-5 (cloth)
ISBN 978-1-4129-5380-1 (pbk.)
    1. School improvement programs--United States. 2. Curriculum enrichment--United States.
I. Reis, Sally M. II. Title.

LB2822.82.R445 2008
375.0010973—dc22   2007022743

This book is printed on acid-free paper.

07   08   09   10   10   9   8   7   6   5   4   3   2   1

Acquisitions Editor:	Allyson P. Sharp
Managing Editor:	David Chao
Editorial Assistant:	Mary Dang
Production Editor:	Libby Larson
Copy Editor:	Julie Gwin
Typesetter:	C&M Digitals (P) Ltd.
Proofreader:	Theresa Kay
Indexer:	Nara Wood
Cover Designer:	Rose Storey

Contents

Acknowledgments

Corwin Press would like to thank the following for their contributions to this work:

Natalie Bernasconi
Gifted and Talented Education Teacher, NBCT
Hillcrest High School
Simpsonville, SC

Sarah Littrell
Director of Instructional Technology and Staff Development
Former Gifted Education Coordinator
Red Oak ISD
Dallas, TX

Cindy Miller
Adjunct Professor
College of Education
University of North Texas
Arlington, TX

Tricia Peña
Principal
Cienega High School
Vail, AZ

Laurie Peterman
Instructional Facilitator
Anoka School District
Lino Lakes, MN

Susan Stewart
Curriculum Coordinator
Ashland University in Ohio
Hartville, OH

About the Authors

 **Dr. Joseph S. Renzulli** is a professor of educational psychology at the University of Connecticut, where he also serves as director of the National Research Center on the Gifted and Talented. His research has focused on the identification and development of creativity and giftedness in young people and on organizational models and curricular strategies for differentiated learning environments that contribute to total school improvement. A focus of his work has been on applying the pedagogy of gifted education to the improvement of learning for all students.

His most recent books include the second edition of *The Schoolwide Enrichment Model*, *The Multiple Menu Model for Developing Differentiated Curriculum*, *The Parallel Curriculum Model*, and *Enriching Curriculum for All Students*. His 1978 article entitled "What Makes Giftedness" has been cited as the most frequently referenced article in the field. Dr. Renzulli is a fellow in the American Psychological Association, is a former president of the Association for the Gifted, and has served on the editorial boards of the *Learning Magazine*, the *Journal of Law and Education*, *Exceptionality*, and most of the national and international journals dealing with gifted education. He was a consultant to the White House Task Force on Education of the Gifted and Talented and has worked with numerous schools and ministries of education throughout the United States and abroad. His work has been translated into several languages and is widely used around the world. His most recent work is a computer-based assessment of student strengths integrated with an Internet-based search engine that matches enrichment activities and resources with individual student profiles (www.renzullilearning.com).

Dr. Renzulli was designated a Board of Trustees Distinguished Professor at the University of Connecticut, and in 2003, he was awarded an Honorary Doctor of Laws Degree from McGill University in Montreal, Canada. The American Psychological Association's *Monitor on Psychology* named Dr. Renzulli among the 25 most influential psychologists in the world. Although Renzulli has obtained more than 30 million dollars in research grants, he lists as his proudest professional accomplishment being the founder of the summer Confratute program at UConn, which began in 1978 and has served thousands of teachers and administrators from around the world.

 **Sally M. Reis** is a professor and the past department head of the educational psychology department at the University of Connecticut, where she also serves as a principal investigator for the National Research Center on the Gifted and Talented. She was a teacher for 15 years, 11 of which were spent working with gifted students at the elementary, junior high, and high school levels. She has authored more than 140 articles, 11 books, 50 book chapters, and numerous monographs and technical reports.

Her research interests are related to special populations of gifted and talented students, including students with learning disabilities, gifted females, and diverse groups of talented students. She is also interested in extensions of the Schoolwide Enrichment Model for both gifted and talented students and as a way to expand offerings and provide general enrichment to identify talents and potentials in students who have not been previously identified as gifted. She is the codirector of Confratute, the longest running summer institute in the development of gifts and talents. She has been a consultant to numerous schools and ministries of education throughout the United States and abroad, and her work has been translated into several languages and is widely used around the world.

She is coauthor of *The Schoolwide Enrichment Model, The Secondary Triad Model, Dilemmas in Talent Development in the Middle Years,* and a book published in 1998 about women's talent development entitled *Work Left Undone: Choices and Compromises of Talented Females.* Ms. Reis serves on several editorial boards, including the *Gifted Child Quarterly,* and is a past-president of the National Association for Gifted Children. She recently was honored with the highest award in her field, Distinguished Scholar of the National Association for Gifted Children, and named a Board of Trustees Distinguished Professor at the University of Connecticut.

To our daughters, Sara Jane and Liza Joe, for whom creativity and joyful learning was our mission, with love and pride for the creative, joyful young women you have become.

What Is "Enrichment" and Why Is It Important in Developing Curriculum in America's Schools?

Those who own the rights to inventions own the world.

—From the political platform of
the Japanese Democratic Party

THE "WHY" QUESTION

"Why," we asked the three visitors from the Japanese Ministry of Education, "are you interested in the work we are doing in the Schoolwide Enrichment Model?" They had come to our research center to learn about the work we do to promote the development of creative productivity in American schools. We reminded them that our education leaders regularly remind us to look east. "You have the highest scores in the world on international achievement comparisons," we said.

We'll never forget the reply! "Very simple, dear professors. We have no Nobel Prize–winners. Your schools have produced a continuous flow of inventors, designers, entrepreneurs, and innovative leaders. We can make anything you invent faster, cheaper, and, in most cases, better. But we want to learn what role this focus on enrichment and high-end learning plays in the production of creative and inventive people." This experience caused us to think about what might be the one great asset of the American education system—an asset that we may be unwittingly losing as attention is turned more and more to cranking up our achievement test scores.

How much are new ideas worth? What are we willing to pay for the persistence, creativity, and task commitment that research scientists or industrial designers devote to following through on innovative ideas with potential high-stakes payoffs? Can we calculate the economic value, job opportunities, and contributions to social and political stability that result from investments in young people whose potential for creativity and innovation will develop new products, find solutions to unsolved problems, and even develop entire new industries?

Innovation resulting from research and development is widely recognized as a key ingredient to productivity, but the United States may be losing its edge in the culture of innovation. A quiet crisis is building that could jeopardize our nation's preeminence and well-being, and this crisis could reverse the global leadership Americans currently enjoy. U. S. productivity growth has slowed significantly since 1973 and continues to grow at a slower rate than our major trading partners, and patent data, one of the best indicators of R&D productivity, also raises concerns about future U.S. competitiveness. Approximately 45% of new U.S. patents are now granted to foreigners and the quality of these patents is strong, especially in the high-technology areas.

Although many factors contribute to a nation's overall productivity, the education system in any country is a prime source for producing the R&D people of the future. In a recent report, the National Science Board (2003) pointed out that the United States faces a major shortage of scientists because too few Americans are entering these fields. We are already experiencing a decline in the indicators that track international comparisons in academic achievement. The recently reported Programme for International Student Assessment (2003) study conducted by the Organisation for Economic Co-operation and Development, a Paris-based group that represents the world's richest countries, ranked the United States 24th out of 29 countries in mathematics. Our most talented American students rank near the bottom of industrialized nations' students in mathematics and science comparisons, and only 39% of recent American university doctorates in engineering were granted to American students.

Thirty-eight percent of all the nation's scientists and engineers with doctorates are now foreign born; however, a recent report from the Institute of International Higher Education (Bollag, 2004) announced a 2.4% decrease in foreign enrollment. The Council of Graduate Schools (2006) reported a 28% decline in international graduate applications between 2003 and 2004 and a 9% decline in the enrollment of first-time international graduate students at the top U.S. universities. The largest drop in applications was in engineering, with a decline of 36%. International students are turning in greater numbers to the higher education systems of our global competitors and are more likely to remain and seek employment in those countries following graduation. Although our capacity to attract top college and graduate students from abroad remains high, employment opportunities in other countries for our most-talented foreign students are increasingly luring these students to return home, and tightening immigration and security regulations threaten to restrict the inflow of foreign students. Even if our net flow of intellectual capital from foreign countries remains high, our domestic development of high-level scientific talent is lagging, and we are relying on inflow, which is increasingly regulated.

Despite these concerns about our declining reservoir of top foreign and domestic talent, massive investments in the American education system are currently directed toward improving the basic skills of struggling learners. No one can argue against this worthy goal, nor is there any attempt here to suggest that we should deviate from our course that attempts to improve the educational opportunities of all students. This investment will pay off in the form of a more-qualified workforce, which is unquestionably an important factor for better preparing the nation's youth for the more demanding jobs required in a knowledge-driven economy. Our $350 billion annual investment in public education, however, has shifted quite dramatically, not only to the detriment of in-depth curriculum at the highest levels in areas such as the sciences and social studies, but also to the detriment of physical well-being (i.e., physical and health education) and creative and artistic development, which are now considered peripheral curricular components. Many states test only math and reading, and they base school and student accountability on these two areas alone.

But what about support for the development of our most creative and innovative young people, the students from all backgrounds and economic classes whose ideas will create the products and the jobs that start the wheels of productivity turning? The federal government provides only $11.2 million for research and model programs that serve our high-potential students. Current estimates of federal education spending indicate that only two cents of every $100 is dedicated to the education of high-potential students.

There has also been a slow but steady decrease in state-level expenditures for this segment of our school population. In the last few years, expenditures for services to gifted and talented students have been severely cut by many state departments of education, and states that formerly were shining examples of high-quality programs for the gifted—Connecticut, Illinois, Michigan, New York, and Oregon to name a few—have completely eliminated all funding. Pressure on school budgets has also resulted in a decline in allocations for special programs at the local level. Almost weekly, we receive yet another phone call or e-mail saying "Our program has been cut." Based on the 2002 U.S. Census survey of local government finances, it appears that of state money allocated to schools, less than one-half of one percent was targeted as categorical funding for enrichment and gifted education programs (on average, across regular K–12 school districts; Evan, Bodman, Cooper, & Kincannon, 2002). Only 2,424 of 10,549 public K–12 school districts (reporting) received categorical grants for such programs from their states. Only about 1,800 K–12 districts received more than $100 per 5% of their enrollment in categorical aid (this excludes states that flow gifted program funds through general funds).

Growth economists believe that improvements in productivity can be linked to a faster pace of innovation and extra investments in human capital, but are we turning our backs on the R&D people of the new century when we fail to support this segment of our school population? Is our education system's current emphasis on just ratcheting up test scores at the expense of promoting creativity and innovative thinking the way to ensure our future as a leading nation in the business of generating original ideas, new knowledge, and even entire new industries?

We have referred to this neglect of America's most gifted and talented youth as a "quiet crisis" because by the time the damage is done, it will be too late to reverse a trend that may place our country in jeopardy. Unchecked, this trend will leave a dearth of scientists, engineers, inventors, entrepreneurs, and creative contributors to all areas of the arts and sciences. These kinds of contributions are precisely the things that made America a prosperous and powerful nation through the twentieth century. Our innovation stimulated a powerful, knowledge-driven economy and shaped a country that made its fame and fortune by creating things rather than merely making them. Neglect of our most gifted and talented students, including those who come from limited economic circumstances, will make it impossible for America to compete in a global economy that is driven by new ideas. Improving the achievement of all students is obviously an important national goal. But let us not turn our back on the one aspect of the American education system that has contributed to our prosperity. Dr. Leon Lederman, the Nobel Prize–winning physicist, said in 1990, "Once upon a time, America sheltered an Einstein, went to the Moon, and gave the world the laser, electronic computer, nylons, television, and the cure for polio. Today, we are in the process, albeit unwittingly, of abandoning this leadership role" (as cited in Larson, 1992, p. 234).

THE "WHAT" QUESTION

The best way to define enrichment is to describe an example of enrichment in action and then to consider the role that various theories of learning play in the curricula that are used in America's schools.

Each week, all of the students at the Bret Harte Middle School in San Jose, California, participate in interest-based enrichment activities designed around a constructivist learning theory that focuses on authentic, high-end learning. Under the guidance of their teacher, David Rapaport, one group of students is identifying, archiving, and preserving documents from the 1800s that were found in an old suitcase belonging to the first pharmacist in Deadwood, South Dakota. Another group, which has strong interests in media, technology, and the graphic arts, is converting the archives into digital format and developing a Web site where this and other student research can be accessed. Some students are using photography and artwork to provide a chronicle of life on the western frontier during the 1800s. Others have prepared articles for publication in a Deadwood magazine.

Teachers at Bret Harte are encouraged to develop enrichment experiences around their own strengths and interests, sometimes working in teams that may involve parents and community members. Students make selections for their participation in various enrichment options based on attractive descriptions that convey the action-oriented learning model that guides this type of curriculum. Enrichment experiences at Bret Harte Middle School and numerous other schools across the nation who use the Schoolwide Enrichment Model are attempting to deal with what many educational leaders believe has become nothing short of a crisis in our schools. As the demands of standardized testing have increased, teachers and administrators have been under almost unrelenting pressure to "get the scores up." This focus on "test prep" has had the effect of squeezing more authentic kinds of high-end learning out of the curriculum, thereby minimizing the one aspect of American education that has contributed to the innovativeness and creative productivity of our culture and our economy, as well as to our leadership role in the world. Improved test scores are important, but a time and a place for the application of knowledge in authentic learning situations is what distinguishes a progressive education system from the perpetual memorization and testing that characterize education in Third World countries.

WHAT EXACTLY IS ENRICHMENT LEARNING AND TEACHING?

All learning exists on a continuum ranging from deductive (didactic) and prescriptive learning on one end to inductive, self-selected, and investigative learning on the other. The essence of inductive or high-end learning is the application of relevant knowledge, thinking skills, and interpersonal skills to the solution of real problems. It involves finding and focusing on a problem, identifying relevant information, categorizing and critically analyzing that information, and synthesizing and effectively communicating the results of an investigation or creative endeavor.

Real-life problems share four criteria. First, a real problem requires a personal frame of reference for the individual or group pursuing the problem. In other words, the problem must involve an emotional or internal commitment in addition to a cognitive interest. A second characteristic of real problems is that they do not have existing or unique solutions for people addressing the problem. If an agreed-on solution or prescribed strategies for solving the problem exist, then it is more appropriately classified as a "training exercise." Even simulations based on approximations of real-world events are considered training exercises if their main purpose is to teach predetermined content or thinking skills.

The third characteristic of a real problem is best described in terms of why people pursue these problems. The main reason is that they want to create new products or provide information that will change actions, attitudes, or beliefs on the part of a targeted audience. For example, a group of young people who gathered, analyzed, and reported on data about television-watching habits in their community were contributing information that was new, at least in a relative way, and that would cause people to think critically about the television-viewing habits of young people.

The final characteristic of real problems is that they are directed toward a real audience. Real audiences consist of people who voluntarily attend to information, events, services, or objects. A good way to understand the difference between a real and a contrived audience is to reflect on what some students did with the results of their local oral history project—a biographical study of all the men from Connecticut who died in Vietnam. Although they presented their findings to classmates, they did so mainly to rehearse presentation skills. Their authentic audiences consisted of members of a local historical society, veterans groups, members of servicemen's families, people who attended a local commemoration of Vietnam veterans, and people who chose to read about their research in the features section of a local newspaper.

Enrichment teaching and learning is purposefully designed to create a learning environment that enhances these kinds of experiences. When pursuing an open-ended problem such as the ones mentioned previously, there are no predetermined content or process objectives, and the teacher's role is decidedly different from the traditional knowledge transmission goals of the regular curriculum. The nature of the problem guides students toward the use of just-in-time knowledge, use of appropriate investigative methods or creative production skills, and professional methods for communicating the results of their work. In this type of learning, students assume roles as firsthand investigators, writers, artists, or other types of practicing professionals. Although students pursue these kinds of involvement at a more junior level than adult professionals, the overriding purpose is to create situations in which young people are thinking, feeling, and doing what practicing professionals do in the delivery of products and services. In this type of learning, standards are important, but in each case, the standards covered are documented at the conclusion of the work. If the standards were laid out beforehand, as is always the case in the didactic or prescribed curriculum, then instruction would inevitably revert to a transmission-or-knowledge approach rather than a genuine investigative and inquiry approach.

This type of learning should be viewed as a vehicle through which students can increase their knowledge base and expand their creative and critical thinking skills, cooperative group work skills, and task commitment by applying their time and energy to problems for which there is no predetermined, correct answer. Enrichment learning should be viewed as the vehicle through which everything, from basic skills to advanced content and processes, comes together in the form of student-developed products, presentations, performances, and services. In much the same way that all the separate but interrelated parts of an automobile come together at an assembly plant, so also do we consider this form of learning to be the assembly plant of the mind. This kind of learning represents a synthesis and an application of content, process, and personal involvement. The student's role is transformed from one of lesson learner to firsthand inquirer, and the role of the teacher changes from an instructor and disseminator of knowledge to a combination of coach, resource procurer, mentor, and guide on the side. Although products play an important role as vehicles in creating authentic learning situations, a major goal of focusing on product development is the application of a wide range of cognitive, affective, and motivational processes.

THE TEACHER AS GUIDE ON THE SIDE

The teacher's role in this kind of learning draws on skills that most teachers already have, especially if they have ever been involved in extracurricular activities, club programs, or any kind of sports and arts programs. As the teachers begin the process of developing learning experiences based on this brand of learning, they should keep in mind four issues:

1. Reversing the teaching equation. The teacher's role in planning and facilitating enrichment experiences is very different from traditional teaching. The more direct teaching that is done, the less likely the teacher will be to turn the responsibility for creative and investigative activity over to the students. Although various planned start-up activities may be part of enrichment activities, too much preplanning will push the instruction toward deductive rather than inductive teaching and learning. A key feature of enrichment clusters is the use of just-in-time (J-I-T) knowledge rather than storehouse or declarative knowledge typically associated with prescribed learning. It is for this reason that we have developed the Renzulli Learning System (described in Chapter Eight) that makes use of electronic assessment and a vast array of high-interest Internet resources. J-I-T knowledge has immediate relevance because it is needed to address a particular problem, and students typically escalate to much higher levels of knowledge than levels found in their grade-level textbooks.

2. **Reversing the role of students.** If teachers are to alter their role from instructor to coach, mentor, referral agent, general contractor, or guide on the side, they must help students see themselves as young professionals. Young people working on an original piece of historical research, creative writing, journalism, or play production become young historians, authors, journalists, and playwrights, scenery designers, or stage managers. This change in how teachers view students is important because it brings with it a different set of expectations for what students do and how teachers help them. Instead of teaching prescribed lessons, teachers will begin to think about how to help a young poet get his or her work published, how to get the shopping mall manager to allow space for a display of models of your town's buildings of historical significance, and how to engineer a presentation by young environmentalists to the state wildlife commission.

3. **Each enrichment learning experience is unique.** As long as the guidelines for inductive teaching are followed, there is not a right or wrong way to plan and facilitate enrichment activities. Differences in interests, personalities, and styles between cluster facilitators are assets that contribute to the uniqueness of this type of learning. Even if the same topic or unit of study is taught to different groups or in different years, each rendition should evolve as a result of different individual and group interests and talents, thus emerging as a unique entity. Inductive teaching is a more natural and, in many ways, easier process than structured teaching, but it also involves breaking some old habits based on traditional teacher roles. Teachers will find that a little experience in an inductive learning environment will help them hone the skills that will become a very natural part of their teaching repertoire.

4. **When in doubt, look outward!** Because teachers are striving for a different brand of teaching and learning, enrichment activities should be modeled after real-world situations. It is a good idea to examine nonclassroom conditions for models of planning, teaching, and patterns of organization. An athletic coach, the advisor for the drama club or school newspaper, or a 4-H Club leader are excellent role models for facilitating enrichment activities. Similarly, tasks and organizational patterns should resemble the activities that take place in a small business, a film studio, a research laboratory, a social service agency, a theater production company, or any organization that must generate real products and services and that always has a target audience in mind as its staff pursue their work. The learning environment should be as different as possible from what happens in a traditional classroom.

THE GOALS OF SCHOOLWIDE ENRICHMENT

The Schoolwide Enrichment Model (SEM) has been described in various ways by a myriad of people who have used it, worked with it, and helped refine it to its current state of effectiveness. Although one commentator referred to it as "elegant common sense" (Renzulli & Reis, 2006), the SEM actually is an empirically tested and carefully chosen blend of research and proven practices, with five main goals. Schools should be enriching places where the mind, spirit, and values of each student are expanded and developed in an atmosphere that is enjoyable, interesting, and challenging.

Goal One

To develop the talent potentials of young people by (a) systematically assessing strengths; (b) providing enrichment opportunities, resources, and services to develop the strengths of all students; and (c) using a flexible approach to curricular differentiation and the use of school time.

A Focus on Talent Development

Schools should be enriching places for talent development. Although knowledge acquisition is unquestionably an important educational goal, other goals such as know-how, creativity, self-fulfillment, and wisdom are equally significant. Schools should not be places where young people merely learn what is already known. Instead, schools should seek a higher mission: creating learning environments in which the knowledge that students bring to school with them is valued. This student-owned knowledge should be viewed as a stepping stone to the creation of new knowledge, to the solutions of unsolved problems, and to invention, artistic production, and examination of ways to improve the quality of life.

Programs such as 4-H, Junior Achievement, the Foxfire Program, Future Problem Solving, Invent America, and a broad range of extracurricular activities consistently have demonstrated that when the application of knowledge is coupled with the acquisition of knowledge, school problems are solved or at least minimized. Observation of 4-H students at work or of a school newspaper staff rushing to publish the next edition allows us to see genuine motivation, engagement, and involvement, as well as cooperativeness, enjoyment, and purpose. These examples of students at work represent the kinds of authenticity in learning that have eluded so much of traditional schooling. These activities also frequently span students' age levels, socioeconomic backgrounds, demographics, and ability levels.

Goal One is targeted directly toward a qualitative change in schools. It is based on a reconceptualized role of the teacher, the curriculum, classroom organization and management, and, most of all, the student. These reconceptualized roles are neither new nor abstract. They have occurred in learning situations throughout history, in classrooms and nonschool learning situations, in extracurricular activities, and in apprenticeships and on-the-job training experiences. We have seen increases in these changing roles of teachers and students as a direct result of applying SEM to a variety of school situations; we know from our field testing of the SEM that this model can fortify a proposal for school change. A goal that focuses on developing talent potentials is not an educational revelation, but the traditional achievement goal always has held supremacy. By making this objective the centerpiece of SEM, we emphasize that what has occurred in the past—a series of scattered, random, and infrequent examples of enriched learning—has the potential to become standard operating procedure for the majority of schools that make a commitment to this plan.

Goal Two

To improve the academic performance of all students in all areas of the regular curriculum and to blend into the standard curriculum those activities that will engage students in meaningful and enjoyable learning.

Indicators and Reasons for Declining Academic Performance

The most obvious and publicized problem facing our schools is poor academic performance—especially the performance of students in poverty. High school and college graduation rates for children in poverty have shown little or no increase over the past several decades. Improving the performance of disadvantaged students continues to be the single most important challenge facing our schools.

Goal Three

To promote continuous, reflective, growth-oriented professionalism on the parts of all school personnel.

What Does It Mean to Be a Professional?

Schools are only as good as the people who work in them. This goal focuses on the crucial but elusive task of improving the professionalism of teachers, administrators, and other school personnel. It might be tempting to dismiss an objective about improved professionalism as idealistic but largely unachievable. However, this objective lies at the heart of school improvement. For this reason, we must examine both failed attempts and promising approaches to professional improvement, and we must use our accumulated knowledge, experience, and wisdom to devise a practical plan to improve the professionalism of personnel in schools using the SEM.

Professionals are people in an occupational category who share a common body of knowledge and standards of practice that allow them to make decisions in the best interests of their clients. The work of true professionals is characterized by the regular use of judgment and nonroutine activities rather than mechanized or prescribed applications of duties. For true professionalism to be achieved, the individual and the institution in which the individual works must be amenable to change. Many reform proposals have recognized the importance of improved professionalism, but they have failed to respect the ground rules of professional work. In short, professionalism is a social contract that requires individuals to acquire and make use of certain competencies and ethics, but the contract also requires that the institution support the application of these competencies and ethics.

Goal Four

To create a learning community that honors ethnic, gender, and cultural diversity; mutual respect and caring attitudes toward one another; respect for democratic principles; and preservation of the Earth's resources.

Schools for a Better Society

Most people in the United States concur that schools should play a role in ameliorating important problems in our society. Our schools originally were invested with the obligation to teach the three R's and to pass on the accumulated knowledge of the past. A rapidly changing world, dramatic changes in the job market, and a host of increasingly complex societal issues placed demands on the educational system that now require an expanded role for the schools. This role can be seen in the curriculum's inclusion of numerous issues that range from driver education and a "life adjustment curriculum" to concerns about war and peace, values and character, and sex and drug education. Each of these issues, and the efforts to address them through additions to the school curriculum, have kindled or rekindled the classic controversies between conservative and liberal ideologies. Although this goal does favor a broader set of beliefs about the role of the school, it is included as a major focus of the SEM because of the rapid changes taking place in our society and the declining well-being of young people in the United States.

Most people would agree that talent development and academic performance are the main responsibilities of schools. However, changes in family structures and a fast-track society have also placed a broader range of responsibilities on schools. Issues such as alarmingly high delinquency rates, substance abuse, racial disharmony, teenage pregnancy, intolerance, wasteful consumerism, and a lack of respect for our fellow human beings have resulted in a generation of young people who are experiencing psychological distress and social alienation as well as declining school performance. Many will argue that school is not the place to address such problems, but these problems and their by-products have ended up on the schoolhouse doorstep. Education alone cannot resolve these problems, but schools can play an important role in fostering the intelligence, persistence, and creativity necessary to bring about needed improvements in both the quality of life for young people and the improvement of the social institutions that are necessary for perpetuating our democratic society.

This goal is not intended to impose a set of political beliefs or social values on schools that use the SEM, but contemporary issues should be part of an enrichment program that attempts to bring relevance and reality into the curriculum. At the same time, we also believe that local decision making must prevail as far as specific topic selection is concerned. Because the focus of this model is on the act of learning, we pursue this goal by concentrating on instructional methods that address more effectively the topics that schools select within broad parameters of this goal. We will also provide references to materials that are available for various kinds of enrichment experiences related to selected topics.

Goal Five

To implement a democratic school governance procedure that includes appropriate decision-making opportunities for students, parents, teachers, and administrators.

The Need for Democratic Governance

Educational leaders across the nation have recognized that decentralized management procedures are a major component of school improvement. This type of management, commonly referred to as site- or school-based management (SBM), has a long and successful history in the private sector. SBM decreases centralized control and encourages high levels of involvement and control from the people who are closest to the creation of products and the delivery of services. Although this goal is evolutionary, maturing over a period of several years, it is essential for any real and lasting school improvement effort.

If a school decides to adopt this (or any other) model or school improvement initiative, the decision must be protected from the biases or predilections of the always-changing personnel who occupy district decision-making positions. In one district with which we are familiar, a new assistant superintendent in charge of curriculum wiped out one of the most successful enrichment programs in the country because of a personality conflict with the program coordinator and her desire to assert authority. Efforts made by a majority of teachers to reinstate the program, including the support of highly satisfied parents in the community, were not strong enough to overcome the amount of power vested in a single person.

Democratic school governance represents a fundamental and systemic organizational change. Like all other changes of this magnitude, and especially changes that include a redistribution of power to make important decisions, the process must be approached with care and thoughtfulness. Training in management and decision-making techniques must be provided to personnel who customarily have been in subordinate roles, just as central office personnel must learn to share power, knowledge, information, and opportunities to influence the reward structure of the school.

Although the previous goals have guided our work in the development of the SEM, it might be worthwhile to point out the overriding reasons why we have developed this systematic plan for infusing more enrichment experiences into the regular school curriculum. First and most important is the enjoyment that students derive from this kind of learning. We all know from our own experiences that anything we enjoy doing we tend to do better. Second, we have found that enrichment learning and teaching promote much higher levels of student engagement, and again, we know from experience as educators that as engagement goes up, boredom goes down. In some ways, you may want to view the SEM as a plan that minimizes and even eliminates boredom by providing numerous opportunities for student engagement and enjoyment! Finally, we have found that all students and teachers benefit from an infusion of enrichment experiences into the regular school curriculum. A radiation of excellence becomes a part of the school culture, and all students and teachers start to take on a more positive attitude toward school. Our theme in applying this pedagogy of high-end learning to traditional teaching is "A Rising Tide Lifts All Ships!" As learning becomes more exciting and engaging for individual students and teachers, so also do others begin to see the excitement and enjoyment that can result from enrichment teaching and learning opportunities.

2

Using the Schoolwide Enrichment Model to Enrich Curriculum for All Students

The Schoolwide Enrichment Model (SEM) gives each teacher the flexibility to develop unique programs for talent development and enrichment based on local resources, student demographics, and school dynamics, as well as faculty strengths and creativity. The major goal of SEM is to promote both challenging and enjoyable high-end learning across a wide range of school types, levels, and demographic differences. Using the SEM, each school faculty can create a repertoire of services that can be integrated into its regular curriculum to extend enrichment for all children to create a "rising tide lifts all ships" approach. This approach enables schools to develop a collaborative school culture that takes advantage of resources and appropriate decision-making opportunities to create meaningful, high-level, and potentially creative opportunities for students to develop their talents.

The SEM suggests that educators examine ways to make schools more inviting, friendly, and enjoyable places that encourage talent development instead of regarding students as repositories for information that will be assessed with the next round of standardized tests. Not only has this model been successful in addressing the problem of high-potential students who have been underchallenged, but it also provides additional important learning paths for gifted and talented students who find success in more traditional learning environments.

The curricular and instructional core of the SEM is the Enrichment Triad Model (Renzulli, 1976), developed in the mid-1970s and initially implemented by school districts primarily in the northeast part of the United States. The model became very popular, and requests were received from throughout the United States for visitations to schools using the triad and for information about how to implement the model. A book about the Enrichment Triad Model (Renzulli, 1977a) was published, and more and more districts began asking for help in implementing this approach. It was at this point that a clear need was established for research about the effectiveness of the model and for practical procedures that could provide technical assistance for interested educators to help develop programs in their schools. We established a training program for teachers at the University of Connecticut called Confratute, which was followed by the development of many more programs based on the Enrichment Triad Model. We became fascinated by the wide range of triad programs developed by different types of teachers in different school districts, including urban, rural, and suburban districts. In some programs, for example, teachers consistently encouraged and developed high levels of creative productivity in students. In other programs, teachers focused on process development and exposure activities but few students engaged in independent, creative, productive-type learning based on their interests. In some districts, many enrichment opportunities were regularly offered to students not formally identified for the program, whereas in other districts, only identified gifted students had access to these different types of enrichment experiences.

In the three decades since the Enrichment Triad Model has been used as the basis for educational programs for gifted and talented students, many diverse examples of creative work have been completed by students whose educational experiences have been guided by this approach. Children have written books; written, produced, and directed plays; conducted sophisticated science experiments; conducted original historical and scientific research; and completed sophisticated computer and technological projects. They have become involved in social projects designed to improve and save the environment and help those in need in their communities.

Perhaps, like others involved in the development of theories and models, we did not fully understand the full implications of the Enrichment Triad Model for encouraging and developing creative productivity in young people. These implications relate most directly to teacher training, resource procurement and management, product evaluation, and other theoretical concerns (e.g., motivation, task commitment, self-efficacy) that probably would have gone unexamined, undeveloped, and unrefined without the favorable results that were reported to us by early implementers of the model. We became increasingly interested in how and why the model was working and how we could further expand the theoretical rationale underlying our work and the population to which services could be provided. We also did not understand the longitudinal implications of enabling children to pursue their interests on their adult choices for postsecondary education and also their careers. Several years of conceptual development followed, which were coupled with our practical experiences, and an examination of the work of other theorists brought us to the further development of the Enrichment Triad Model and the resulting SEM, representing approximately 30 years of field testing, research, evolution, and dissemination.

In this chapter, an overview of the conception of giftedness on which this model is based is presented, as is a description of the original Enrichment Triad Model with a brief overview of how the model has expanded and changed. All components of the SEM are introduced, followed by more in-depth chapters about each of these separate services. Selected research about the SEM is discussed and a brief summary of the research dealing with the SEM is provided.

EXPANDING CONCEPTIONS OF GIFTS AND TALENTS: THE THEORY UNDERLYING THE SEM

The study of how to develop gifts and talents, like any other specialized area of study, represents a spectrum of ideologies that exists along a continuum ranging from conservative to liberal points of view. *Conservative* and *liberal* are not used here in their political connotations, but rather according to the degree of restrictiveness that is used in determining who is eligible for special programs and services. Restrictiveness can be expressed in two ways; first, a definition can limit the number of specific performance areas that are considered in determining eligibility for special services. A conservative definition, for example, might limit eligibility to academic performance only and exclude other areas such as music, art, drama, leadership, public speaking, social service, creative writing, or skills in interpersonal relations. Second, a definition can limit the degree or level of excellence that one must attain by establishing extremely high cutoff points.

Although liberal definitions have the obvious advantage of expanding the conception of giftedness, they also open up two theoretical concerns by introducing (a) a values issue (How do we define broader conceptions of giftedness?) and (b) the age-old problem of subjectivity in measurement. In recent years, the values issue has been largely resolved. Very few educators cling tenaciously to a "straight IQ" or purely academic definition of giftedness. *Multiple talent* and *multiple criteria* are almost the bywords of the present-day attempts to identify high potential, and most people have little difficulty in accepting a definition that includes most areas of human activity that are manifested in socially useful forms of expression.

TWO KINDS OF GIFTEDNESS

It is generally accepted that intelligence is not a unitary concept, but rather there are many kinds of intelligence, and, therefore, single definitions cannot be used to explain this multifaceted phenomenon. The confusion and inconclusiveness about present theories of intelligence have led Sternberg (1984) and others to develop new models for explaining this complicated concept. Sternberg's "triarchic" theory of human intelligence consists of three main kinds of giftedness: analytic, synthetic, and practical abilities. Gardner (1983) proposed seven distinctive types of intelligent behavior that he called linguistic, logical/mathematical, spatial, bodily/kinesthetic, musical, interpersonal, and intrapersonal, as well as the recently added naturalist intelligence.

This recent work, coupled with our own research described in this chapter, suggests that at the very least, attributes of intelligent behavior must be considered in the context of cultural and situational factors. There is no ideal way to measure intelligence, and, therefore, we must avoid the typical practice of believing that if we know a person's IQ score, we also know his or her intelligence. The historical difficulty of defining and measuring intelligence highlights the even larger problem of isolating a unitary definition of giftedness. To help in this analysis, two broad categories of giftedness are described: high-achieving or schoolhouse giftedness and creative-productive giftedness. Before describing each type, we want to emphasize the following:

1. Both types are important.

2. There is usually an interaction between the two types.

3. Special programs should make appropriate provisions for encouraging both types of giftedness as well as the numerous occasions when the two types interact with each other.

High-Achieving (Schoolhouse) Giftedness

High-achieving giftedness might also be called test-taking or lesson-learning giftedness. It is the kind most easily measured by IQ or other cognitive ability tests, and for this reason, it is also the type most often used for selecting students for entrance into special programs. The abilities people display on IQ and aptitude tests are exactly the kinds of abilities most valued in traditional school learning situations. In other words, the tasks required in ability tests are similar in nature to tasks that teachers require in most lesson-learning situations. A large body of research tells us that students who score high on IQ tests are also likely to get high grades in school, and that these test-taking and lesson-learning abilities generally remain stable over time. The results of this research should lead us to some very obvious conclusions about high-achieving giftedness: It exists in varying degrees, it can be identified through standardized assessment techniques, and we should therefore do everything in our power to make appropriate modifications for students who have the ability to cover regular curricular material at advanced rates and levels of understanding. Curriculum compacting (Reis, Burns, & Renzulli, 1992; Renzulli, Smith, & Reis, 1982) is a procedure described in Chapter Five used for modifying standard curricular content to accommodate advanced learners. Other acceleration techniques should represent essential parts of every school program that strives to respect the individual differences that are clearly evident from classroom performance or scores yielded by cognitive ability tests.

Creative-Productive Giftedness

If scores on IQ tests and other measures of cognitive ability only account for a limited proportion of the common variance with school grades, we can be equally certain that these measures do not tell the whole story when it comes to making predictions about creative-productive giftedness. Before defending this assertion with some research findings, we briefly review what is meant by this second type of giftedness, the important role that it should play in programming, and, therefore, the reasons we should attempt to assess it in our identification procedures—even if such assessment causes us to look below the top 3% to 5% on the normal curve of IQ scores.

Creative-productive giftedness describes those aspects of human activity and involvement in which a premium is placed on the development of original material and products that are purposefully designed to have an effect on one or more target audiences. Learning situations that are designed to promote creative-productive giftedness emphasize the use and application of information (content) and thinking skills (process) in an integrated, inductive, and real-problem-oriented manner. The role of the student is transformed from that of a learner of prescribed lessons to one in which he or she becomes a firsthand inquirer. This approach is quite different from the development of lesson-learning giftedness, which tends to emphasize deductive learning, structured training in the development of thinking processes, and the acquisition, storage, and retrieval of information. In other words, creative-productive giftedness is simply putting one's abilities to work on problems and areas of study that have personal relevance to the student and that can be escalated to appropriately challenging levels of investigative activity. The roles that both students and teachers should play in the pursuit of these problems have been described elsewhere (Renzulli, 1977a, 1982) and have been embraced in general education under a variety of concepts such as constructivist theory, authentic learning, discovery learning, problem-based learning, and performance assessment.

Why is creative-productive giftedness important enough for us to question the tidy and relatively easy approach that has traditionally been used to select students on the basis of test scores? Why do some people want to rock the boat by challenging a conception of giftedness that can be numerically defined by simply giving a test? The answers to these questions are simple and yet very compelling. A review of the research literature (Renzulli, 1986, 2005) shows that there is much more to identifying human potential than the abilities revealed on traditional tests of intelligence, aptitude, and achievement. Furthermore, history shows that it has been the creative and productive people of the world, the producers rather than consumers of knowledge, the reconstructionists of thought in all areas of human endeavor, who have become recognized as truly gifted individuals. History does not remember people who merely scored well on IQ tests or those who learned their lessons well. The definition of giftedness (see Figure 2.1) that characterizes creative-productive giftedness and serves as part of the rationale for the SEM is the three-ring conception of giftedness (Renzulli, 1978, 1986, 2005), in which giftedness is defined as an interaction among three basic clusters: being above average in general in ability, high levels of creativity, and task commitment.

Gifted behavior consists of behaviors that reflect an interaction among three basic clusters of human traits—above-average ability, high levels of task commitment, and high levels of creativity. Individuals capable of developing gifted behavior are those possessing or capable of developing this composite set of traits and applying them to any potentially valuable area of human performance. People who manifest or are capable of developing an interaction among the three clusters require a wide variety of educational opportunities and services that are not ordinarily provided through regular instructional programs (Renzulli & Reis, 1997, p. 8).

Students with these potentials can develop this composite set of potentials with a variety of educational opportunities and services offered in addition to regular instructional programming. We believe that gifted behaviors can be developed through the systematic enrichment opportunities described in the SEM.

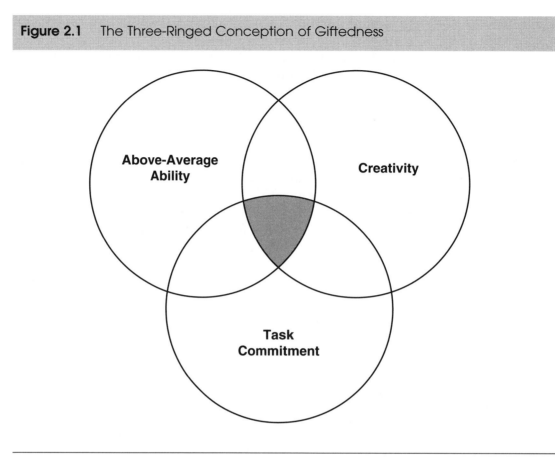

Figure 2.1 The Three-Ringed Conception of Giftedness

Above-Average
Ability

Creativity

Task
Commitment

SOURCE: Courtesy of Creative Learning Press.

AN OVERVIEW OF THE ENRICHMENT TRIAD MODEL

The Enrichment Triad Model was designed to encourage creative productivity on the part of young people by exposing them to various topics, areas of interest, and fields of study, and to further train them to apply advanced content, process-training skills, and methods training to self-selected areas of interest. Three types of enrichment are included in the Triad Model (see Figure 2.2).

Type I enrichment is designed to expose students to a wide variety of disciplines, topics, occupations, hobbies, people, places, and events that would not ordinarily be covered in the regular curriculum. In schools that use this model, an enrichment team consisting of parents, teachers, and students often organizes and plans Type I experiences by contacting speakers; arranging minicourses, demonstrations, or performances; or ordering and distributing films, slides, videotapes, or other print or nonprint media.

Type II enrichment consists of materials and methods designed to promote the development of thinking and feeling processes. Some Type II training is general and is usually carried out both in classrooms and in enrichment programs. Training activities include the development of the skills outlined in Figure 2.3: (a) cognitive

Figure 2.2 The Enrichment Triad Model

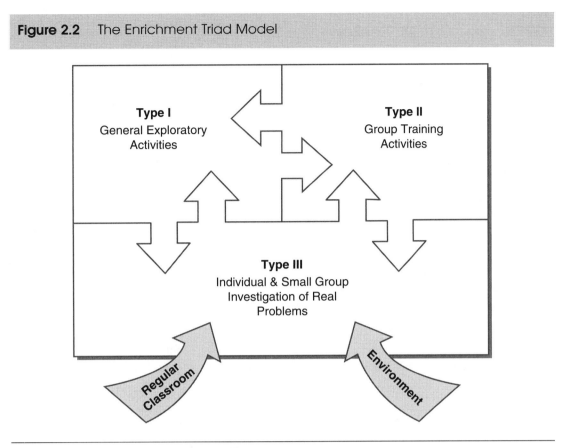

SOURCE: Courtesy of Creative Learning Press.

thinking and problem solving, critical thinking, and affective processes; (b) character development and affective skills; (c) a variety of specific learning-how-to-learn skills; (d) appropriate use of advanced-level reference materials; and (e) written, oral, and visual communication skills. Other Type II enrichment is specific, as it cannot be planned in advance and usually involves advanced methods instruction in an interest area selected by the student. For example, students who become interested in botany after a Type I experience might pursue additional training in this area by doing advanced reading in botany; compiling, planning, and carrying out plant experiments; and seeking more advanced methods training if they want to go further.

Type III enrichment involves students who become interested in pursuing a self-selected area and are willing to commit the time necessary for advanced content acquisition and process training, in which they assume the role of a firsthand inquirer. In Type III enrichment, teachers

- provide opportunities for applying interests, knowledge, creative ideas, and task commitment to a self-selected problem or area of study;
- help students acquire advanced-level understanding of the knowledge (content) and methods (process) that are used in particular disciplines, artistic areas of expression, and interdisciplinary studies;
- coach students to develop authentic products that are primarily directed toward bringing about a desired effect on a specified audience;

Figure 2.3 Taxonomy of Cognitive and Affective Processes

I. Cognitive Thinking Skills	K–3	4–8	9–12
A. Creative Thinking Skills			
B. Creative Problem-Solving and Decision Making			
C. Critical and Logical Thinking			

II. Character Development and Affective Process Skills	K–3	4–8	9–12
A. Character Development			
B. Interpersonal Skills			
C. Intrapersonal Skills			

III. Learning-How-to-Learn Skills	K–3	4–8	9–12
A. Listening, Observing, and Perceiving			
B. Reading, Note Taking, and Outlining			
C. Interviewing and Surveying			
D. Analyzing and Organizing Data			

IV. Using Advanced Research Skills and Reference Materials	K–3	4–8	9–12
A. Preparing for Research and Investigative Projects			
B. Using Library and Electronic References			
C. Finding and Using Community Resources			

V. Written, Oral, and Visual Communication Skills	K–3	4–8	9–12
A. Written Communication Skills			
B. Oral Communication Skills			
C. Visual Communication Skills			

SOURCE: Courtesy of Creative Learning Press.

- help students learn self-directed learning skills in the areas of planning, organization, resource utilization, time management, decision making, and self-evaluation; and
- work with students to develop task commitment, self-confidence, and feelings of creative accomplishment.

THE REVOLVING DOOR IDENTIFICATION MODEL: IDENTIFYING STUDENTS FOR THE SEM

As our experience with triad programs grew, our concern about the students who were being identified to participate and those who were not being included in these programs also grew. We became increasingly concerned about students who were not able to participate in enrichment programs because they did not score in the top 1% to 3% of the population in achievement or intelligence tests. Research conducted by Torrance (1962, 1974) had demonstrated that students who were rated highly on creativity measures do well in school and on achievement tests but are often not selected for gifted programs because their scores are often below the cutoff for admission. Some of our own research (Reis & Renzulli, 1982) indicated that when a broader population of students (15% to 20% of the general population, called the "talent pool") was able to participate in Types I and II enrichment experiences, they produced equally good Type III products as the traditional gifted students (the top 3% to 5%). This research produced the rationale for the Revolving Door Identification Model (RDIM; Renzulli, Reis, & Smith, 1981), in which a talent pool of students receives regular enrichment experiences and the opportunity to "revolve into" Type III creative productive experiences. In the RDIM, we recommended that students be selected for participation in the talent pool on the basis of multiple criteria, which includes indices of creativity, motivation, and other traits, because we believe that one of the major purposes of gifted education is to develop creative thinking and creative productivity in students. Once identified and placed in the talent pool through the use of test scores; teacher-, parent-, or self-nomination; and examples of creative potential or productivity, students are observed in classrooms and enrichment experiences for signs of advanced interests, creativity, or task commitment. We have called this part of the process "action information" and have found it to be an instrumental part of the identification process in assessing students' interest in and motivation to become involved in Type III creative productivity. Further support for expanding identification procedures through the use of these approaches has recently been offered by Kirschenbaum (1983) and Kirschenbaum and Siegle (1993), who demonstrated that students who are rated or test high on measures of creativity tend to do well in school and on measures of achievement. The development of the RDIM led to the need for a guide dealing with how all of the components of the previous triad and the new expanded identification could be implemented. The resulting work was entitled *The Schoolwide Enrichment Model* (Renzulli & Reis, 1985, 1997).

THE SEM

All schools implement the SEM in a way that fits with their own vision of enrichment and talent development. In some schools, the entire student population is considered the talent pool, whereas in others, a talent pool of 10% to 15% of above-average-ability and high-potential students is identified through a variety of measures, including achievement tests, teacher nominations, assessment of potential for creativity and task commitment, as well as alternative pathways of entrance (self-nomination, parent nomination, etc.). High achievement test and IQ test scores usually warrant inclusion of a student in the talent pool, enabling those students who are underachieving in their academic schoolwork to be included.

Once students are identified for the talent pool, they are eligible for several kinds of services; first, interest and learning style assessments are used with talent-pool students. Informal and formal methods are used to create or identify students' interests and to encourage students to further develop and pursue these interests in various ways. Learning style preferences that are assessed include projects, independent study, teaching games, simulations, peer teaching, programmed instruction, lecture, drill and recitation, and discussion. Second, curriculum compacting is provided to all eligible students for whom the regular curriculum is modified by eliminating portions of previously mastered content. This elimination or streamlining of curriculum enables above-average students to avoid repetition of previously mastered work and guarantees mastery while simultaneously finding time for more appropriately challenging activities (Reis, Burns, & Renzulli, 1992; Renzulli, Smith, & Reis, 1982). A form, entitled the Compactor (Renzulli & Smith, 1978), is used to document which content areas have been compacted and what alternative work has been substituted. Third, the Enrichment Triad Model offers three types of enrichment experiences. Types I, II, and III enrichment are offered to all students; however, Type III enrichment is usually more appropriate for students with higher levels of ability, interest, and task commitment.

Separate studies on the SEM demonstrated its effectiveness in schools with widely differing socioeconomic levels and program organization patterns (Olenchak, 1988; Olenchak & Renzulli, 1989). A brief research summary is included at the end of this chapter. The SEM has been implemented in thousands of school districts across the country (D E. Burns, 1987), and interest in this approach continues to grow.

Components of the SEM

The present reform initiatives in general education have created a more receptive atmosphere for more flexible approaches that challenge all students, and accordingly, the SEM addresses the ways in which we can provide challenging and enriching learning experiences for all students by (see Figure 2.2)

- offering a continuum of special services that will challenge students with demonstrated superior performance or the potential for superior performance in any and all aspects of the school and extracurricular programs;

- infusing into the general education program a broad range of activities for high-end learning that will (a) challenge all students to perform at advanced levels and (b) allow teachers to determine which students should be given extended opportunities, resources, and encouragement in particular areas in which superior interest and performance are demonstrated; and

- funding the positions of an enrichment specialist to carry out the first two goals.

THE REGULAR CURRICULUM

The regular curriculum consists of everything that is a part of the predetermined goals, schedules, learning outcomes, and delivery systems of the school. The regular curriculum might be traditional, innovative, or in the process of transition, but its predominant feature is that authoritative forces (i.e., policy makers, school councils, textbook adoption committees, state regulators) have determined that the regular curriculum should be the centerpiece of student learning. Application of the SEM influences the regular curriculum in three ways. First, the challenge level of required material is differentiated through processes such as curriculum compacting and textbook content modification procedures. Second, systematic content intensification procedures should be used to replace eliminated content with selected in-depth learning experiences. Third, the types of enrichment recommended in the Enrichment Triad Model (Renzulli, 1977a) are integrated selectively into regular curriculum activities. Although our goal in the SEM is to influence rather than replace the regular curriculum, application of certain SEM components and related staff development activities has resulted in substantial changes in both the content and instructional processes of the entire regular curriculum.

THE ENRICHMENT CLUSTERS

The enrichment clusters, a second component of the SEM, are nongraded groups of students who share common interests and who come together during specially designated time blocks during school to work with an adult who shares their interests and who has some degree of advanced knowledge and expertise in the area. The enrichment clusters usually meet for a block of time weekly during a semester. All students complete an interest inventory developed to assess their interests, and an enrichment team of parents and teachers tallies all of the major families of interests. Adults from the faculty, staff, parents, and community are recruited to facilitate enrichment clusters based on these interests, such as creative writing, drawing, sculpting, archeology, and other areas. Training is provided to the facilitators who agree to offer the clusters, and a brochure is developed and sent to all parents and students that discusses student interests and select choices of enrichment clusters. A sample cluster title and description of a cluster in a school using the SEM follows:

Invention Convention

Are you an inventive thinker? Would you like to be? Brainstorm a problem, try to identify many solutions, and design an invention to solve the problem, as an inventor might give birth to a real invention. Create your invention individually or with a partner under the guidance of Bob Erikson and his students, who work at the Connecticut Science Fair. You may decide to share your final product at the Young Inventors' Fair on March 25th, a statewide daylong celebration of creativity.

Students select their top three choices for the clusters, and scheduling is completed to place all children into their first or, in some cases, second choice. Like extracurricular activities and programs such as 4-H and Junior Achievement, the main rationale for participation in one or more clusters is that students and teachers want to be there. All teachers (including music, art, physical education, etc.) are involved in teaching the clusters, and their involvement in any particular cluster is based on the same type of interest assessment that is used for students in selecting clusters of choice.

The model for learning used with enrichment clusters is based on an inductive approach to solving real-world problems through the development of authentic products and services. Unlike traditional, didactic modes of teaching, this approach, known as enrichment learning and teaching (described fully in a later section), uses the Enrichment Triad Model to create a learning situation that involves the use of methods, develops higher-order thinking skills, and authentically applies these skills in creative and productive situations. Enrichment clusters promote cooperation in the context of real-world problem solving, and they also provide superlative opportunities for promoting self-concept. "A major assumption underlying the use of enrichment clusters is that *every child is special if we create conditions in which that child can be a specialist within a specialty group*" (Renzulli, 1994, p. 70).

Enrichment clusters are organized around the various characteristics of differentiated programming for gifted students on which the Enrichment Triad Model (Renzulli, 1977a) was originally based, including the use of major disciplines, interdisciplinary themes, or cross-disciplinary topics (e.g., a theatrical and television production group that includes actors, writers, technical specialists, and costume designers). The clusters are modeled after the ways in which knowledge utilization, thinking skills, and interpersonal relations take place in the real world. Thus, all work is directed toward the production of a product or service. A detailed set of lesson plans or unit plans are not prepared in advance by the cluster facilitator; rather, direction is provided by three key questions addressed in the cluster by the facilitator and the students:

1. What do people with an interest in this area (e.g., filmmaking) do?

2. What knowledge, materials, and other resources do they need to do it in an excellent and authentic way?

3. In what ways can the product or service be used to have an effect on an intended audience?

Enrichment clusters incorporate the use of advanced content, providing students with information about particular fields of knowledge, such as the structure of a field as well as the basic principles and the functional concepts in a field

(Ward, 1960). Ward (1960) defined functional concepts as the intellectual instruments or tools with which a subject specialist works, such as the vocabulary of a field and the vehicles by which people in the field communicate with one another. The method used in a field is also considered advanced content by Renzulli (1988a), involving the use of knowledge of the structures and tools of fields, as well as knowledge about the methods of particular fields. This knowledge about the methods of fields exists both for the sake of increased knowledge acquisition and also for the utility of that know-how as applied to the development of products, even when such products are considered advanced in a relative sense (i.e., age, grade, and background considerations).

The enrichment clusters are not intended to be the total program for talent development in a school or to replace existing programs for talented youth. Rather, they are one vehicle for stimulating interests and developing talent potentials across the entire school population. They are also vehicles for staff development, in that they provide teachers an opportunity to participate in enrichment teaching and subsequently to analyze and compare this type of teaching with traditional methods of instruction. In this regard, the model promotes a spillover effect by encouraging teachers to become better talent scouts and talent developers, and to apply enrichment techniques to regular classroom situations.

THE CONTINUUM OF SPECIAL SERVICES

A broad range of special services is the third school structure in the SEM, and a diagram representing these services is presented in Figure 2.4 and elaborated on in Chapter Three. Although the enrichment clusters and the SEM-based modifications of the regular curriculum provide a broad range of services to meet individual needs, a program for total talent development still requires supplementary services that challenge our most academically talented young people, who are capable of working at the highest levels of their special interest and ability areas. These services, which cannot ordinarily be provided in enrichment clusters or the regular curriculum, typically include providing individual or small-group counseling, allowing various types of acceleration, giving direct assistance in facilitating advanced-level work, arranging for mentorships with faculty or community members, and making other types of connections between students, their families, and out-of-school people, resources, and agencies.

Direct assistance also involves setting up and promoting student, faculty, and parental involvement in special programs such as Future Problem Solving (http://www.fpsp.org), Odyssey of the Mind (http://www.odysseyofthemind.com), the Model United Nations program (http://www.un.org/cyberschoolbus/modelun/index.asp), and state and national essay competitions and mathematics, art, and history contests. Another type of direct assistance consists of arranging out-of-school involvement for individual students in summer programs, on-campus courses, special schools, theatrical groups, scientific expeditions, and apprenticeships at places where advanced-level learning opportunities are available. Provision of these services is one of the responsibilities of the enrichment specialist or an enrichment team of teachers and parents who work together to provide options for advanced learning. Most enrichment teaching specialists spend two days a week in a resource capacity to the faculty and three days providing direct services to students.

Figure 2.4   The Continuum of Services for Total Talent Development

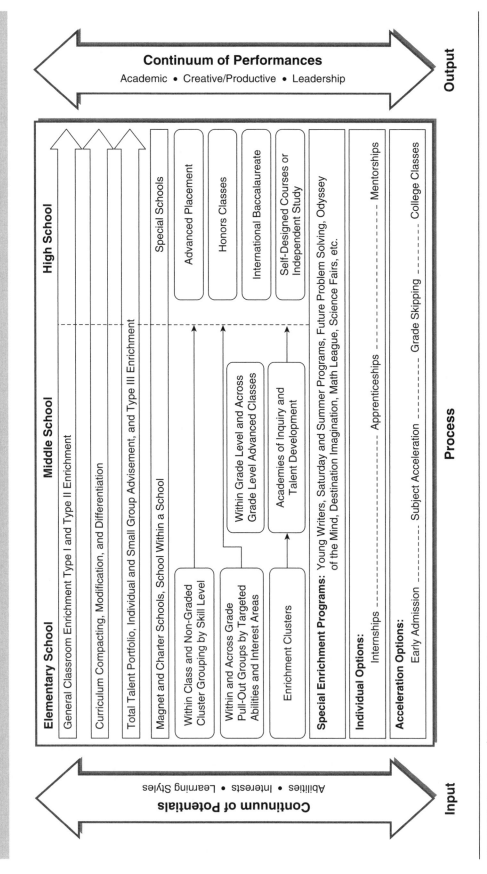

SOURCE: Courtesy of Creative Learning Press.

THE SERVICE DELIVERY COMPONENTS

The Total Talent Portfolio

The SEM targets specific learning characteristics that can serve as a basis for talent development. Our approach to targeting learning characteristics uses both traditional and performance-based assessment to compile information about three dimensions of the learner—abilities, interests, and learning styles. This information, which focuses on strengths rather than deficits, is compiled in a management form called the "Total Talent Portfolio," described more fully in Chapter Four and shown in Figure 2.5. It is used to make decisions about talent development opportunities in regular classes, enrichment clusters, and in the continuum of special services. The major purposes of the Total Talent Portfolio are

1. To collect several different types of information that portray a student's strength areas and to regularly update this information.

2. To classify this information into the general categories of abilities, interests, and learning styles, as well as related markers of successful learning such as organizational skills, content area preferences, personal and social skills, preferences for creative productivity, and learning-how-to-learn skills.

3. To periodically review and analyze the information to make purposeful decisions about providing opportunities for enrichment experiences in the regular classroom, the enrichment clusters, and the continuum of special services.

4. To negotiate various acceleration and enrichment learning options and opportunities between teacher and student through participation in a shared decision-making process.

5. To use the information as a vehicle for educational, personal, and career counseling and for communicating with parents about the school's talent development opportunities and their child's involvement in them.

This expanded approach to identifying talent potentials is essential if we are to make genuine efforts to include more underrepresented students in a plan for total talent development. This approach is also consistent with the more flexible conception of developing gifts and talents that has been a cornerstone of our work and our concerns for promoting more equity in special programs.

Curriculum Compacting and Differentiation Techniques

The next service delivery component of the SEM is a series of curriculum modification techniques, described more fully in Chapter Five, that are designed to (a) adjust levels of required learning so that all students are challenged, (b) increase the number of in-depth learning experiences, and (c) introduce various types of enrichment into regular curricular experiences. The procedures used to carry out curriculum modification are curriculum compacting, textbook analysis and surgical removal of repetitive material from textbooks, and a planned approach for introducing greater depth into regular curricular material.

Figure 2.5 The Total Talent Portfolio

Joseph S. Renzulli

Abilities	Interests	Style Preferences			
Maximum Performance Indicators	Interest Areas	Instructional Styles Preferences	Learning Environment Preferences	Thinking Styles Preferences	Expression Style Preferences
Tests • Standardized • Teacher-Made Course Grades Teacher Ratings **Product Evaluation** • Written • Oral • Visual • Musical • Constructed (Note differences between assigned and self-selected products) Level of Participation in Learning Activities Degree of Interaction With Others Ref: Renzulli, 1997	Fine Arts Crafts Literary Historical Mathematical/Logical Physical Sciences Life Sciences Political/Judicial Athletic/Recreation Marketing/Business Drama/Dance Musical Performance Musical Composition Managerial/Business Photography Film/Video Computers Other (Specify) Ref: Renzulli, 1997	Recitation & Drill Peer Tutoring Lecture Lecture/Discussion Discussion Guided Independent Study* Learning/Interest Center Simulation, Role Playing, Dramatization, Guided Fantasy Learning Games Replicative Reports or Projects* Investigative Reports or Projects* Unguided Independent Study* Internship* Apprenticeship* *With or without a mentor Ref: Renzulli & Smith, 1978	**Inter/Intra Personal** • Self-Oriented • Peer-Oriented • Adult-Oriented • Combined **Physical** • Sound • Heat • Light • Design • Mobility • Time of Day • Food Intake • Seating Ref: Amabile, 1989; Dunn, Dunn, & Price, 1978; Gardner, 1983	Analytic (School Smart) Synthetic/Creative (Creative, Inventive) Practical/Contextual (Street Smart) Legislative Executive Judicial Ref: Sternberg, 1984, 1988, 1992	Written Oral Manipulative Discussion Display Dramatization Artistic Graphic Commercial Service Ref: Kettle, Renzulli, & Rizza, 1998; Renzulli & Reis, 1985

SOURCE: Courtesy of Creative Learning Press.

Students who are candidates for curriculum compacting and differentiation often have strengths, such as reading and language scores that range several years above grade level. This presents teachers with a common problem: how to instruct and challenge students like this. Compacting curriculum means that teachers pre-assess (using instruments or tests such as the appropriate unit tests for the grade level in the Basal Language Arts program) and excuse targeted students from completing the activities and worksheets in the units where they show proficiency. Students with high potential may participate in language arts lessons one or two days a week, and they spend the balance of the time with alternative projects, some of which are self-selected. This strategy may eliminate up to six or eight hours a week of language arts skills that are beneath these students' level. When pretests indicate that students do not have the required skills, they then participate in class instruction. In the time saved through compacting, students can engage in a number of enrichment activities. If, for example, science is an area of strength area or interest, students may conduct a science fair project on growing plants under various conditions or another area in which they have an interest. Teachers who use the system of compacting well explain that compacting curriculum actually saves time that would have been spent correcting papers that did not need to be assigned. The Compactor, as can be seen in Figure 2.6, can also be used as a vehicle for explaining to parents how specific modifications are being made to accommodate advanced achievement level and interests. A copy of the Compactor should also given to the next grade-level teacher, as conferences between teachers help ensure continuity in dealing with the child's special needs.

Enrichment Learning and Teaching

The third service delivery component of the SEM, which is based on the Enrichment Triad Model, is enrichment learning and teaching, which has roots in the ideas of a small but influential number of philosophers, theorists, and researchers such as Jean Piaget (1975), Jerome Bruner (1960, 1966), and John Dewey (1913, 1916). The work of these theorists, coupled with our own research and program development activities, has given rise to the concept we call enrichment learning and teaching. The best way to define this concept is in terms of the following four principles:

1. Each learner is unique; therefore, all learning experiences must be examined in ways that take into account the abilities, interests, and learning styles of the individual.

2. Learning is more effective when students enjoy what they are doing; therefore, learning experiences should be constructed and assessed with as much concern for enjoyment as for other goals.

3. Learning is more meaningful and enjoyable when content (i.e., knowledge) and process (i.e., thinking skills, methods of inquiry) are learned in the context of a real and present problem; therefore, attention should be given to opportunities to personalize student choice in problem selection, the relevance of the problem for individual students at the time the problem is being addressed, and authentic strategies for addressing the problem.

4. Some formal instruction may be used in enrichment learning and teaching, but a major goal of this approach to learning is to enhance knowledge and thinking skills, which are gained through formal instruction with applications of knowledge and skills that result from students' own construction of meaning (Renzulli, 1994, p. 204).

Figure 2.6 The Compactor

INDIVIDUAL EDUCATIONAL PROGRAMMING GUIDE

The Compactor

Prepared by Joseph S. Renzulli
Linda M. Smith

NAME _____ AGE _____ TEACHER(S) _____

SCHOOL _____ GRADE _____ PARENT(S) _____

Individual Conference Dates
and Persons Participating in Planning of IEP

_____ _____

CURRICULUM AREAS TO BE CONSIDERED FOR COMPACTING Provide a brief description of basic material to be covered during this marking period and the assessment information or evidence that suggests the need for compacting.	PROCEDURES FOR COMPACTING BASIC MATERIAL Describe activities that will be used to guarantee proficiency in basic curricular areas.	ACCELERATION AND/OR ENRICHMENT ACTIVITIES Describe activities that will be used to provide advanced level learning experiences in each area of the regular curriculum.

☐ Check here if additional information is recorded on the reverse side.

The ultimate goal of learning that is guided by these principles is to replace dependent and passive learning with independence and engaged learning. Although all but the most conservative educators will agree with these principles, much controversy exists about how these (or similar) principles might be applied in everyday school situations. A danger also exists that these principles might be viewed as yet another idealized list of glittering generalities that cannot be manifested easily in schools that are entrenched in the deductive model of learning; developing a school program based on these principles is not an easy task. Over the years, however, we have achieved success by gaining faculty, administrative, and parental consensus on a small number of easy-to-understand concepts and related services and by providing resources and training related to each concept and service delivery procedure. Numerous research studies and field tests in schools with widely varying demographics have been conducted (Renzulli & Reis, 1994), and these are described in the following, as are studies that document that the SEM can be implemented in a wide variety of settings and used with various populations of students, including high-ability students with learning disabilities and high-ability students who underachieve in school.

NONNEGOTIABLES ABOUT IMPLEMENTING ENRICHMENT IN THE SEM

The many changes taking place in general education have resulted in some unusual reactions to the SEM that might best be described as the good news/bad news phenomenon. The good news is that many schools are expanding their conception of giftedness, and they are more willing than ever to extend a broader continuum of enrichment and differentiated learning services to larger proportions or even the entire school population. More good news also suggests that many schools are using enrichment services as a theme to provide these types of services for all students in the school. The bad news is that the motivation for these changes is often based on mistaken beliefs that we can adequately serve high-potential students without some forms of instructional grouping and that we don't need enrichment teachers, as classroom teachers can do all of this in the contexts of their classrooms without the special training that is necessary to understand how to implement enrichment programming. Accordingly, the following are some nonnegotiables about the SEM.

First, although we have advocated a larger talent pool than traditionally has been the practice in gifted education, and a talent pool that includes students who gain entrance on both test and nontest criteria (Renzulli, 1988b), we firmly maintain that the concentration of services necessary for the development of high-level potentials cannot take place without targeting and documenting individual student abilities, interests, and learning styles. Targeting and documenting does not mean that we will simply play the same old game of classifying students as "gifted" or "not gifted," and let it go at that. Rather, targeting and documenting are part of an ongoing process that produces a comprehensive and always evolving Total Talent Portfolio about student abilities, interests, and learning styles. The most important thing to keep in mind about this approach is that all information should be used to make individual programming decisions about present and future activities and about ways we can enhance and build on documented strengths. Documented information will (a) enable us to recommend enrollment in advanced courses or special programs (e.g., summer programs, college courses, etc.) and (b) provide direction in taking extraordinary steps to develop specific interests and resulting projects within topics or subject-matter areas of advanced learning potential.

Enrichment specialists must devote a majority of their time to working directly with targeted students, and this time should mainly be devoted to facilitating individual and small-group investigations (i.e., Type IIIs). Some of their time with talent pool students can be devoted to stimulating interest in potential Type IIIs through advanced Type I experiences and advanced Type II training that focuses on learning research skills necessary to carry out investigations in various disciplines. To do this, we must encourage more classroom teachers to become involved in talent development through both enrichment opportunities and in curriculum modification and differentiation in their classrooms. We must also encourage more classroom teachers to participate in enrichment teams that work together to provide talent development opportunities for all students in the school, enabling the enrichment specialists to work with more-advanced students.

A second nonnegotiable is that SEM programs must have specialized personnel to work directly with talent pool students, to teach advanced courses, and to coordinate enrichment services in cooperation with a schoolwide enrichment team. The old cliché, "Something that is the responsibility of everyone ends up being the responsibility of no one," has never been more applicable than when it comes to enrichment specialists. The demands made on regular classroom teachers, especially during these times of mainstreaming and heterogeneous grouping, leave precious little time to challenge our most-able learners and to accommodate interests that clearly are above and beyond the regular curriculum. In a study recently completed by researchers at the National Research Center on the Gifted and Talented, it was found that in 84% of regular classroom activities, no differentiation was provided for identified high-ability students. Accordingly, time spent in enrichment programs with specialized teachers is even more important for high-potential students.

Related to this nonnegotiable are the issues of teacher selection and training as well as the scheduling of special program teachers. Providing unusually high levels of challenge requires advanced training in the disciplines that one is teaching, in the application of process skills, and in the management and facilitation of individual and small-group investigations. It is these characteristics of enrichment specialists, rather than the mere grouping of students, that have resulted in achievement gains and high levels of creative productivity on the parts of special-program students.

Every profession is defined in part by its identifiable specializations, according to the tasks to be accomplished, but specialization means more than the acquisition of particular skills. It also means affiliation with others who share common goals; the promotion of one's field; participation in professional activities, organizations, and research; and contributions to the advancement of the field. It also means the kinds of continued study and growth that make a difference between a job and a career. Now, more than ever, it is essential to fight for the special-program positions that are falling prey to budget cuts and the "heterogenization" of education. All professionals in the field should work for the establishment of standards and specialized certification for enrichment specialists. They should also help parents organize a task force that will be ready at a moment's notice to call in the support of every parent (past as well as present) whose child has been served in a special program.

RESEARCH ON THE SEM

The SEM (Renzulli, 1977a; Renzulli & Reis, 1985, 1997) has been widely implemented as an enrichment program used with academically gifted and talented students and as a magnet school theme for all students who are using talent development experiences. Separate studies of the SEM have demonstrated its effectiveness in schools with students of widely differing socioeconomic levels and varied program organization patterns (Olenchak, 1988; Olenchak & Renzulli, 1989), as summarized in Appendix A.

The SEM has been implemented in more than 2,500 schools across the country (D. E. Burns, 1987), and programs using this approach have been widely implemented internationally. The effectiveness of the model has been studied in more than 20 years of research and field testing about (a) the effectiveness of the model as perceived by key groups, such as principals (Cooper, 1983; Olenchak, 1988); (b) research related to student creative productivity (D. E. Burns, 1987; Delcourt, 1988; Gubbins, 1982; Newman, 1991; Reis & Renzulli, 1982; Starko, 1986b); (c) research relating to personal and social development (Olenchak, 1991; Skaught, 1987); (d) the use of the SEM with culturally diverse or special-needs populations (Baum, 1985, 1988; Baum, Renzulli, & Hébert, 1995; Emerick, 1988; Taylor, 1992); (e) research on student self-efficacy (Schack, 1986; Schack, Starko, & Burns, 1991; Starko, 1986b; Stednitz, 1985); (f) the use of the SEM as a curricular framework (Karafelis, 1986; Reis & Fogarty, 2006; Reis, Gentry, & Park, 1995); (g) research relating to learning styles and curriculum compacting (Imbeau, 1991; Reis et al., 1993; Smith, 1976; Stewart, 1979); and (h) longitudinal research on the SEM (Delcourt, 1988; Hébert, 1993; Westberg, 1999). This research on the SEM suggests that the model is effective at serving high-ability students in a variety of educational settings and in schools serving diverse ethnic and socioeconomic populations. These studies also suggest that the pedagogy of the SEM can be applied to various content areas, resulting in higher achievement when implemented in a wide variety of settings and used with diverse populations of students, including high-ability students with learning disabilities and those who underachieve.

Specific studies that investigated achievement include a study on curriculum compacting that found that when teachers eliminated as much as 50% of the regular curriculum for gifted students, students who had their curriculum compacted scored as well or better in the out-of-level postachievement tests, using the Iowa Test of Basic Skills (1990). For example, students whose curriculum was eliminated in science scored significantly higher on science achievement tests than did the control group whose curriculum was not compacted. Students whose curriculum was compacted in mathematics scored significantly higher on the math concepts Iowa Test than did control group students whose curriculum was not compacted in mathematics.

Another study used the SEM in reading (Reis et al., 2005), as described in Chapter Seven, to investigate the effects of an enrichment approach to reading on elementary school students' reading achievement and attitudes toward reading. Researchers found that when they eliminated five hours of regular grouped reading instruction and replaced it with short conferences and enriched reading based on interests, significant differences were found in reading fluency and achievement as well as attitudes for students using this enriched reading approach.

In another study (Baum et al., 1995), teachers guided 17 gifted, underachieving students (ages 8–13) in the completion of creative products based on their interests as part of the SEM. Positive gains were made by 82% of the students, who were no longer underachieving in their school setting at the end of the intervention. Another study (Reis, Gentry, & Maxfield, 1998) investigated the effect of providing one type of gifted education pedagogy, enrichment clusters, to the entire population of two urban elementary schools. Enrichment clusters provided a regularly scheduled weekly time for students to work with adult facilitators to complete a product or provide service in a shared interest area. Teaching practices of classroom teachers who participated as cluster facilitators were affected both in the enrichment clusters and in regular classrooms. More challenging content was integrated into 95% of the clusters through teaching specific and authentic methods, advanced thinking, and problem-solving strategies. Starko (1986a) found that students involved in SEM enrichment groups reported more than twice as many creative projects per student as those in a comparison group and that they showed greater diversity and sophistication in projects (see Appendix A for a research summary of studies related to the SEM and Renzulli Learning).

SUMMARY

The SEM provides a detailed plan to develop talents and gifts and encourage creative productivity in students. Each school that has the SEM program has the flexibility to develop its own unique programs based on local resources, student demographics, and school dynamics, as well as faculty strengths and creativity. The idea is to create a repertoire of services that can be integrated in such a way to create a "rising tide lifts all ships" approach. The model includes a continuum of services, enrichment opportunities, and three distinct services: curriculum modification and differentiation, enrichment opportunities of various types, and opportunities for the development of individual portfolios, including interests, learning styles, product styles, and other information about student strengths. Not only has this model been successful in addressing the problem of high-potential students who have been underchallenged, but it also provides additional important learning paths for gifted and talented students who find success in more traditional learning environments. Each of these components is more fully described in subsequent chapters.

There may never have been a time when so much debate about what should be taught has existed in American schools. The current emphasis on testing, the standardization of curriculum, and the drive to increase achievement scores has produced major changes in education during the last two decades. Yet at the same time, our society continues to need to develop creativity in our students. As overpopulation, disease, pollution, and starvation increase both here and throughout the rest of the world, the need for creative solutions to these and other problems seems clear. The absence of opportunities to develop creativity in all young people, and especially in talented students, is troubling. In the SEM, students are encouraged to become responsible partners in their own education and to develop a passion and joy for learning. As students pursue creative enrichment opportunities, they learn to acquire communication skills and to enjoy creative challenges. The SEM provides the opportunity for students to develop their gifts and talents and to begin the process of lifelong learning, culminating, we hope, in creative, productive work of their own selection as adults.

3

Challenging All Students With a Continuum of Enrichment Services

The overall mission of any approach to enrichment is to escalate the level and quality of learning experiences for all students in any and all areas of the curriculum. As part of this mission, the SEM provides guidance for the development of challenging and appropriate educational opportunities for all young people, regardless of differences in demographic and economic backgrounds or differences in the rates, styles, and levels at which they learn. We believe that true equity can only be achieved when we acknowledge individual differences in the students we serve and when we recognize that high-achieving students have as much right to accommodations in their schooling as do students who are experiencing learning difficulties. We also believe that equity is not the product of identical learning experiences for all students; rather, it is the product of a broad range of differentiated experiences that take into account each student's unique strengths.

As the SEM is based on a belief that we can develop gifts and talents in children (Renzulli, 1986), it focuses on the many kinds of aptitudes, talents, and potentials for advanced learning and creative productivity that exist in all school populations. The goal is not to certify some students as gifted and others as nongifted, but to provide every student with the opportunities, resources, and encouragement necessary to achieve his or her maximum potential. In the SEM, the "language" of the model is that of labeling the services, not the student. Examples of labeled services are a special minicourse for all fourth graders in how to access the Internet, an Advanced Placement (AP) course in chemistry, a multigrade cluster group in mathematics for high-achieving students, a special enrichment cluster for all students interested in filmmaking, assigned time in a resource room to work on a research project, and curriculum compacting for students who have already mastered the material to be covered in an upcoming unit of study.

Young people display or have the potential to display their individuality and uniqueness in many ways. Some students learn at faster rates and higher levels of comprehension than others. Sometimes this learning may be in one or two subjects, and in other cases, it may be across the entire curriculum. Similarly, some students are more creative or artistic than others, and still others may demonstrate potentials for excellence in leadership, organizational skills, or interpersonal relations.

We believe that the many and diverse talent potentials of young people can be enhanced through the broad continuum of services briefly described in Chapter One. These specified activities might take place in regular classrooms on an individual or small-group basis, in special grouping arrangements that are purposefully formed because of advanced achievement levels, high levels of interest in particular subjects or problems, or strong motivation to pursue the development of a common product or service. Advanced opportunities can also take place outside the school in special internship or mentorship situations, in magnet schools or special-theme high schools, at cultural institutions, in summer programs or programs offered by colleges or universities, or anywhere else where highly capable and motivated youth can gain knowledge and experience that are not ordinarily available in the regular school program. We also believe that all regular curricular material should be subject to modification according to the learning rates and learning styles of individual students.

A total talent approach to education should give special consideration to schools that serve young people who may be at risk because of limited English proficiency, economically limited circumstances, or attendance at poor-quality schools, or because they just learn in a different way from the majority. We believe that it is in these schools and among these student populations that extraordinary efforts, indeed heroic efforts, should be made to identify and cultivate the high-level talents of young people, talents that historically have gone unrecognized and underdeveloped, and these should be incorporated into a broad continuum of services.

BACKGROUND TO THE ESTABLISHMENT OF A CONTINUUM OF SERVICES

In the last decade, many promising practices have been implemented to challenge and engage all students, and we believe that the development of a continuum of services in the SEM can incorporate these practices to meet the diverse learning and affective needs of all students at all grade levels (see Figure 3.1). This continuum provides services that range from general enrichment for all students across all grade levels to curriculum differentiation procedures, including enrichment and acceleration for rapid learners, as well as individualized research opportunities for identified gifted and talented students. Some services are relatively inexpensive and some involve considerable time and funds, whereas others have no cost, as they involve strategies for grouping and regrouping students, based on interests and achievement levels.

Figure 3.1 SEM Cube

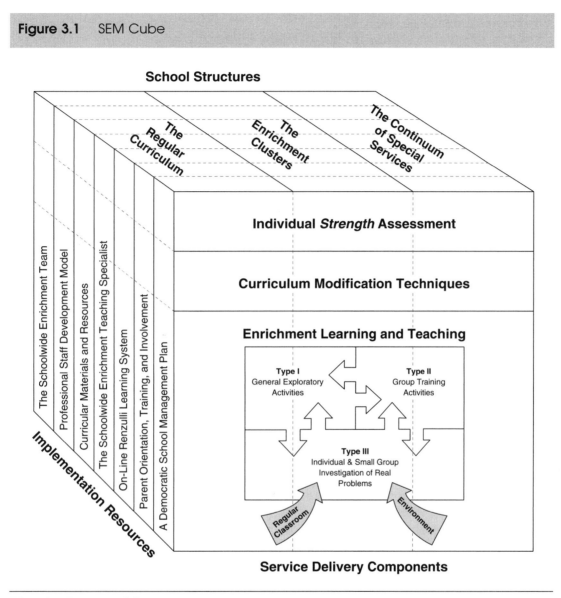

SOURCE: Courtesy of Creative Learning Press.

Some services involve advanced knowledge acquisition, and the use of higher-level thinking skills is important, but the benefits of a continuum of services when implemented as a high-end learning theory is the application of knowledge and authentic methods of inquiry to firsthand investigative activities and the pursuit of creative endeavors. Related to this assumption is the interconnectedness of services provided by the model. Thus, for example, a presentation on fashion design or depletion of the ozone layer above the Earth (Type I enrichment), or training in brainstorming or how to design a questionnaire (Type II enrichment), are valuable experiences in and of themselves, but the best payoff from such activities is maximized when individuals or small groups decide to follow up these general enrichment experiences with self-selected investigative and creative involvements that are guided by the specification for Type III enrichment. Even curriculum compacting, that part of the SEM that accommodates students who can cover material at accelerated levels, plays into the enrichment end of the model by allowing advanced students to "buy time" for possible Type III investigations.

THEORETICAL AND ORGANIZATIONAL MODELS

Two categories of models guide the special services that are a part of the development of a continuum of services: theoretical (or pedagogical) models and organizational (or administrative) models. When most people are asked what model is being used to guide their special program, they almost always answer in terms of organizational models. Although we believe that both types of models play important roles in guiding program quality and effectiveness, theoretical models should be the first and most essential consideration in program planning.

Theoretical models include the principles and derivative experiences and activities that are designed to accomplish particular kinds of learning. Theoretical models usually draw on the work of leading philosophers, researchers, and learning theorists, and they are located somewhere on a continuum of learning theories ranging from highly didactic or prescriptive learning on one end to highly inductive or investigative learning on the other. The works of Pavlov, Thorndike, and Skinner are examples of didactic theories, whereas inductive or constructivist theories are represented by writers such as Dewey, Pestalozzi, Piaget, and Montessori. Theoretical models should be the first and most important consideration when examining the quality of services for gifted students, and we have briefly summarized in the previous section the high-end learning theory that underlies the SEM.

Organizational models, on the other hand, are concerned with how we group students, move them around between and among various service delivery options, plan schedules and events, allocate time blocks, assign teachers, and do other things that contribute to the efficient and effective use of student time and human and material resources. Examples in this category are pullout programs, full-time special classes, cluster grouping, afterschool programs, Saturday programs, grade skipping, advanced classes, college courses, special schools, and differentiation in the regular classroom. Organizational models are obviously important, but they do not tell us why or how we present learning experiences in any of the organizational models mentioned previously that are qualitatively different from the learning experiences that take place in regular education. A special class for gifted students could, for example, be very didactic or prescriptive in its approach to learning, or it could be an environment in which students engage in self-selected investigative activities using the authentic methods of practicing professionals, even if their method is at a more junior level than adult scientists, writers, or other professionals. The most important consideration is that students in the special class are thinking, feeling, and doing what real-world investigators and problem solvers do, as opposed to being consumers of knowledge who are mainly involved in accumulating information and practicing thinking skills, albeit at a faster level. The same theoretical distinctions can be made for all of the types of organizational models listed previously. It is not when or where we do it, or even with whom we do it. The key issue is *how* we do it!

We believe that what makes a model a model is that services provided are based on sound theory and research and can be replicated in a variety of situations. A good SEM model must have two salient features. The first feature is that there should be consensus about the underlying learning theory and service delivery procedures on the part of the majority of people who are responsible for providing services. Without agreement on common goals, people providing services can do whatever they want to do, and this approach may end up with people actually working at cross-purposes with one another. The second feature of a model is that each school or program develops its own unique means for delivering services and its own unique continuum of services, as long as the means are consistent with the agreed-on underlying theory and common goals. This feature prevents models from becoming too prescriptive and, at the same time, allows the creativity of program personnel and the availability of unique local resources to be brought to bear on the program. It also enables program modification and renewal, and the infusion of new ideas and resources, so long as any and all modifications are compatible with the goals of the model.

AN INTEGRATED CONTINUUM OF SPECIAL SERVICES

The SEM delivers enrichment and acceleration through an integrated continuum of services (see Figure 3.2). The word *integrated* is emphasized because maximum payoff is achieved when a service provided through one component of the model enables students who show superior performance or advanced interest to escalate their experience through options that might be available through other service delivery components. Services provided by the model range from general enrichment for both wide-ranging and targeted subgroups to highly individualized curriculum modification procedures for rapid learners and firsthand investigative opportunities for highly motivated individuals and small groups. The model also includes a broad array of specific grouping arrangements based on commonalities in abilities, interests, learning styles, and preferences for various modes of expression.

Services based on the Enrichment Triad Model form the core of the enrichment dimension of the SEM, but the model also includes various acceleration options (e.g., grade skipping, enrollment in college classes) and numerous supplementary program options that provide opportunities for talent development in specialized areas (e.g., Math League, Invention Convention, and National History Day Competition, to mention only a few of the hundreds of available options). Other components of the model include performance-based assessment of student strengths, individual and group counseling, and various special placement options (in and outside the school) based on high degrees of proficiency and potential.

The continuum of services provides a graphic overview of the integrated continuum of services. The arrow on the left-hand side of the figure, Continuum of Potentials (Input), is intended to convey the broad range of abilities, interests, and learning styles that exist in any population and subpopulation of students. Even in highly targeted groups (e.g., advanced math students), there is always a range of abilities, interests, and learning styles, and this range requires that differentiated learning experiences must be provided to accommodate individual differences. Although it has become somewhat of a cliché, there are in fact as many differences in a selected group of students as exist between gifted students and the population in general.

The arrow on the right-hand side of Figure 3.2, Continuum of Performances (Output), is intended to illustrate the range of performances and modes of expression that will result from differentiated learning experiences. When considering this range of performances, we should take various modes of expression into consideration as well as levels of ability. Graphic, dramatic, artistic, spatial, and other forms of expression should be considered in addition to traditional written and spoken expression styles. We should also take into consideration various levels of evaluation

40

Figure 3.2 The Continuum of Services for Total Talent Development

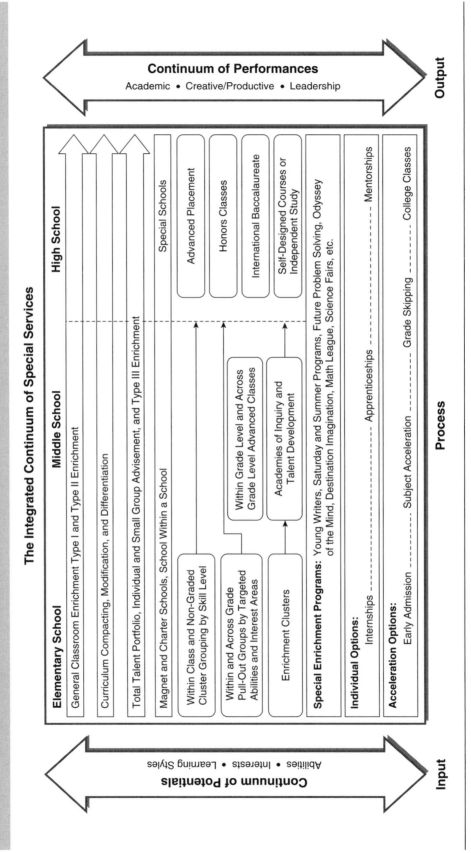

SOURCE: Courtesy of Creative Learning Press.

criteria when providing feedback related to student achievement and creative productivity. Traditional, norm-referenced evaluations (e.g., test scores, letter or number grades) may suffice when evaluating standard and advanced lesson learning activities, but creative and productive products need to be considered by using alternative modes of assessment (see, for example, the Student Product Assessment Form [Reis & Renzulli, 1982]). The assessment of creative products should always take into consideration evaluation by internal criteria of what is important to the creator (Bloom, Englehart, Furst, Hill, & Krathwohl, 1956), as well as external criteria that focus on how others will evaluate one's work. Placing value on internal criteria helps students develop a sense of what they think is important and unique about their work. We would not, for example, foster the uniqueness of a writer such as Langston Hughes if his writing was evaluated with the external criteria typically used to evaluate standard prose.

The center section of Figure 3.2 (Process) represents many of the organizational methods for delivering services to students. An important consideration is that any and all services provided through various organizational approaches are integrated or interconnected, so that an experience in one organizational setting can be capitalized on by connecting it with options from another organizational component. Let us assume for a moment that one component of a comprehensive program offers general enrichment for all students in the regular classroom. Let us further assume that two or three students have had a remarkably positive reaction to, for example, a Type I (general exploratory) presentation and demonstration on robotics. We might want to form a special enrichment cluster for these students, arrange for a mentorship experience, provide them with Internet access to explore robotics, or give them information on a national or international robotics competition. The most advanced students might subsequently be provided with a summer mentorship experience on a college campus or in an internship at a robotics manufacturing company.

Another example of integrated services deals with the most advanced students in a particular subject area. Let us assume that there are 8 or 10 primary-age students across two or three grade levels who have demonstrated extremely high achievement in mathematics. Classroom teachers should ideally be providing curriculum compacting services for such students, and teachers should be using the time gained through compacting to provide in-class acceleration and mathematics enrichment opportunities. But equally important is the need to arrange a special grouping situation that allows these students to interact with their mathematically able peers on a regular basis. Both compacting and cluster grouping will be further enhanced if the classroom teachers and the people providing instruction to the special group are in close communication about the respective activities in classroom and special group situations.

These few examples of integrated services from the continuum presented in Figure 3.2 are little more than common sense, and yet a good deal of the time and energy of previous decades has been devoted to arguments about the supremacy of one approach over all others. It is our hope that emphasis in the future will be devoted to answering questions about how we escalate learning options for our most potentially able students in and among interconnected services, rather than what is the one best approach to providing for the gifted. It is also our hope that there will be integration between and among the three main considerations of special programming—identification (input), programming (process), and output (product). One of our biggest challenges for the future is to create logical and defensible relations between where and in which ways a young person is located on the continuum of potentials (identification) and how this information can guide us in making the most appropriate decisions for maximizing this person's assets (programming).

HOW AND WHEN ENRICHMENT ACTIVITIES TAKE PLACE

A broad continuum of special services encompasses enrichment and acceleration options that take place in or through

1. Regular classrooms or clusters of classes from one or more grade levels during special grouping arrangements in classrooms, across grade levels, or in afterschool and out-of-school programs

2. Special schools such as magnet or high schools that focus on advanced learning opportunities in particular curricular areas

3. Arrangements made for individual students at colleges, summer programs, internship opportunities, or special counseling services

The continuum also ranges across both general and targeted groups of students. A general enrichment experience on a topic such as local history might be presented to all students at a particular grade level, or it might be provided on an invitational basis to students who have a special interest in history. In a later chapter, we will discuss how general enrichment for all students serves as a stepping stone for more intensive follow-up on the parts of students who develop advanced interest in topics that were originally introduced through general enrichment.

Age and grade levels also play a role in making decisions about special services. Abilities, interests, and learning styles tend to become more differentiated among students and more focused on the parts of individual children as students grow older. There is, therefore, more justification for interest and achievement level grouping as students progress through the grades. It may be difficult to have a special class in mathematics, for example, at the primary or elementary grade levels. But a within-class cluster group or a nongraded cluster group of the highest achieving math students is one way of ensuring advanced levels of challenge for students with unusually high levels of achievement in mathematics. At the middle and secondary school levels, achievement in various subjects becomes more differentiated, and interests become more focused; thus, there is greater justification for advanced classes or special services such as a math club or a competitive math league group.

The nature of the subject matter and the degree to which classroom teachers can reasonably differentiate instruction also play a role in making decisions about grouping students for participation in activities on the continuum of special services. Subjects that are highly structured and linear-sequential in content (e.g., algebra, chemistry, physics) tend to be taught in a more unalterable fashion than subjects more conducive to variations in speed and level. Language arts and social studies, for example, lend themselves to greater within-topic differentiation of the complexity of the material; therefore, individual differences can be accommodated more easily in heterogeneous groups. Of course, age or grade level and the subject matter area interact with one another in making decisions about grouping students for special services. Within-class differentiation in literature, for example, is easier to accomplish at the elementary or middle school levels, but an advanced literature class is a more specialized option at the high school level.

Options such as special schools at the high school level, the number of AP courses offered, and enrollment in college courses are a function of school and district size and geographic location. The continuum of special services can also be expanded as more offerings become available through increased availability of electronic media and distance learning. Although the enrichment clusters and the SEM-based modifications of the regular curriculum provide services to meet individual and group needs, a program for total talent development still requires a range of ancillary services that challenge young people who are capable of working at the highest levels of their special interests and abilities. The continuum of special services might be viewed as the talent development counterpart to the kinds of special services that schools have always made available to students with remedial or compensatory educational needs.

These services, which cannot ordinarily be provided in enrichment clusters or the regular curriculum, are familiar to most educators and have been in place in some schools for many years. Some of these services are represented by the extracurricular program; in other cases, they may be part of special class options or existing internship or work-study programs. A continuum of special services that focuses on talent development typically includes

- Individual or small-group counseling
- Direct assistance in facilitating advanced-level work
- Mentorships with faculty members or community persons
- Within- and across-grade cluster groups for students with extremely advanced performance in a particular area
- Connections between students and out-of-school people, resources, and agencies

KEYS TO DEVELOPING A COMPREHENSIVE CONTINUUM OF SERVICES

There are three keys to developing a comprehensive continuum of special services:

1. Identifying the types of programs and opportunities available for students of varying age levels in certain geographic areas

2. Obtaining information about how schools can access these programs and opportunities

3. Enlisting school personnel and parent volunteers who are willing to devote time to organizing and managing special service options

Many of the programs and opportunities available for young people can be located by contacting professional organizations and societies. *The Encyclopedia of Associations* (Burek, 1990), which is available in most university and large public libraries, lists thousands of organizations by both topic and geographic area, and almost all professional organizations and special interest groups can now easily be located through the World Wide Web. Some organizations have databases that list special opportunities for students by category and age or grade levels. The Council for Exceptional Children, for example, conducts computer searches for special summer program opportunities for a modest fee. *The Educational Opportunity Guide* published by the Duke University Talent Program lists hundreds of opportunities for students to explore an area of interest.

ORGANIZING SERVICES IN THE CONTINUUM

The overall responsibility for organizing a broad-based continuum of special services is usually assumed by the schoolwide enrichment teaching specialist working in cooperation with the schoolwide enrichment team. At the middle and secondary school levels, these teams are frequently organized within departments—special services that represent the individual interests of department members or the department as a whole. Examples could include the following:

- A social studies teacher with a particular interest in world peace encouraged his students to prepare essays and submit them to a contest sponsored by the U.S. Institute for Peace.
- An entire mathematics department served as coaches for a Math League team in their school.
- An industrial arts teacher, working in cooperation with a local craftsman, assisted a group of interested students in the construction of furniture for display at a state fair.
- A group of parent volunteers at an elementary school organized and conducted a series of afterschool enrichment courses that focused on a wide range of student interests. Some of these courses were so popular that they later were used as the basis for forming enrichment clusters.

The establishment of a continuum of special services is an excellent way to use inexpensive and often neglected resources that contribute to talent development. The continuum is also a good vehicle for using cultural institutions and private-sector resources as well as promoting more community involvement in the schools. A well-planned program of special services may take several years to develop, but as the program expands to include a full range of offerings, all students can benefit from the diversity of resources encompassed in this component of the SEM. The self-selection of special services also helps students work with other young people and adults who share common interests. This factor alone is a powerful force in promoting group acceptance, developing self-concept, and helping students develop respect for one another.

THE ROLE OF GROUPING AND TRACKING IN A CONTINUUM OF SERVICES

Grouping is a complex and often polarizing issue that has become highly politicized. The debate that surrounds this issue is a distraction from providing appropriate and meaningful learning activities for all students. Accordingly, it is important to confront this topic now and clarify its role with respect to the SEM. Grouping is an intensely debated, controversial practice. The pendulum between homogeneous and heterogeneous grouping has swung back and forth since the beginning of public education. Before presenting recommendations about grouping in the context of the SEM, we discuss some of the concerns that make grouping such a contentious issue.

It is crucial to make a very clear distinction between grouping and tracking. We view tracking as the general and usually permanent assignment of students to classes that are taught at a certain level and that are usually taught using a whole-group instructional model. Tracking is most prevalent at the secondary school level, and there are several features about tracking that have made it a detrimental procedure, especially for students who end up in low tracks. A concentration of low-achieving students in one classroom almost always results in a curriculum that emphasizes remediation, isolated and repetitive practice of skills such as phonics and computation at the expense of problem solving and comprehension, and low expectations for all students in the group (Oakes, 1985; Slavin, 1987, 1990).

Critics of tracking argue that students frequently are locked into all low-track or "general" track classes. Unlike college or vocational tracks, these classes have a dead-end orientation rather than an orientation toward postsecondary education or entrance into the skilled labor market. This lack of purposefulness frequently results in low student motivation and self-esteem, underachievement, behavior problems, absenteeism, and school dropouts. Low-track classes are usually taught in such a way that they become ends in themselves, rather than places where students are being prepared to move into higher track classes. Economically disadvantaged students are disproportionately represented in low-track classes, and this practice further reinforces their sense of failure and feelings about the limited value of a formal education.

In contrast, at the elementary level, within-class instructional groups are common practice, and they serve an important purpose in accommodating different levels of achievement in the classroom. It is essential, however, to have a built-in review process so that students who are ready to progress to a more advanced group do not get locked into a lower group for reasons of mere convenience. Without such a review process, instructional groups can serve as de facto tracks; as such, they play a role in the cumulative development of underachievement.

Our first recommendation, therefore, is purposefully intended to prevent grouping from becoming tracking by initiating a systematic practice of the consistent use of flexible grouping. We recommend regularly scheduled formal and informal assessments should be used—regardless of the types of grouping arrangements a school uses—so students can progress to achievement-level groups that offer maximum challenges. Students and parents should be informed about the group jumping and flexible grouping policy (in writing), and information about group placement should be routinely provided.

THE POLITICS OF GROUPING

The argument over grouping has been long and passionate, and every faction rattles off its cache of research studies while simultaneously pointing out the shortcomings of research presented by the opposition. Like all of the armies that ever took up weapons, each group is convinced that rightness is on its side. Adversaries even lay claim to the same study by adding their own surplus interpretation or procedure for reanalyzing the data. The only thing certain about the research on ability grouping and its relation to achievement is that there are well-documented arguments on both sides of the issue (Kulik, 1992; Oakes, 1985; Rogers, 1991; Slavin, 1987, 1990).

Gifted and special education programs may be conceived of as one form of ability grouping, but they also involve many other changes in curriculum, class size, resources, and goals that make them fundamentally different from comprehensive ability grouping plans. Slavin (1987) has pointed out that

> studies of special programs for the gifted tend to find achievement benefits for the gifted students . . . and others, would give the impression that ability grouping is beneficial for high achievers and detrimental for low achievers. However, it is likely that characteristics of special accelerated programs for the gifted account for the effects of gifted programs, not the fact of separate grouping per se. (p. 307)

Slavin (1987) presents a clear message: If positive growth is the result of curriculum adaptations, class size, resources, and goals, why then cannot we apply the same explanation to cases in which growth is not shown? More important, shouldn't we be using the know-how of educational practices that emerges from studies of favorable achievement to explore ways of promoting better performance in lower achieving students? This is exactly the rationale that underlies the SEM. But the grouping issue, rather than a focus on what must be done to create favorable acts of learning, has taken center stage, and it is offered as a quick-fix approach to improving our schools. Gutiérrez and Slavin (1992), pursuing the same distinctions pointed out previously, offers an alternative to traditional forms of ability grouping:

> In the nongraded plan, students are flexibly grouped for major subjects (especially reading and math) across class and age lines, so that the resulting groups are truly homogeneous on the skills being taught. Further, by creating multi-age groups from among all students in contiguous grade levels, it is possible for teachers to create entire reading or math classes at one or, at most, two levels, so that they need not devote much class time to follow-up. (p. 339)

The research summarized by Gutiérrez and Slavin (1992) clearly indicates that multiage grouping based on the skills being taught has proven to be an effective practice. But we also believe that even in a homogeneous skill-level group, provisions must also be made for curriculum compacting and cluster grouping that are based on other considerations (e.g., interests, learning styles) as well as achievement levels. We also believe that group jumping should be the goal of all group assignments. Like the Boy Scout and Girl Scout merit badge program, the goal should be to demonstrate competence in a skill area, after which the individual moves on to a more advanced level of involvement.

NONGRADED INSTRUCTIONAL GROUPING AND WITHIN-CLASSROOM CLUSTER GROUPING

In the SEM, grouping is viewed as a much more flexible (i.e., less permanent) arrangement of students than the frequently unalterable group arrangements that characterize tracking. Although we will present recommendations for various types of instructional and cluster groups, note that there are many other factors about grouping that should be taken into consideration in addition to achievement level, and sometimes in place of achievement level. These factors include motivation, general interests (e.g., drama) and specific interests in a general area (e.g., writing plays, acting, directing), complementary skills (e.g., an artist who might illustrate the short stories of students in a creative writing group), career aspirations, and even friendships that might help promote self-concept, self-efficacy, or group harmony. In the real world, which serves as the rationale for many of the procedures that guide the SEM, the most important reason people come together is because they are pursuing a common goal. In most cases, the effectiveness of the group is a function of the different assets that are brought to bear on a mutual purpose. The major criteria for group effectiveness are commonality of purpose, reciprocal respect and harmony, group and individual progress toward goals, and individual enjoyment and satisfaction. It is these criteria that helped to create the rationale for the enrichment clusters as well as the enrichment learning and teaching strategies that will be described in detail in Chapter Five.

Another factor that should be taken into consideration is the age level of students and the material being taught. Many elementary-level students begin to fall behind and have difficulty catching up when they are placed in lower level groups. Although nongraded instructional groups and cluster groups in the classroom may be necessary to accommodate varying achievement levels in basic skills, variations in teaching style can also be used to deal with diversity in students' knowledge and skills. In studies of Asian teachers, Stigler and Stevenson (1991) point out how Asian teachers thrive in the face of diversity and indicate that some teaching practices actually depend on diversity for their effectiveness.

Stigler and Stevenson (1991) credit the highly skilled professionalism of Asian teachers for their remarkable success and the widespread excellence of their lessons. They also point out that the techniques used by Asian teachers are not foreign or exotic. Although one of the goals of the SEM is to provide professional training that allows teachers to expand their repertoire of teaching practices, the range of diversity in American schools and our educational traditions will continue to make grouping an issue in school improvement.

Although curriculum compacting and other modification techniques are important procedures in the SEM for meeting individual differences in achievement levels, we also recommend that instructional groups be formed *within* the classroom and across grade levels. There is both research support (Gutiérrez & Slavin, 1992; Kulik, 1992; Rogers, 1991) and a commonsense rationale for forming advanced instructional groups for students who are achieving several years above grade level.

Two criteria, however, should guide the formation of advanced instructional groups. First, a course description rather than a group label should be used, and the course should be defined by the level of instruction and the amount of material to be covered. This approach avoids the stigma of calling it an honors or gifted group. Defining advanced classes by the level and amount of material ensures that certain predetermined standards will be met, that we will avoid watering down the course, and that success in the course is dependent on certain expectations. A detailed description of the amount of material, the rate of coverage, reading and writing assignments, homework expectations, and evaluation criteria should be provided.

The second criterion for advanced instructional groups is that standardized test scores should not be a factor in determining admittance. If, after examining the course description and understanding the expectations of the teacher, a student expresses an interest in enrolling, that student should be given an opportunity, regardless of test scores and previous grades. High motivation on the part of a student, coupled with supplementary assistance from a teacher or other adult, may very well enable a lower achieving student to maintain the level of standards that define the course. A key issue related to this second criterion is that students may volunteer to take a course. Consider the procedure used with AP courses. The content, standards, and examinations are set, but taking the AP exam is not required. In addition to its attractiveness to some students (and the teachers who offer AP courses), the benefits of such courses are more in the nature of incentives and bonuses rather than penalties. Students get credit for passing an AP course, and there is an additional bonus if they pass the official AP exam at a level that earns them advanced standing in participating colleges.

A good example of how carefully defined standards for rigorously demanding, high-level classes can have an effect on at-risk students can be found in the multira-cial San Diego High School. A program based on the International Baccalaureate curriculum was developed at this inner-city school that serves a mainly low socio-economic, minority population. Students can select from among nine academic requirements that include traditional courses; an interdisciplinary course in the philosophy of knowledge; participation in a creative, aesthetic, or social service activity; and an extended essay based on independent research. Students' performance is evaluated through written and oral external examinations that are used worldwide, and oral presentations, lab books, portfolios, and research papers are also evaluated externally. The academic performance of all students at San Diego High School improved dramatically, and three years after instituting the International Baccalaureate, 85% of the graduating class went on to college. The school became a "hot" recruiting place for many Ivy League colleges seeking to increase their minority student enrollments.

If we are serious about improving the standards of American education and providing greater access to advanced courses for students who traditionally have been locked into lower tracks, it will also be necessary to concentrate on basic skills achievement at lower grade levels. We also need to have alternative routes to advanced courses for those students who have the motivation to enroll but who lack some of the skills necessary for high-level instruction. Transitional preparatory classes and individual or small-group tutoring are ways of helping motivated students prepare for more-advanced classes. These approaches, however, should not fall into the remedial range of instruction. If, for example, students are preparing for an advanced literature class, the focus should be on literature rather than more practice on grammar.

MANAGING WITHIN-CLASSROOM CLUSTER GROUPS

Although the use of cluster grouping in classes is a major improvement over tracking or large-group instruction, in practice, this approach is usually less effective than it could be because students are often placed in clusters on the basis of a single criterion. In most classrooms that use cluster grouping, all high-achieving math students or all low-achieving reading students are typically members of the same group. The students in this small group are usually given the same instruction and assignments, despite the fact that high-achieving or low-achieving students can differ from one another with respect to their strengths and weaknesses in the various strands or subdisciplines in a given subject area.

For example, two students who score in the 95th percentile on the math subtest of a norm-referenced achievement test score may be markedly different in their achievement with respect to fractions, decimals, problem solving, or measurement skills. One student in the high-achieving group may need more help on fractions but less assistance with problem solving. By using an average score to reflect individual achievement in a subject area, and grouping students according to this number, we continue to "wash out" the differences between students and in the subject area. When this happens, the potential benefits of small-group teaching as a means of maximizing individual student performance are decreased because individual differences between the students and in each of the ability groups are not addressed. As a result, teachers may not see increased achievement for students who were placed in such groups when compared with students who were taught similar objectives through large-group instruction. In other words, the use of small groups for instruction will not, in and of itself, guarantee student achievement (Kulik & Kulik, 1987; Slavin, 1987; Walberg, 1984).

The quality of small-group instruction depends on what goes on in the cluster groups. More specifically, the achievement of students in these groups depends on the ability of the teacher to group students flexibly and then adapt the learning objectives, teaching strategies, modeling activities, practice materials, and pacing to match the students' needs. Flexible cluster grouping allows students to participate in group instruction when the unit pretesting reveals wide differences among students with regard to mastery of learning objectives for a given unit of study. Once groups of students are formed for instruction, characteristics of individuals comprising the cluster dictate the learning objectives, the type of modeling, the type and amount of practice materials, and the pacing.

Although cluster grouping and concomitant instructional changes represent common sense with respect to teaching practices, cluster grouping should not dominate classroom instruction. Instead, a balance between whole-class and cluster grouping is determined by the teacher according to the purpose of instruction and the degree to which students differ with respect to various curricular objectives. Large-group activities such as storytelling, discussions, debriefings, class meetings, audiovisual aids, visitations, lectures, and demonstrations are used to motivate students, to introduce or extend a curriculum unit, or to teach content or skills that are new for all students. Individual or small-group activities are used for intensive study or exploration of specific topics in the unit that reflect strong personal interest or when wide differences exist among students with respect to mastery of learning objectives in a given unit of study.

When teachers implement small-group instruction, classroom management issues inevitably arise. "What will I do with the other students in the room?" "How will I know they are meaningfully engaged while I am working with the small groups?" In the 1950s, the answer to these questions was to assign seatwork to the students who were not meeting in a small group. In too many cases, worksheets were used as busywork to fill students' time. This seatwork involved ineffective and uninteresting drill and repetition that bore little resemblance to the way the skills were actually used and applied in real-world situations.

One possible solution is offered by the practice of using flexible skill groups in the regular classroom (Hoover, Sayler, & Feldhusen, 1993). In these instances, teachers help students in each small group work cooperatively to practice and apply the skill or objective that was the focus of the teacher-led group instruction. By working cooperatively, students are not reduced to practicing the kind of repetitive drill that the old seatwork approach produced. These cooperative practice groups meet and work with the teacher on a rotating basis; specifically, teachers meet with two to four groups a day to evaluate student progress, provide instruction or new scaffolding to support students' learning, and assess the appropriateness of grouping arrangements and reassign (e.g., "group jump") students accordingly. This application of cooperative learning principles ensures that all students in a small group are supporting and helping one another and that they are all striving to achieve a common objective that is appropriate for all group members.

Still other students can be allowed to use interest centers, learning centers, classroom libraries, and software and technology (such as Renzulli Learning) to pursue individual interests or to extend and enrich a curriculum unit. Students provided with these enrichment options demonstrate mastery of curriculum objectives in the assessment of student knowledge that preceded instruction. Class meetings are used to explain enrichment options and to teach the skills necessary for students to work independently. Student logs can be used to provide the teacher with information about what each student does each day, and contracts can be written by students and teachers, using compromise and consensus, to ensure that each student has a relevant and realistic plan for his or her enrichment time.

CONCLUDING THOUGHTS ON GROUPING

It is easy to point out the social consequences of grouping, the grouping practices followed in other nations, and the level of professionalism required for teachers to accommodate the diversity that is always present when two or more students come together. Our schools are a reflection of the society at large and the educational traditions that this society has created. Schools do, indeed, play a role in shaping society; however, they have thus far been an abysmal failure at influencing larger societal issues such as housing, health care, and equal job opportunities. These larger societal issues also are forms of grouping that must be addressed at the same time that we struggle with the most equitable forms of grouping that should take place in our schools. Schools cannot shoulder the entire burden of shaping and improving our multicultural society. Until these larger issues are addressed, and until dramatic changes take place in the funding of education, in the levels of preparation of our teachers, and in developing a national commitment to improve standards for all students, grouping will continue to be a practice for accommodating the broad range of diversity that characterizes our school population. We believe that grouping per se is not the issue. Rather, the issue is what is done *within* groups, regardless of how they are organized, to help all students maximize their potentials and view learning as both a valuable and enjoyable experience. It is for this reason that the SEM focuses on the act of learning rather than the types of administrative arrangements that have been offered as school reform paradigms. By concentrating on what and how we teach, grouping becomes incidental to the overall process of school improvement. The most important issue to remember is that whatever is done in groups, regardless of how they are organized, should be focused on helping all students maximize their potentials and view learning as both a valuable and enjoyable experience.

ESTABLISHING A CONTINUUM OF SERVICES IN SCHOOL-BASED OR DISTRICT-LEVEL ENRICHMENT PROGRAMS: GETTING STARTED

Establishing opportunities for enrichment across the grade levels and differentiation in all classrooms is the easiest way to begin the development of a continuum of services that could range from some level of service in the regular classroom setting to a separate school or center for our most advanced learners. School-based gifted programs offer a diverse set of learning opportunities. Resource room programs enable teachers to send students from their regular classrooms to spend time with other high-potential students and to enable them to work on independent study projects and group projects in their interest areas. The following practical examples highlight the levels of a continuum of services used in districts and schools in varying areas of the country.

In some districts, students have the opportunity to travel to a center one day each week to work with other identified gifted and talented students on advanced curriculum or to pursue individual interests. For example, the Center for Creative Learning in St. Louis County, Missouri, directed by Dr. Linda Smith, was established in 1990 as part of Rockwood's commitment to meeting the learning needs of its most advanced students (http://www.rockwood.k12.mo.us/gifted/elementary.htm). The center supplements the regular school program by providing differentiated educational opportunities for academically gifted students in Grades K–5. Students spend one day each week at the center, and while at their home schools, these same students receive enrichment and acceleration experiences through the efforts of regular classroom teachers. Still other gifted programs incorporate innovative mentorship opportunities in which a bright student is paired with a high school student or adult who has an interest in the same area.

Cluster grouping is widely used in many different districts' continuum of services. Some schools use cluster grouping to enable students who are gifted or academically advanced in a certain content area to be grouped in one classroom with other students who are talented in the same area. When cluster grouping is used, one fifth-grade teacher may have a group of six very advanced math students clustered in a classroom, instead of having these students distributed among four different fifth-grade classrooms. Research by both Marcia Gentry (1999) and James Kulik (1992) has found that cluster grouping and other forms of instructional grouping benefit gifted and talented students and also help to challenge other students across lower levels of achievement. Many principals and superintendents urge classroom teachers to use differentiated instruction and curriculum compacting across all grade levels to ensure sufficient challenge to all students and to eliminate content that students have already mastered. Some schools provide afterschool enrichment programs or send talented students to Saturday programs offered by museums, science centers, or local universities.

Various forms of acceleration are also used in schools, including the most common form, grade skipping, as well as early entrance to kindergarten or first grade, content-level acceleration (enabling students who are advanced in reading to work at an advanced level that is commensurate with their reading comprehension level), and curriculum compacting. A recent report by Nicholas Colangelo, Susan Assouline, and Miraca Gross (2004) at the University of Iowa entitled *A Nation Deceived* provides research support for the many different types of acceleration that are successful with gifted learners. A policy on acceleration from Ohio provides a comprehensive example of how one state department of education suggests that various forms of acceleration can be implemented in schools (Ohio Department of Education, 2006).

A continuum of services for gifted and high-potential learners can also include a number of challenging curriculum content options implemented in classrooms. Several research-based curriculum and instructional options have been developed under the auspices of the federal Jacob Javits Education Act, which also produced the most recent federal report on what is happening with academically talented students in America ("National Excellence," 1993). Dr. Katherine Gavin and her colleagues have developed research-based, exciting math curriculum for talented elementary students (http://www.gifted.uconn.edu/projectm3/). A team of researchers has worked with us to develop research-based strategies to challenge gifted and talented readers at the elementary and middle school levels (http://www.gifted.uconn.edu/SEMR/). Curriculum in science and social studies has been developed by Professors Sandra Kaplan at the University of Southern California (http://www-rcf.usc.edu/~skaplan/javits.html) and Joyce VanTassel-Baska at the College of William and Mary.

OTHER ENRICHMENT OPTIONS

National programs have also been developed for high-ability students, such as Future Problem Solving (http://www.fpsp.org), conceived by Dr. E. Paul Torrance of the University of Georgia. These types of programs have enabled hundreds of thousands of students to apply problem-solving techniques to real-world problems in society and in their communities. Although not intended solely for academically talented and advanced students, Future Problem Solving is widely used in gifted programs because of the curricular freedom and academic challenge associated with the problems that students pursue. Likewise, programs such as Odyssey of the Mind (http://www.odysseyofthemind.com) encourage teams of students to use creative problem solving to design structures, vehicles, and solutions to problems such as designing a vehicle that uses a mousetrap as its primary power source. Many gifted students have the opportunity to participate in National History Day (http://www.nationalhistoryday.org), in which they work individually or in small groups on a historical event, a person from the past, or an invention related to a theme that is determined each year. Using primary source data such as diaries or other archives gathered in libraries, museums, and interviews, students prepare research papers, projects, media presentations, or performances as entries. Many districts and states have also developed innovative programs that include a variety of services for high-potential and gifted learners, such as mentorships, Saturday programs, and summer internships.

The latest innovation to challenge gifted and talented learners in classrooms and in separate gifted programs is a new online system (www.renzullilearning.com) designed to use strengths-based assessment and differentiated learning experiences for gifted and talented students. Renzulli Learning provides a computer-based diagnostic assessment and then creates an individual profile of each student's academic strengths, interests, learning styles, and preferred modes of expression. The online assessment, which takes about 30 minutes, results in a printed profile that highlights individual student strengths, which is accompanied by a differentiation search engine that selects hundreds of resources that relate specifically to each student's interests, learning styles, and product styles. The search engine matches student strengths and interests to an enrichment database of 15,000 enrichment activities, materials, resources, contests and competitions, independent studies, and opportunities for research and follow-up. A project management tool, called the Wizard Project Maker, guides students and teachers to use specifically selected resources for assigned curricular activities, independent or small-group investigative projects, and research studies.

Summer Programs and Schools for Gifted Students

A national program called the Center for Talented Youth at Johns Hopkins (http://cty.jhu.edu/) actively recruits and provides testing and program opportunities for precocious youth. These students generally have scored highly on standardized tests, are recommended by teachers or counselors to participate in early assessment, and may be eligible for multiple options including summer programs, acceleration, and college courses. Other summer programs focus on in-depth investigative experiences for students in the summer under the mentorship of doctoral-level researchers (http://www.gifted.uconn.edu/mentor).

Several states have created separate schools for academically talented students in math and science such as the North Carolina School for Science and Mathematics (http://www.ncssm.edu/). Some large school districts have established magnet schools to serve the needs of academically talented students. In St. Paul, Minnesota, for example, several magnet and themed schools are available for gifted learners, including a school that is a full-time program for academically gifted and talented students with a focus on critical and creative thinking skills (http://capitolhill.spps.org/).

In other states, advanced, intensive summer programs are provided by Governor's Schools in different content areas. Many colleges and universities offer summer programs for advanced and gifted learners (for more information, see the Web site of the National Association for Gifted Children, www.nagc.org, and the link to the diverse listing of summer programs for high-potential and gifted students).

The goal for each administrator and enrichment specialist is to work with teachers and parents to develop a continuum of services that is appropriate for each individual school, taking into account the unique learning needs of the students, the programs and services already in place, and what is needed to challenge and enrich every child's education.

4

Developing Talent Portfolios for All Students

Every child has strengths or potential strengths, and our work on the Schoolwide Enrichment Model (SEM) capitalizes on these strengths by helping every student develop a portfolio of strengths in the areas of abilities, interests, and learning styles. The SEM pays equal attention to interests and learning styles as well as to the cognitive abilities that have been traditionally used for educational decision making. Assets related to these three clusters of learner characteristics are documented in these student portfolios, and the information is used to make decisions about various types of student involvement in the full continuum of regular curriculum and enrichment opportunities that are available in schools using the SEM.

Although information obtained from formal assessment is a part of student portfolios, additional information gained through informal, performance-based assessment is equally valuable in maximizing the use of the portfolio. The ways to capitalize on student performance are to

1. Provide opportunities for participation in a broad range of activities in and across interest areas.

2. Observe and document performance, satisfaction, and enthusiasm.

3. Make decisions about subsequent activities that will capitalize on positive reactions to previous experiences.

Student portfolios are used to document strengths, interests, and talents. Regularly scheduled meetings with staff members, parents, and students are used to make decisions about appropriate follow-up, needed resources, and the development of future performance assessment situations. Whereas the traditional diagnostic-prescriptive learning model focuses on remediating student weaknesses, this approach accentuates the positive, because it uses positive reactions to learning experiences as vehicles for attacking deficiencies in basic skill learning. For example, a child who has developed a spirited interest in dolphins but who also experiences difficulties in reading and basic language skills is far more likely to read background material and improve written and oral language skills when he or she works on a research project based on this abiding interest in dolphins. All cognitive behavior is enhanced as a function of the degree of interest present in an act of learning, wherever that cognitive behavior may be on the continuum from basic skill learning to higher levels of thinking and creative productivity. For this very reason, the SEM uses performance-based assessment in the context of student interests as well as in basic skill learning.

WHAT IS THE TOTAL TALENT PORTFOLIO?

The paper-based version of Total Talent Portfolio is described in this chapter, and the electronic version is described in Chapter Eight on Renzulli Learning. Either version of a Total Talent Portfolio can be used to gather and record information systematically about students' abilities, interests, and learning styles. The major dimensions of the portfolio and the specific items that guide data gathering in each dimension are presented in Figure 4.1, and a discussion about the use of Renzulli Learning for Electronic Talent Portfolios is introduced in Chapter Seven. The Total Talent Portfolio centers on a key issue: creating learning experiences that encourage the development of strong interests. How did the student in the example develop the interest in dolphins that served as a launching pad for subsequent activity? This interest might have been discovered through formal assessment such as responses to items on an instrument called the Interest-a-lyzer (discussed later in this chapter), or it might have resulted from purposefully planned interest development activities. We receive dozens of examples of Total Talent Portfolios (see Figures 4.1A, B, C, D, and E) and notice that each version is unique and that teachers have a great deal of pride and ownership in this process.

Identifying interests through formal or performance-based activities is only a first step, however, because other strategies must be implemented for nurturing interests and examining the ways in which the student might like to pursue interests. We also need to give teachers guidance and resources necessary to escalate the level of student productivity. Two unique features about the Total Talent Portfolio that distinguish it from other compilations of student records are discussed next.

STATUS AND ACTION INFORMATION

The portfolio consists of both status information and action information. Status information is anything we know or can record about a student prior to the instructional process that tells us something about learner characteristics. Examples of status information are test scores, course grades, teacher ratings of various learning behaviors, and formal and informal assessments of interests and learning styles.

Figure 4.1 Examples of Different Total Talent Portfolios

Total Talent Portfolio

Joseph S. Renzulli

(A)

Abilities	Interests	Style Preferences			
Maximum Performance Indicators	Interest Areas	Instructional Styles Preferences	Learning Environment Preferences	Thinking Styles Preferences	Expression Style Preferences
Tests • Standardized • Teacher-Made Course Grades Teacher Ratings **Product Evaluation** • Written • Oral • Visual • Musical • Constructed (Note differences between assigned and self-selected products) Level of Participation in Learning Activities Degree of Interaction With Others	Fine Arts Crafts Literary Historical Mathematical/Logical Physical Sciences Life Sciences Political/Judicial Athletic/Recreation Marketing/Business Drama/Dance Musical Performance Musical Composition Managerial/Business Photography Film/Video Computers Other (Specify) Ref: Renzulli, 1997	Recitation & Drill Peer Tutoring Lecture Lecture/Discussion Discussion Guided Independent Study* Learning/Interest Center Simulation, Role Playing, Dramatization, Guided Fantasy Learning Games Replicative Reports or Projects* Investigative Reports or Projects* Unguided Independent Study* Internship* Apprenticeship* *With or without a mentor Ref: Renzulli & Smith, 1978	**Inter/Intra Personal** • Self-Oriented • Peer-Oriented • Adult-Oriented • Combined **Physical** • Sound • Heat • Light • Design • Mobility • Time of Day • Food Intake • Seating Ref: Amabile, 1989; Dunn, Dunn, & Price, 1978; Gardner, 1983	Analytic (School Smart) Synthetic/Creative (Creative, Inventive) Practical/Contextual (Street Smart) Legislative Executive Judicial Ref: Sternberg, 1984, 1988, 1992	Written Oral Manipulative Discussion Display Dramatization Artistic Graphic Commercial Service Ref: Kettle, Renzulli, & Rizza, 1998; Renzulli & Reis, 1985

(Continued)

Figure 4.1 (Continued)

(B)

Me, Myself and I!

A Total Talent Portfolio

_____   _____   _____
My Name   My Teacher's Name   My Grade

This booklet is about you! We would like your mom or dad to help you fill out this interest inventory. An interest inventory is a series of questions about subjects you like best in school and activities you prefer to do outside of school. Your parent or guardian is to help you understand what is being asked and help you think about all of the activities that you do on your own. The answers to the questions should be <u>your</u> answers, not your mom's or dad's. The reason we are asking you to complete this inventory is so we can get to know you better. If we know what fascinates you and how you like to learn best, we can help to make your days in school more interesting and successful. Please take your time as you complete this booklet. Think carefully about the questions; there is no need to rush! We would love to have you return this booklet to your teacher in about two weeks. Thank you and have fun!

(C)

School Subjects	Interests
Circle the smiley face that shows best how you feel about each of the subjects listed below:	Use numbers to rank the areas below. Put a 1 next to your favorite activity, a 2 next to your second favorite, etc.

School Subjects		Interests
Art	☹ ☹ ☺ ☺ ☺	Acting
Geography	☹ ☹ ☺ ☺ ☺	Arts & Crafts
Gym	☹ ☹ ☺ ☺ ☺	Cartooning
Math	☹ ☹ ☺ ☺ ☺	Creative Writing
Music	☹ ☹ ☺ ☺ ☺	Community Service
Reading	☹ ☹ ☺ ☺ ☺	Dancing
Science	☹ ☹ ☺ ☺ ☺	Geography
Social Studies	☹ ☹ ☺ ☺ ☺	History
Writing	☹ ☹ ☺ ☺ ☺	Music
		Science Experiments
		Technology/Computers
		Other _____

Here are some topics that I would love to learn more about:

_____

_____

(D)

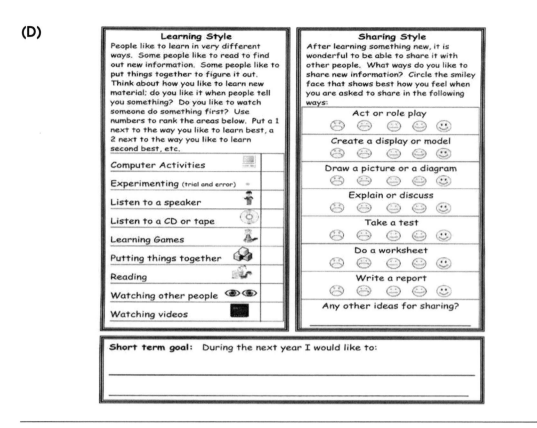

Learning Style

People like to learn in very different ways. Some people like to read to find out new information. Some people like to put things together to figure it out. Think about how you like to learn new material; do you like it when people tell you something? Do you like to watch someone do something first? Use numbers to rank the areas below. Put a 1 next to the way you like to learn best, a 2 next to the way you like to learn second best, etc.

Computer Activities	
Experimenting (trial and error)	
Listen to a speaker	
Listen to a CD or tape	
Learning Games	
Putting things together	
Reading	
Watching other people	
Watching videos	

Sharing Style

After learning something new, it is wonderful to be able to share it with other people. What ways do you like to share new information? Circle the smiley face that shows best how you feel when you are asked to share in the following ways:

Act or role play

Create a display or model

Draw a picture or a diagram

Explain or discuss

Take a test

Do a worksheet

Write a report

Any other ideas for sharing?

Short term goal: During the next year I would like to:

_____

_____

(E)

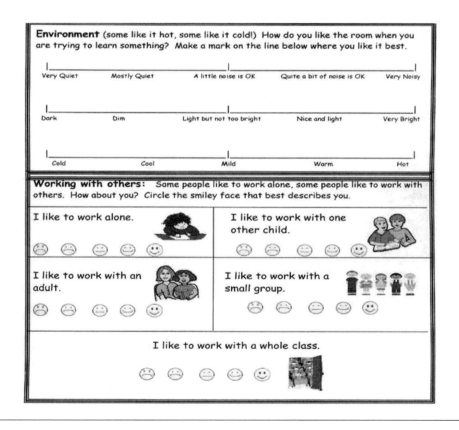

Environment (some like it hot, some like it cold!) How do you like the room when you are trying to learn something? Make a mark on the line below where you like it best.

| Very Quiet | Mostly Quiet | A little noise is OK | Quite a bit of noise is OK | Very Noisy |

| Dark | Dim | Light but not too bright | Nice and light | Very Bright |

| Cold | Cool | Mild | Warm | Hot |

Working with others: Some people like to work alone, some people like to work with others. How about you? Circle the smiley face that best describes you.

I like to work alone.

I like to work with one other child.

I like to work with an adult.

I like to work with a small group.

I like to work with a whole class.

Action information consists of annotated recordings of events that take place in the instructional process. Action information, by definition, cannot be recorded beforehand because it is designed to document the ways in which students react to various learning experiences as well as other experiences that take place outside the formal learning environment. Documentation procedures such as the Action Information Message (see Figure 4.2) and staff development techniques related to the use of this form are designed to capture episodes in which remarkable interests, unusual insights, or other manifestations of learning are displayed. By seizing the moment to record this information, teachers and students have a vehicle for documenting what might be starting points to high levels of follow-up activity.

Action information also includes annotated work samples of completed assignments and other performance-based observations and assessments. These annotations can be both informal notes and more structured analyses of student work.

Figure 4.2 Action Information Message

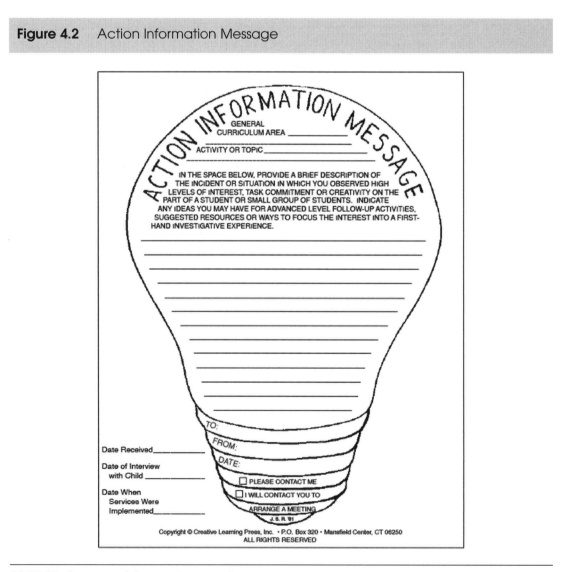

SOURCE: Courtesy of Creative Learning Press.

FOCUS ON STRENGTHS

The second unique feature of the Total Talent Portfolio is its focus on strengths and high-end learning behaviors. An educational tradition has caused us to use student records mainly for spotting deficiencies. Our adherence to the medical (i.e., diagnostic-prescriptive) model has almost always been pointed in the negative direction: "Find out what's wrong with them and fix it up!" Total talent assessment emphasizes the identification of the most positive aspects of each student's learning behaviors. Documentation based on the categories in Figure 4.1 should be carried out by inserting any and all information in the portfolio that calls attention to strong interests, preferred styles of learning, and high levels of motivation, creativity, and leadership, as well as the academic strengths that can lead to more advanced learning activities.

Portfolios of any type are only as valuable as the use to which they are put. Portfolios as prime examples of performance-based assessment are receiving a great deal of attention in the professional literature; they are being considered as supplements to or replacements for traditional evaluation procedures such as standardized tests. Although the information gathered in a Total Talent Portfolio can be used for program evaluation purposes, the primary use of the portfolio in the context of the SEM is to make educational programming decisions for individual students or for small groups of students who share common abilities, interests, or learning styles.

PORTFOLIO ENGINEERING: CREATING A TOTAL TALENT PORTFOLIO

Through a process that might best be described as *portfolio engineering*, examples of positive performance are accumulated on a continuing basis, and regularly scheduled reviews are used to make decisions about subsequent talent development activities. These decisions may relate to guidance regarding the selection of enrichment clusters, within-class special projects, curriculum compacting, group jumping, or individual learning opportunities that are a part of the continuum of special services discussed earlier.

Portfolio engineering also involves conducting conferences among groups of teachers and specialists, meeting with parents, and conveying information about student strengths to subsequent-year teachers, college admission officers, and prospective employers. The theme of the Total Talent Portfolio might best be summarized in the form of two questions: First, what are the very best things we know and can record about a student? Second, what are the very best things we can do to capitalize on this information? The first question is addressed in the following three sections that deal with student abilities, interests, and learning styles. The second question is addressed in the remaining chapters of the book.

GATHERING AND RECORDING INFORMATION ABOUT ABILITIES

Abilities, or maximum performance indicators, as traditionally defined in the psychometric literature, deal with competencies that represent the highest level of performance a student has attained in a particular area of aptitude or scholastic achievement. This dimension of school performance has traditionally been evaluated by tests or course grades. School performance can be documented by these conventional assessments, but can also be explained by a number of additional procedures by which maximum performance can be examined. These procedures may not be as reliable and objective as traditional tests, but they do have the advantage of letting us know how students perform on more complex tasks and on tasks that require the application of knowledge to assigned or self-selected learning activities.

The merits of formal testing versus alternative forms of assessment have been debated extensively in the literature, and it is not our purpose here to reexamine this debate or to argue for one approach or the other. We believe that any and all sources of information are valuable if they improve our understanding of potential for future performance and if they provide direction for enhancing future performance. We do believe, however, that alternative forms of assessment are equal in value to formal tests, and that a Total Talent Portfolio that does not include alternate assessment information will seriously limit the purposes of this component of the SEM.

Standardized Tests and Teacher-Made Tests

The concept of ability implies the measurement of competencies in terms of maximum performance. The traditional use of the term *ability*, at least in educational settings, has almost always been linked with standardized test scores and expressed in a normative or comparative fashion with the scores of other students in the same age or grade group. Arguments about the value of standardized tests have existed since the time these instruments came onto the educational scene, and the tests themselves are a reality in our schools. In those cases in which the tests meet the criteria of reliability, validity, objectivity, and audience appropriateness, they can provide us with useful information if used properly in the context of the SEM. At the risk of dwelling on a cliché, the tests are not as much of a problem as the uses to which they are put.

Although standardized test scores are gathered and recorded in the Total Talent Portfolio, these scores are only one source of information about students' abilities. The most important use of standardized test scores is to identify which general area or areas are a student's greatest strengths. To do this, we need only look at one student's scores, and we should avoid comparative information such as percentiles or other norms based on national or even local comparisons. Instead, we focus on this question: In which curricular areas or aptitudes does this student show his or her greatest strengths?

Teacher-made assessments usually are designed to assess the degree of mastery of a specific unit that has been taught and to evaluate competence in an entire course or a segment thereof. Objective teacher-made tests (e.g., multiple-choice, matching, short answer) provide information about knowledge acquisition, the mastery of basic skills, and, in some cases, problem-solving strategies. This information is valuable for determining general levels of proficiency, but the most valuable kind of teacher-made assessments, so far as the purposes of the Total Talent Portfolio are concerned, are those that elicit open-ended or extended responses.

Responses of this type enable teachers to gain insight into complex student abilities such as constructing convincing arguments, using expressive written or oral language, generating relevant hypotheses, applying creative solutions to complex problems, and demonstrating deep levels of understanding. Open-ended responses also provide excellent opportunities for students to demonstrate artistic and scientific creativity and to display advanced abilities such as analysis, generalization, and evaluation. Whenever teacher-made tests result in a student's exemplary manifestations of these more complex learning abilities, the tests should be copied, annotated, and entered into the student's portfolio.

The majority of teacher-made assessments generally fall into the short-answer, recognition, or recall category. For this reason, there is a need to provide teachers with guidance in constructing and evaluating questions that elicit more complex responses. Fortunately, a good deal of new technology is available for this purpose, mainly as a result of advances that have been made in the area of performance-based assessment.

Grades

The grades students have received in previously completed courses can also provide information about particular strength areas. When grades reflect both performance on teacher-made assessments and other accomplishments in less-structured situations, they provide a more comprehensive picture of student abilities than can be derived from test scores alone. The advantages and disadvantages of course grades are well documented in the literature on tests and measurements, and all teachers have had experiences related to the grading process and the usefulness of grades. The value of course grades in the Total Talent Portfolio is similar to standardized and teacher-made assessments: They all provide a quick overview of general strengths that may be capitalized on when making decisions about possible modifications in the regular curriculum, enrichment cluster placement, or access to special opportunities that are available in the continuum of special services.

For example, Mark, a sixth-grade student with consistently poor grades and a lack of interest in all subjects except science, was placed in a science enrichment cluster. This placement may seem obvious, but prior to the initiation of a SEM program, the only supplementary services made available to him related to his deficiencies. Special science opportunities were actually denied to Mark because he did not measure up in other curricular areas. The enrichment program was also the catalyst for curricular modifications. Decisions made in meetings of Mark's middle school teachers provided him opportunities to substitute nonfiction and science fiction reading selections for other required reading in language arts, and creative writing assignments were replaced with writing that focused on scientific interests. The social studies teacher also allowed him to replace regular assignments with reports about scientific people and events in the countries they were studying, and the enrichment specialist arranged for Mark to assist the computer specialist by repairing equipment.

Teacher Ratings

One of the instruments that has been a longstanding part of the SEM is a series of rating scales used to identify behavioral characteristics reflecting superior learning potentials. The Scales for Rating the Behavioral Characteristics of Superior Students (SCRBSS; Renzulli, Smith, White, Callahan, & Hartman, 1976; Renzulli et al., 2002) have been used widely for special program assessment; however, their use in the Total Talent Portfolio is not intended to label students. Rather, the purpose of the scales, like all other items in the portfolio, is to contribute information that will result in a comprehensive picture of a student's strengths. The SCRBSS consists of the following 10 scales, each of which is named for the specific ability area it is designed to evaluate: Learning, Motivation, Creativity, Leadership, Art, Music, Dramatics, Communication (Precision), Communication (Expressiveness), and Planning. Each scale is composed of a series of items derived from the research literature dealing with specific manifestations of superior abilities in the 10 areas.

When using the SCRBSS, it is important to analyze students' ratings on each of the selected scales separately. The 10 dimensions of the instrument represent relatively different sets of behavioral characteristics, and, therefore, no attempt should be made to add the subscores together to form a total score. Because of variations in student populations, the range of learning options that may be available in a particular school, and the availability of other types of data, it is impossible to recommend a predetermined set of superior scores for the scales. The best norm or frame of reference for SCRBSS is the individual student.

Like all information in the Total Talent Portfolio, SCRBSS ratings should be used in conjunction with other information as part of a comprehensive system for identifying student strengths. Every effort should be made to capitalize on individual strengths revealed by the ratings by devising learning experiences that develop these capacities. For example, a student who achieves high ratings on the Motivation Scale will probably profit from experiences that provide opportunities for self-initiated pursuits and an independent study approach to learning. A student with high scores on the Leadership Characteristics Scale should be given opportunities to organize activities and to assist the teacher and his or her classmates in developing plans of action for carrying out projects. Thus, a careful analysis of scale ratings can assist teachers in their efforts to develop more individualized learning experiences for individual and small groups who share common strengths.

GATHERING AND RECORDING INFORMATION ABOUT STUDENT INTERESTS

The second dimension of the Total Talent Portfolio is student interests. If there is a keystone in the overall structure of the SEM, it is student interests. All cognitive behavior is enhanced as a function of the degree of interest that is present in an act of learning, wherever that cognitive behavior may be on the continuum from basic skill learning to higher levels of conceptualization and creative productivity. The relationship between interest and learning was undoubtedly recognized by the first humans on Earth, but it became a topic of scientific inquiry in the nineteenth century, when philosophers recognized the close relationship between interest and learning (James, 1885). Dewey (1913) and Thorndike (1921) called attention to the important role that interests play in all forms and levels of learning. They also recognized the importance of the interestingness of tasks and objects as well as the personal characteristics of the learner. Numerous empirical studies have also demonstrated that individual interests have profound influences on learning (Krapp, 1989; Renninger, 1989, 1990; Schiefele, 1989), and developmental theorists have also acknowledged the importance of interests. "It is primarily in those areas in which one takes a deep personal interest and has staked a salient aspect of one's identity that the more individualized and 'creative' components of one's personality are engaged and expressed" (Albert & Runco, 1986, p. 335). Gruber (1986) argued that the main force in the self-construction of the extraordinary is the person's own activities and interests. Research studies that have examined the long-range effects of participation in enrichment-based programs have indicated that the single best indicator of college majors and expressions of career choice on the parts of young adults have been intensive involvement in projects based on early interests (Hébert, 1993). Studies have also shown that students who participated in a SEM program for five years or longer and exhibited higher levels of creative productivity than their peers displayed early, consistent, and more intense interests (Renzulli & Reis, 1994).

The Interest-a-lyzer

Building educational experiences around student interests is probably one of the single most effective ways to guarantee that enrichment practices will be introduced into a school. In numerous evaluation studies of SEM programs, student comments about most-favored practices almost always dealt with greater freedom to select at least part of the work they pursued. A planned strategy for helping students examine their present and potential interests is based on an instrument called the Interest-a-lyzer.

Sample items from the Interest-a-lyzer:

- Imagine that your class has decided to create its own video production company. Each person has been asked to sign up for his or her first, second, or third choice for one of the listed jobs such as actor/actress, director, prop person, scenery designer, etc.
- Computers and telephone technology allow us to communicate with people all over the world. Imagine that your school has installed an Internet or telephone system that will allow you to communicate with anyone in the world. With whom would you correspond?
- Imagine that you have the opportunity to travel to a new and exciting city. You can select three places to visit (art gallery, symphony orchestra, court room, zoo, stock market, historical sites). Select three places to visit.

This instrument has been used with students in Grades 4 through 9, and it has also been adapted for use with younger children (McGreevy, 1982), secondary students (Hébert, Sorenson, & Renzulli, 1997), and adults (Renzulli, 1977b). The items consist of a variety of real and hypothetical situations to which students are asked to respond in terms of the choices they would make (or have made) were they involved in these situations. The main purpose of the Interest-a-lyzer is to open up communication both within the student and between students and teachers. It also is designed to facilitate discussion between groups of students with similar interests who are attempting to identify areas in which they might like to pursue advanced-level studies.

Field tests of the Interest-a-lyzer have shown that this instrument can serve as the basis for lively group discussions or in-depth counseling sessions with individual students. Field tests have shown, also, that the self-analysis of interests is an ongoing process that should not be rushed and that certain steps should be taken to avoid peer pressure that may lead to group conformity or stereotyped responses. An attempt has been made to overcome some of these problems by developing a careful set of directions for the instrument; however, teachers should allow students maximum freedom of choice in deciding how and with whom they would like to discuss their responses.

Another concern that came to our attention during field tests of the Interest-a-lyzer was that young children often have only limited exposure to certain topics. One item, for example, deals with a hypothetical situation in which students are asked to indicate their preferences for working on various feature sections of a newspaper. Because many students involved in the field test were unfamiliar with the diversity of feature sections, a brainstorming activity was planned in which students were asked to identify and cut out many different parts of newspapers. The clippings were displayed in the form of a bulletin board collage, and group discussions were used to call attention to the nature and function of each section. This activity helped students respond to the questionnaire item in a more meaningful way. It is recommended that people using this instrument consider each item in relation to the age and maturity of students with whom they are working and that activities such as the one described here be organized whenever there is any doubt as to students' familiarity with the content of the respective items. Teachers may also want to modify or add their own items to the instrument, especially when dealing with very young children or students from culturally diverse populations.

The Interest-a-lyzer is not the type of instrument that yields a numerical score; rather, it is designed in a way that allows for pattern analysis. The major patterns or factors that might emerge from the instrument are as follows:

1. Fine Arts

2. Scientific and Technical

3. Creative Writing and Journalism

4. Legal, Political, and Judicial

5. Mathematical

6. Managerial

7. Historical

8. Athletic and Outdoor-Related Activities

9. Performing Arts

10. Business

11. Consumer Action and Environment-Related Activities

Remember that (a) these factors represent general fields or families of interest and (b) numerous ways exist in which an individual may be interested in any particular field. Thus, identifying general patterns is only the first step in interest analysis. General interests must be refined and focused so that students eventually identify specific problems in a general field or a combination of fields. Additional preferences that we should look for in discussions based on the Interest-a-lyzer are as follows:

- Activities that require precision and accuracy (e.g., editing, scientific experiments, observation, musical conducting)
- Preferences for meeting and dealing with people (e.g., teaching, organizing a clean-up-the-environment campaign)

- Activities that show preferences for helping people (e.g., serving as a volunteer at a daycare center or kindergarten classroom; becoming a doctor, dentist, or veterinarian)
- Preferences for activities that involve color, materials, artistic products that have eye appeal, and any and all types of design (e.g., costumes, clothing play sets, landscape, jewelry, metal sculpture)
- Preferences for working with machines, tools, or precision equipment (e.g., photography, building scenery, refinishing furniture)
- Activities that involve creative expression through music, writing, drawing, or movement (e.g., cartooning, writing plays, composing, choreography)
- Preferences for leadership, making money, or "running things" (e.g., play director, business manager, officer in an organization)
- A concern for legal, moral, or philosophical issues (e.g., circulating a petition to start an animal shelter, campaigning for equal participation of girls in sports activities)
- Activities that show a preference for working with computational and numerical problems (e.g., using calculators, computers, or Internet resources; inventing mathematical games or puzzles; working on brain teasers)
- Activities that show a preference for outdoor work (e.g., growing things, camping, studying wildlife)

Many interrelationships and areas of overlap exist in these examples; a great deal of the art of good teaching is to sort out interests with the greatest potential for further and, we hope, more intensive follow-up. Information and conclusions that result from the analysis of student interests should be noted on the Interest-a-lyzer or similar documents and then placed in the Total Talent Portfolio.

Individualization and the Role of Learning Styles

One of the major assumptions underlying the SEM is that total respect for the individual learner must also take into consideration how the child would like to pursue a particular activity, as well as the rate of learning and the child's preference for a particular topic or area of study. This is not to say that complete freedom of choice can or should exist for all educational activities. On the contrary, there are certain basic skill areas that are taught more appropriately by one approach than another. The number of such cases, however, is more limited than current practices would suggest, and additional steps toward individualization for learning style seem warranted.

Research studies are currently available that support a concept of learning that educators have known about and talked about for years. The concept is that students usually learn more easily and enjoyably when they are taught in a manner consistent with their preferred style of learning. Preferences may vary within the individual according to content area and interest in certain topics; however, if some effort is not made to identify and accommodate these preferences, a valuable opportunity to improve both student achievement and enjoyment for learning will be wasted. As Torrance (1965) has pointed out, "Alert teachers have always been aware of the fact that when they change their method of teaching, certain children who had appeared to be slow learners or even nonlearners become outstanding achievers" (p. 253).

A large number of studies have concluded that matching students with various learning environments affects cognitive outcomes and student satisfaction with different types of educational processes (Brophy & Good, 1974; Hunt, 1971; Kagan, 1966; Smith, 1976). Overall, the findings from these investigations suggest that an effort to match teaching strategies to students' learning-style preferences can be beneficial. Learning-style matching approaches were found not only to give students an opportunity to become involved in planning their educational experiences, but also to enhance students' attitudes toward the subject matter under consideration, and, in some cases, to increase scores on end-of-unit examinations. These positive findings, combined with the growing concern about the importance of learning styles, lead us to suggest that a comprehensive model must pay serious attention to the assessment and analysis of styles as well as abilities and interests. This concern is even more relevant today because of greater efforts to organize learning experiences that pay greater attention to multicultural differences among the school population.

Accordingly, the third dimension of the Total Talent Portfolio is a series of indicators of student preferences for learning. They consist of instructional-style preferences, learning environment preferences, thinking-style preferences, and preferences for various types of product styles and formats. These indicators provide information about what individuals are likely to do in a variety of learning situations. Whereas maximum performance indicators and interests are usually specific to a particular aptitude or content domain, preferences for performance cut across content domains, interpersonal relations, and various ways in which schools are organized for learning. Preferences represent the characteristic ways in which students adapt and organize the assets they bring to various learning situations. For example, the student mentioned earlier who was interested in dolphins may prefer to pursue this interest through a group project or aquarium internship rather than through a lecture, discussion, or simulation format.

Although we recognize that it is impossible to accommodate all of these preferences in the context of standard classroom operation, we believe that an understanding of the factors in general, and familiarity with at least some of their manifestations in students, will greatly enhance those opportunities when teachers can introduce enrichment experiences into the schedule. Even in more-flexible school structures such as the enrichment clusters and the continuum of special services, it may not be possible to accommodate the full range of individual attributes represented in the four style-preference categories of Figure 4.1A. Nevertheless, using as much of this information as possible, whenever possible, should be a major goal of all learning situations. It is only through the use of these types of information that schools can break through the barrier of depersonalization that makes these institutions uninviting places and learning unimportant for so many of our students.

INSTRUCTIONAL STYLES PREFERENCES

The third column of Figure 4.1A lists a broad range of instructional style preferences that are familiar to most teachers. In some cases, these instructional techniques or styles can also be found in the literature under the title of *learning styles*. Although several definitions of instructional styles can be found in the educational and psychological literature (Smith, 1976), the definition we recommend focuses on (a) the specific and identifiable techniques for organizing learning for individuals or for groups of varying size and (b) the degree of structure inherent in any instructional technique. Our definition and related descriptions of instructional-style alternatives have been adopted in an attempt to remove some of the mystery that surrounds the notion of learning styles. By focusing on instructional practices familiar to most teachers, we overcome the drawback of working with a "psychological middleman" that requires teachers to second-guess how certain psychological concepts (e.g., abstract-random learner) might be used in a learning situation. Although alternative conceptions have value with respect to stimulating follow-up research that could eventually affect educational practice, our concern is for a theoretically sound, yet practical, approach that has direct and immediate implications for classroom practice.

Examination of the third column of Figure 4.1A reveals that the several instructional styles listed exist on a continuum, beginning with highly structured approaches to learning and progressing to less-structured learning situations. Entire books have been devoted to the study of various instructional techniques, and it is beyond the scope of this book to present a comprehensive analysis of this literature. However, for the purpose of providing a common frame of reference for the discussion that follows, we will present a brief description of the progression from structured to unstructured techniques.

Recitation and Drill

This traditional and widely used approach to instruction involves a teacher asking questions and calling on students to respond with the appropriate information. In contrast to discussion, where students are called on to think about the relationships among facts, recitation typically entails questions that can be answered by statements of fact. The responses that students provide for these questions are evaluated in terms of the correctness of facts. Recitation is usually preceded by assignment of a topic and rote study on the parts of students.

Programmed and Computer-Assisted Instruction

This type of instruction is based on students working alone on material that has been sequenced to teach a particular concept. The material characteristically consists of short statements that terminate with a question or a blank to be filled in. The statements are presented electronically or in a textbook or workbook. Other features of programmed instruction include a provision for immediate feedback, students' determination of their own rates of progress, highly organized content, and low rate of student error. A good deal of computer software has been developed in recent years, and it tends to take one of three forms: tutorial, in which the computer presents new information; drill and practice, in which the computer is used for remediation; and simulations, which involve the learner in relatively complex problem solving.

Peer Tutoring

This technique involves the use of students as teachers of other students. The tutoring situation can be highly structured (e.g., the teacher assigns a tutor to a particular child and defines the content to be covered) or it can be relatively unstructured (e.g., students select their own tutors and cover material that they determine). Although peer tutoring can involve upper-grade students tutoring younger children, the practice is usually limited to cooperative arrangements in a classroom.

Lecture

Lecture refers to a verbal presentation in which the teacher or another individual perceived as an expert in a particular area communicates the ideas and concepts to be acquired. The lecture method is usually marked by a lack of discussion or interchange between teacher and students; the teacher talks to students. The lecturer organizes and presents the material in the sequence and style he or she prefers.

Discussion

Discussion is characterized by two-way interaction between teacher and students or among students. As opposed to the straight lecture method, group discussion involves a greater degree of active participation on the parts of students. Ideally, discussion as a technique requires students to think about the relationships among facts and concepts, to weigh the significance of facts and concepts, and to engage in critical analysis of them. Varying degrees of teacher domination are found, ranging from instances in which the teacher plays a nondirective, mediating role to ones in which the teacher asks most of the questions and provides the agenda and procedures to be followed.

Teaching Games and Simulations

Teaching games are activities that are fun for students to participate in and, at the same time, involve content that the teacher wants students to learn. Teaching games do not need to be realistic to be effective. They can involve the entire class or be geared to individual students or small groups of students. Simulations, on the other hand, are constructed around real-world situations that are used to teach content and skills through role playing. Generally, a specific concept, problem, or social process is outlined, and students are asked to role play in this context. The student-player must make decisions on the spot. These decisions, in turn, affect the next move of other players. The function of the teacher in this context is generally to coordinate the proposed actions. Realism is a primary concern in the development of simulations. Indeed, the more a simulation reflects real-world circumstances, the more successful the learning experience will be. The growing concern in recent years to introduce more realism into the curriculum has resulted in greater popularity for this technique and an accompanying increase in the availability of simulation materials. Interactive computer software has also added new opportunities for problem solving through the use of simulations.

Independent Study

Independent study can be based on independent choice of a topic, independence from the classroom at large, or both. Independent study can be highly structured (as in cases in which a course guide, assignments, and proficiency tests are prescribed), or less structured, allowing students to pursue topics or areas of their own choice. Less-structured independent study is characterized by freedom from constant supervision, although there is interaction with others when needed. Typically, the student chooses an area of study, develops his or her own approach to gathering information, and produces some kind of outcome, such as an oral presentation or a research paper. If students cover a regular course or unit through independent study, they are usually held accountable using the same evaluation criteria as students who take the course through traditional procedures. Using a combination of guided and unguided independent study is an excellent way to allow individuals or small groups to cover material at a faster pace than the pace of a classroom in general. Self-directedness, effective time management skills, and the ability to work cooperatively with others are characteristic of people who prefer this style of learning.

Projects

The project method, also described in the literature as the group investigation model, shares several characteristics with unguided independent study. This method will be dealt with at greater length in our discussion of Type III enrichment in Chapter Six. The project method is characterized by individual pursuits or by groups of students working together. In some cases, the project may fulfill the requirements of an assignment, and students frequently extend their work beyond the original requirements to create a product with real-world applications. In other cases, the project may originate with the students. In all cases, the project results in a final product or service that can be shared with other students. Students work with varying degrees of direction from the teacher or other adults, but, typically, the major responsibility for project management rests with students.

Internships, Apprenticeships, and Mentorships

Learning experiences in this category usually involve placing individuals or small groups of students in workplace situations under the direction of adults with high degrees of expertise in a particular profession or area of study. This approach to learning dates back to ancient times and was the forerunner of formal schools. The degree of structure in these situations varies according to the amount of control exercised by adults with whom young people work; however, the use of internships, apprenticeships, and mentorships has been found to be a highly successful method for students who do not adjust well to formal classroom situations and for students who have already developed high levels of interest, motivation, and achievement in a particular area.

LEARNING ENVIRONMENT PREFERENCES

Environmental preferences have not been investigated to the same extent as preferences for instructional style; however, a small body of research and a large measure of common sense suggest that the social and physical aspects of the environment affect various kinds of school performance. Amabile (1983) reviewed research dealing with social and environmental factors that influence creativity in school-age learners. The social contexts in which people operate reflect their preferences for closeness and interaction with others. When a person is given freedom of choice, the extent to which he or she pursues group affiliation is almost always an indicator of social-style preferences. Some students thrive in small or large peer group situations, others prefer to work with a single partner, and still others prefer to work alone or with an adult. Environmental preferences, like the instructional preferences discussed earlier, may vary as a function of the material being taught, the nature of the task to be accomplished, and the social relationships that exist in any given group of students. Most modern classrooms provide variations in the learning environment, but these variations are usually offered to students on a one-choice-at-a-time basis. In other words, a teacher may alternate among organizational arrangements such as individual seatwork, cooperative learning groups, and sustained silent reading; however, students are usually not given a choice outside the organizational arrangement selected by the teacher. Although a predominant organizational arrangement may be necessary for purposes of efficiency and classroom control, we recommend that some attention be given to modification or "waivers" when it is clear that some students will benefit from a variation in the learning environment.

Dunn and Dunn (1992, 1993) investigated factors that affect learners in four general categories. The first category consists of environmental influences such as sound, light, temperature, and the physical design of the learning environment. The second category consists of emotional factors such as motivation, persistence, responsibility, and the degree of structure in learning situations. The third category focuses on the sociological needs of learners and is based on preferences for learning-group arrangements (e.g., self, pair, small group, large group, with or without adults). The fourth category comprises factors related to the physical environment, such as perceptual modality preferences (e.g., auditory, visual, tactile, and kinesthetic), food intake, time of day, and the amount of mobility that is permitted in the learning environment. A 100-item instrument, entitled the Learning Style Inventory (Dunn, Dunn, & Price, 1975, 1978, 1979), provides factor scores and profiles for each of the four categories described earlier, and the authors have provided numerous practical suggestions for designing educational environments that take maximum advantage of individual learning styles.

A series of instruments designed by Henderson and Conrath (1991) uses a computerized assessment format to provide individual student profiles for modality preferences (visual, auditory, bodily/kinesthetic), group preferences (individual, group), expression preferences (oral, written), and preferences for linear, sequential activities or random, intuitive activities.

BENEFITS OF THE TOTAL TALENT PORTFOLIO

The main purpose of the portfolio is to provide as comprehensive a picture as possible about each student's strengths in the areas of abilities, interests, and styles. The easiest way to use the portfolio is to prepare a folder for each student, and include in the folder a copy of Figure 4.1A. Circling items that reflect strength areas on this figure provides a comprehensive picture of strengths that can be capitalized on in various learning situations. Circled items should be backed up by including in the folder examples of student work that are illustrative of the circled items. More detailed profiles can be prepared by simply pasting each of the six columns in Figure 4.1A on the left-hand side of blank pages and using the remainder of each page to record anecdotal notes, observations, and references to work samples included in the portfolio. Note that the categories listed in each column are only guides for recording certain types of information. Additional types of proficiency information may be included as a result of particular learning opportunities that may exist in certain schools or classrooms, or because of certain behavioral strengths displayed by students that fall outside of the categories and items specified in the columns of Figure 4.1A. This figure, or any form derived from it, is designed to call attention to documented student characteristics, to provide an overview of all information in the portfolio, and to serve as the basis for discussions geared toward making programming decisions. Student work, selected by teachers and students, should be placed in the portfolio, and examples of particular strengths in a work sample should be marked and annotated with attached notes or marginal comments by the teacher and student.

Portfolios should be reviewed by teams of teachers at least four times a year, and portfolios should also serve as focal points for meetings with parents. The cover sheet of the portfolio should include summary notations about particular accomplishments in each of the school structures at which the SEM is targeted. The portfolio should travel with students from year to year and should serve as the basis for briefing subsequent-year teachers about individual student strengths and accomplishments.

For the Total Talent Portfolio to achieve maximum effectiveness, it is necessary to avoid three pitfalls that have characterized other systems for gathering and recording information about student performance. These pitfalls are

1. The escalation of needless paperwork

2. The tendency to look at discrete items in student records

3. The focus on deficiencies that characterizes so much of school record keeping

Any process for recording information about students can easily turn into another "paperwork nightmare" for teachers. When this happens, the original intent of vehicles such as the portfolio becomes lost in yet another round of record-keeping overkill and resistance on the part of teachers to use the information in positive ways. We can avoid this pitfall by not converting the portfolio into another set of boxes, checklists, numerical ratings, or percentile scales. Even when the portfolio does include information derived from instruments that yield psychometric scores, we should not take this information too seriously. Most psychometric reporting is based on normative scales that are designed to compare groups of students in categories (e.g., age, grade, gender, socioeconomic level). The Total Talent Portfolio is intended to look at individual students in a noncomparative way. We do not want to know how a student stacks up against other students. Rather, we want to know how particular abilities, interests, and styles stack up in the student himself or herself, and we want to know this in a very general way. "Liza's best academic area is math" is a statement that allows us to make educational decisions that capitalize on strengths. We do not need complex, comparative statistics to make these decisions for us.

The second pitfall, focusing on discrete items, can best be avoided by noting the interactions among several items in the portfolio that result in a comprehensive picture of student performance and potential. "Liza's best academic area is math, she seems to like science and computers best, she likes to work in small groups, and she likes to draw" is a rich source of information that extends far beyond any individual element of the statement. A teacher may not be able to accommodate all of these strengths, interests, and preferences all of the time, or even most of the time, but if they are not accommodated at least part of the time, an exceptional opportunity is lost to capitalize on those things that make Liza a unique person and a unique learner. The payoff that results when we make adjustments that accommodate each student's uniqueness is not only in terms of better performance but also in higher motivation and greater enjoyment of learning.

A focus on deficiencies is the most serious pitfall of student record-keeping systems. The Total Talent Portfolio differs from traditional permanent record folders in both the use and the psychology of the portfolio as well as the information contained in it. Most permanent records are used for class placement in schools in which ability grouping is practiced and for placement in skill-level groups within classrooms. They also are notorious for calling attention to learning deficiencies and to personal, social, or family problems. In most instances, when a permanent record folder is pulled during the school year, it is almost always in connection with a present or impending problem. We do not want this psychology of deficit and rehabilitation to be cast over the Total Talent Portfolio; therefore, we recommend that it not become a part of the traditional permanent record folder. Nor do we recommend that it become a replacement for existing records. Our focus on positive attributes should remain unmixed from information about problems and deficits because the power of negative information about students always seems to predominate, and, therefore, circumscribe the positive focus that the portfolio is designed to accentuate. A ground rule when reviewing and discussing portfolios is, therefore, that their only use should be for making decisions about specific and positive actions that will further a student's strength areas.

No one is naive enough to believe that in the foreseeable future schools will magically convert from a curricular decision-making process that is externally driven and group oriented to one that is tailored to the broad range of characteristics documented in the Total Talent Portfolio. The complexity of the educational system and the many masters that teachers are required to serve make it difficult to accommodate the broad array of abilities, interests, and styles that characterize individual learners, but the widespread and well-documented dissatisfaction with schools in general suggests that the opportunity is ripe for experimentation and small steps toward organizing learning environments that are more responsive to the uniqueness of individual students. Systemic educational reform should begin in the classroom, where learners, teachers, and curriculum interact, rather than in yet another set of regulations or list of standards and outcomes. The Total Talent Portfolio, either in paper or electronic format, is a tool that can help focus attention on the enjoyment of learning for all students, student's strengths, and the positive interactions that represent engaging acts in learning.

5

Curriculum Compacting and Differentiation

A major service delivery component of the Schoolwide Enrichment Model consists of a series of procedures and recommendations for curriculum modification and differentiation so that the abilities and interests of all students can be served. This chapter consists of a step-by-step procedure for modifying existing curriculum. To accommodate for the needs of students across so many different levels of academic achievement, many teachers have adopted a variety of within-classroom strategies collectively referred to as *differentiated instruction*. Differentiation is an attempt to address the variation of learners in the classroom through multiple approaches that modify instruction and curriculum to match the individual needs of students (Tomlinson, 2000). Tomlinson (1995) emphasized that when teachers differentiate curriculum, they stop acting as dispensers of knowledge and, instead, serve as organizers of learning opportunities. Differentiation of instruction and curriculum suggests that students can be provided with materials and work of varied levels of difficulty with scaffolding, diverse kinds of grouping, and different time schedules (Tomlinson, 2000).

Renzulli (1977a, 1988a; Renzulli & Reis, 1997) defined differentiation as encompassing five dimensions: content, process, products, classroom organization and management, and the teacher's own commitment to change himself or herself into a learner as well as a teacher. The differentiation of *content* involves adding more depth to the curriculum by focusing on structures of knowledge, basic principles, functional concepts, and methods of inquiry in particular disciplines. The differentiation of *process* incorporates the use of various instructional strategies and materials to enhance and motivate various students' learning styles. The differentiation of *products* enhances students' communication skills by encouraging them to express

75

themselves in a variety of ways. To differentiate *classroom management*, teachers can change the physical environment and grouping patterns they use in class and vary the allocation of time and resources for both groups and individuals.

Classroom differentiation strategies can also be greatly enhanced by using the Internet in a variety of creative ways. Last, teachers can differentiate *themselves* by modeling the roles of athletic or drama coaches, stage or production managers, promotional agents, and academic advisers. All these roles differ qualitatively from the role of teacher as instructor. Teachers can also inject themselves into the material through a process called *artistic modification* (Renzulli, 1988a). This process guides teachers in the sharing of direct, indirect, and vicarious experiences related to personal interests, travel experiences, collections, hobbies, and teachers' extracurricular involvements that can enhance content.

Curriculum compacting is a differentiation strategy that incorporates content, process, products, classroom management, and teachers' personal commitment to accommodating individual and small-group differences. This approach can benefit teachers of all grades in most content areas and addresses the demand for more challenging learning experiences designed to help all students achieve at high levels and realize their potential.

CURRICULUM COMPACTING: DEFINITIONS AND STEPS FOR IMPLEMENTATION

Curriculum compacting streamlines the grade-level curriculum for high-potential students to enable time for more challenging and interesting work. This differentiation strategy was specifically designed to make appropriate curricular adjustments for students in any curricular area and at any grade level. The procedure involves (a) defining the goals and outcomes of a particular unit or block of instruction, (b) determining and documenting the students who have already mastered most or all of a specified set of learning outcomes, and (c) providing replacement strategies for material already mastered through the use of instructional options that enable a more challenging, interesting, and productive use of the student's time.

Most teachers indicate that they are committed to meeting students' individual needs. Yet many teachers do not have background information to put this commitment into practice. Related research demonstrates that many talented students receive little differentiation of curriculum and instruction and spend a great deal of time in school doing work that they have already mastered (Archambault et al., 1992; Reis et al., 1993; Westberg, Archambault, Dobyns, & Salvin, 1992). Too often, for example, some of our brightest students spend time relearning material they already know, which can lead to frustration, boredom, and, ultimately, underachievement. Curriculum compacting has been effective in addressing underachievement when the compacted regular curriculum is replaced with self-selected work in a high-interest area, making schoolwork much more enjoyable (Baum, Renzulli, & Hébert, 1995; Reis et al., 1993).

Curriculum compacting, as presented in this chapter, has been field tested since 1975. It has been used with individuals and groups of students with above-average ability in any academic, artistic, or vocational area. Most important, research demonstrates that compacting can dramatically reduce redundancy and challenge gifted students to new heights of excellence (Reis et al., 1993). It can be particularly meaningful for high-ability students who are underachieving because it provides one clear way to streamline work that may be too easy and replace that work with more challenging work and also with self-selected opportunities in that area or in another area of interest.

Many educators would like to adapt the regular curriculum for their above-average students. Accomplishing this, however, is no small task. Too little time, too many curricular objectives, and poor organizational structures all can take their toll on even the most-dedicated professionals. This brief chapter overview is designed to help teachers overcome those obstacles. Targeted for elementary and middle-level educators, it explains how to streamline or compact curriculum through a practical, step-by-step approach. Readers will learn the skills required to modify curriculum, as well as techniques for pretesting students and preparing enrichment options. Practical issues such as record keeping and administrative support are also included. Both efficient and complete, these guidelines will save valuable classroom time for both teachers and students.

DEFINING CURRICULUM COMPACTING

An overview of the curriculum compacting process is best provided by the use of the management form "The Compactor," as presented in Figure 5.1. It serves as both an organizational and record-keeping tool. Teachers usually complete one form per student or one form for a group of students with similar curricular strengths. Completed compactors should be kept in students' academic files and updated regularly. The form can also be used for small groups of students who are working at approximately the same level (e.g., a reading or math group) and as an addendum to an Individualized Education Plan (IEP) in states in which services for gifted students fall under special education laws.

The Compactor is divided into three columns:

• The first column includes information on learning objectives and student strengths in those areas. Teachers should list the objectives for a particular unit of study, followed by data on students' proficiency in those objectives, including test scores, behavioral profiles, and past academic records.

• In the second column, teachers should list the ways in which they will pre-assess whether students already know the skills that will be taught in class. The pretest or preassessment strategies they select, along with results of those assessments, should be listed in this column. The assessment instruments can be formal measures such as tests, or informal measures such as performance assessments based on observations of class participation and written assignments. Specificity of knowledge and objectives is important; recording an overall score of 85% on 10 objectives, for example, sheds little light on what portion of the material can be compacted, because students might show limited mastery of some objectives and high levels of mastery of others.

• Column Three is used to record information about acceleration or enrichment options. To determine these options, teachers must consider students' individual interests and learning styles. They should not uniformly replace compacted regular curriculum work with harder, more-advanced material that is solely determined by

Figure 5.1 The Compactor

INDIVIDUAL EDUCATIONAL PROGRAMMING GUIDE

The Compactor

Prepared by Joseph S. Renzulli
Linda M. Smith

NAME _____ AGE _____ TEACHER(S) _____

Individual Conference Dates
and Persons Participating in
Planning of IEP

SCHOOL _____ GRADE _____ PARENT(S) _____

_____ _____ _____ _____

CURRICULUM AREAS TO BE CONSIDERED FOR COMPACTING Provide a brief description of basic material to be covered during this marking period and the assessment information or evidence that suggests the need for compacting.	PROCEDURES FOR COMPACTING BASIC MATERIAL Describe activities that will be used to guarantee proficiency in basic curricular areas.	ACCELERATION AND/OR ENRICHMENT ACTIVITIES Describe activities that will be used to provide advanced level learning experiences in each area of the regular curriculum.

☐ Check here if additional information is recorded on the reverse side.

the teacher. Many years of research and field testing have helped us learn that when teachers do this, students will learn a major lesson. They learn that if they do their best work, they are rewarded with more, harder work. Instead, we recommend that students' interests should be considered. If, for example, a student loves working on science fair projects, time to work on these projects can be used to replace material already mastered in a different content area. Teachers should be careful to help monitor the challenge level of the material being substituted. Too often, talented students do not understand the nature of effort and challenge because everything they encounter in school is too easy for them. Teachers must attempt to replace the compacted material with work that is engaging and challenging.

HOW TO USE THE COMPACTING PROCESS

The first of three phases of the compacting process consists of defining the goals and outcomes of a given unit or segment of instruction. This information is readily available in most subjects because specific goals and outcomes are included in teachers' manuals, curriculum guides, scope-and-sequence charts, and some of the new curricular frameworks that are emerging in connection with outcome-based education models. Teachers should examine these objectives to determine which represent the acquisition of new content or thinking skills as opposed to reviews or practice of material that has previously been taught. The scope and sequence charts prepared by publishers or a simple comparison of the table of contents of a basal series will provide a quick overview of new versus repeated material. A major goal of this phase of the compacting process is to help teachers make individual programming decisions; a larger professional-development goal is to help teachers be better analysts of the material they are teaching and better consumers of textbooks and prescribed curricular materials.

The second phase of curriculum compacting is to identify students who have already mastered the objectives or outcomes of a unit or segment of instruction that is about to be taught. Many of these students have the potential to master new material at a faster than normal pace, and knowing one's students well is, of course, the best way to begin the assessment process. Standardized achievement tests can serve as a good general screen for this step because they allow us to list the names of all students who are scoring one or more years above grade level in particular subject areas.

Being a candidate for compacting does not necessarily mean that a student knows all of the material under consideration. Therefore, the second step in identifying candidates involves the use of assessment techniques to evaluate specific learning outcomes. Unit pretests or end-of-unit tests that can be given as pretests are appropriate for this task, especially when it comes to the assessment of basic skills. An analysis of pretest results enables the teacher to document proficiency in specific skills and to select instructional activities or practice material necessary to bring the student up to a high level on any skill that may need some additional reinforcement.

The process is slightly modified for compacting content areas that are not as easily assessed as basic skills and for students who have not mastered the material but are judged to be candidates for more rapid coverage. First, students should understand the goals and procedures of compacting, including the nature of the replacement process. Underachieving students often regard compacting as a bargain as they may able to compact out of a segment of material that they already know (e.g., a unit that includes a series of chapters in a social studies text), and the procedures for verifying mastery at a high level should be specified. These procedures might consist of answering questions based on the chapters, writing an essay, or taking the standard end-of-unit test. The amount of time for completion of the unit should be specified, and procedures such as periodic progress reports or log entries for teacher review should be discussed and selected.

PROVIDING ACCELERATION AND ENRICHMENT OPTIONS FOR TALENTED STUDENTS

The final phase of the compacting process can be one of the most exciting aspects of teaching because it is based on cooperative decision making and creativity on the parts of both teachers and students. Time saved through curriculum compacting can be used to provide a variety of enrichment and acceleration opportunities for the student.

Enrichment strategies might include a variety of strategies such as those included in the Enrichment Triad Model (Renzulli, 1977a), which provide opportunities for exposure to new topics and ideas, methods training and creative and critical thinking activities, and opportunities to pursue advanced independent or small-group creative projects. This aspect of the compacting process should also be viewed as a creative opportunity for a teacher to serve as a mentor to one or two students who are not working up to potential. We have also observed another interesting occurrence that has resulted from the availability of curriculum compacting. When some previously bright but underachieving students realized that they could both economize on regularly assigned material and "earn time" to pursue self-selected interests, their motivation to complete regular assignments increased; as one student put it, "Everyone understands a good deal!" Several strategies have been suggested for differentiating instruction and curriculum for talented or high-potential students. They range from substitution of regular material for more advanced material to options such as independent-program or specific-content strategies (e.g., Great Books or Literature Circles). Many of these strategies can be used in combination with compacting or as replacement ideas after the students' curriculum has been compacted, as can acceleration, which enables students to engage in content that is appropriately challenging (Southern & Jones, 1992; Stanley, 1989) by joining students in a higher grade-level class or by doing advanced curricular materials while in the same class, a form of content acceleration.

ROSE: A SAMPLE COMPACTOR FORM

Rose is a fifth grader in a self-contained classroom. Her school, which is very small, is located in a lower socioeconomic, urban school district. Although Rose's reading and language scores range between 2 and 5 years above grade level, most of her 29 classmates are reading 1 to 2 years below grade level. This presented Rose's teacher with a common problem: What was the best way to instruct Rose? He agreed to compact her curriculum. Taking the easiest approach possible, he administered all of the unit and level tests in the Holt Basal Language Arts program and excused Rose from completing the activities and worksheets in the units where she showed proficiency (80% and greater). If Rose missed one or two questions, the teacher would quickly check for trends in those items: If an error pattern emerged, instruction would be provided to ensure concept mastery. Rose usually took part in language arts lessons 1 or 2 days a week. The balance of the time she spent with alternative projects, some of which she selected. This strategy spared Rose up to 6 or 8 hours a week of language arts instruction that was simply beneath her level. She joined the class instruction only when her pretests indicated she had not fully acquired the skills.

In the time saved through compacting, Rose engaged in a number of enrichment activities. First, she enjoyed as many as 5 hours a week in a resource room for high-ability students. This time was usually scheduled during her language arts class, benefiting both Rose and her teacher; he didn't have to search for enrichment options because Rose went to the resource room, and she didn't have make-up assignments because she was not missing essential work. Rose also visited a regional science center. Science was a second strength area for Rose, and based on the results of her Interest-a-lyzer, famous women were a special interest. Working closely with her teacher, Rose chose seven biographies of noted women in the science field. All of the books were extremely challenging and locally available. Three were even adult level, but Rose had no trouble reading them.

Rose's Compactor, which covered an entire semester, was updated in January. Her teacher remarked that compacting her curriculum had actually saved him time—time he would have spent correcting papers needlessly assigned! The value of compacting for Rose also convinced him that he should continue the process.

PROVIDING SUPPORT FOR TEACHERS TO IMPLEMENT COMPACTING

In our experiences with curriculum compacting professional development, we have learned that most teachers can implement compacting, but this process is easier for some teachers than for others. Some teachers see the form and read the previous brief explanation and are ready to start. Others require more coaching and help, and for that reason, we provided an eight-step process in a book we wrote with our colleague, Deborah Burns, about compacting.

Step One: Select Relevant Learning Objectives in a Subject Area or Grade Level

To select curricular content and learning objectives, teachers may refer to the formal curriculum guides issued by school districts or states, or the informal guides provided by textbook publishers. After locating the objectives, teachers must focus on those that are appropriate for their students. Often, there is a discrepancy between the objectives noted in the curriculum guides and those actually tested by the school districts. Other objectives may be redundant or overly ambitious, and so teachers should ask the following:

a. To what extent do these objectives represent new learning?
b. Which objectives will best help students increase their use of this content area?
c. Which objectives can be applied to the workplace?
d. Which objectives deal with developing skills or concepts, as opposed to merely memorizing facts?
e. Which objectives are important for high-ability students to understand?
f. Which objectives cannot be learned without formal or sustained instruction?
g. Which objectives reflect the priorities of the school district or state department of education?

After the objectives are selected, they should be listed by priority. Because of their importance, the higher ranked items are the ones teachers will concentrate on with the entire class, whereas the less-relevant ones are prime candidates for compacting. Simply having a set of learning objectives does not tell a teacher how or if these objectives can be adapted to meet students' individual needs. Teachers must know the subject matter, as well as their students' learning styles. Step Two in the compacting process can help teachers make these evaluations.

Step Two: Find an Appropriate Way to Pretest the Learning Objectives

Pretesting, as its name implies, is intended to measure students' skills and talents before instruction begins. It should provide teachers with precise information on

a. Which objectives students have already met
b. Which objectives students have not yet attained
c. Any problems that may prevent student progress with the objectives

Ideally, a pretest should demonstrate whether a student has full, partial, or little mastery of an objective. Objective-referenced tests can do that effectively, as they usually assess one objective at a time through short-answer or multiple-choice responses. On a practical level, these paper-and-pencil tests appeal to teachers because they can be administered in large-group settings, require little time to oversee or correct, and are readily available from textbook publishers or testing companies, allowing teachers to keep records of students' progress.

Performance-Based Assessment

Performance-based assessment is a popular alternative to objective-referenced tests. By asking students to do oral, written, or manipulative work in front of them, teachers can observe and evaluate the process students use to arrive at an answer. This procedure is especially successful with younger children who are not yet ready for paper-and-pencil tests. Students may be evaluated individually or in small groups, or through conferences, interviews, or portfolios of completed work. As with objective-referenced tests, this requires preplanning. Teachers must take the time to locate or create the performance tests, making sure that they are aligned with the desired learning objectives.

Step Three: Identify Students Who Should Take the Pretests

In Step Three, teachers identify students who should participate in the pretesting activity. To do this, teachers must first discern students' specific strengths. This step is critical for two reasons. First, it ensures that when students are excused from class for enrichment activities, they are absent only during their curricular strength times. Second, it eliminates the need to assign make-up work when the students return to the classroom. Academic records, standardized tests, class performance, and evaluations from former teachers are all effective means of pinpointing candidates for pretesting. Another method is observation. Teachers should watch for students who complete tasks quickly and accurately, finish reading assignments ahead of their peers, or seem bored or lost in daydreams. Some students will even tell their teachers that the work assigned is too easy.

Achievement and aptitude tests can be a valuable gauge of academic ability. By comparing students' subtest scores with local or national norms, educators can see which youngsters fall into the above-average ranges. Because these students usually know more or learn faster than their peers, it is safe to assume that they may benefit from pretesting. National test results confirm the fact that bright students do not necessarily excel in all subject areas. For example, those who score well in math will not always show equal ability in vocabulary. Likewise, students with good vocabulary skills are not always those who do best in reading comprehension. This underscores the importance of using more than one test and relying on a battery of data to evaluate students' strengths and weaknesses in specific content areas. Teachers must get a total academic picture.

Teachers must also remember that this information leads only to likely candidates for compacting. In other words, just because students perform well in a given area does not mean they have mastered all the learning objectives in that area. What's more, all test instruments are flawed to some degree. Establishing cutoff scores, then, is not an exact science. When it comes to measuring achievement, the debate still rages over "how high is high?" Overall, students who place above the 85th percentile on subtests of norm-referenced achievement tests may be considered viable candidates for compacting. Some teachers may decide that they want to pretest all students in the classroom. These pretests results can be used to organize ad hoc, small groups of students with common instructional needs.

Step Four: Pretest Students to Determine Mastery Levels

Pretests, both formal and informal, help teachers determine student mastery of course material. But what constitutes mastery? Because definitions of mastery vary so much, teachers in the same school should strive to reach a consensus. Deciding how and when to pretest students can be a time-intensive exercise. One shortcut is to increase the number of students or objectives examined at one time; for example, if a chapter in a math text covers 10 objectives, a small group of students, or the entire class, could be tested on all 10 objectives in one sitting. If small-group testing is not feasible, teachers can follow the same procedures with individual students. Some educators may want to install a permanent "testing table" for this purpose; others may let students score and record their own test results to save time.

Performance-Based Testing

Some teachers may want to use performance-based testing. If they choose this form of pretesting, they should observe students closely by taking notes, tracing thought patterns, and posing open-ended questions to assess proficiency with the objectives. Let's assume, for example, that the assignment is to write a persuasive essay. The instructions could be to actually create and submit an essay, which teachers would read and analyze for content; teachers could also ask students how they went about organizing their thoughts to see if they truly understand the assignment. Similar sessions can be held to assess other abilities, such as decoding rules, solving problems, or processing science skills. Through these evaluations, many teachers will discover the value of performance-based testing as a supplement to pretesting.

Pretests may also be administered to the entire class. Although it may entail more work for the teacher, it provides the opportunity for all students to demonstrate their strength in an area. In fact, involving everyone in the process can boost individual confidence and build a stronger sense of community in the classroom. Equipped with a matrix of learning objectives, teachers can fill in the test results and form small, flexible groups based on skill needs.

Mastery levels are bound to fluctuate among students. Youngsters with learning disabilities, visual or hearing impairments, or who speak English as a second language must often be evaluated differently than their peers. Consider, for example, a student who demonstrates superior understanding of science concepts. If the goal of compacting is to develop the potential talents of all students, then shouldn't she too be allowed to take part in alternative learning activities, even if her spelling and language arts skills are low? There are, in fact, several ways to accomplish this:

a. Try to compact the students in their best content area, even though performance may be below grade level in another content area. Students can spend classroom time, as well as some recess, lunch, or afterschool time, in alternative activities.

b. Place the students in enrichment programs during the language arts period, because language arts are incorporated into most other subjects. Although students may not be working with the same set of skills as those being taught, they would apply other language arts skills during research, problem-solving, and project-sharing exercises.

Implementing curriculum compacting for special-needs students may be difficult for many teachers, but studies show that the rewards justify the hours spent. Engaging these students in the process can elevate self-esteem, foster positive attitudes toward learning, and, in the long-term, improve performance. There are a number of resources that teachers can use to help conduct pretests:

• Parent volunteers, aides, and tutors can lend a hand administering tests.
• Reading, math, and other curriculum specialists can assist in identifying learning objectives and student strengths.
• District consultants and teachers of gifted children may be available to help with pretests and other aspects of compacting. This service is especially vital during the first few years, when teachers are trying to organize and implement the compacting program.
• Companies are developing new computer technology to pretest and provide individual instruction to targeted students.

Step Five: Streamline Practice or Instructional Time for Students Who Show Mastery of the Objectives

Students who have a thorough grasp of the learning objectives should be allowed to take part in enrichment or acceleration activities. This exposes them, during class time, to material that is not only new and stimulating, but more closely aligned to their learning rates and abilities. For illustration purposes, let's say that a student has mastered three out of five objectives in a given unit. It follows, then, that the student should not take part in the classroom instruction of those three objectives. Depending on the teacher, some students may be excused from specific class sessions (for example, the Monday and Wednesday portions of vocabulary building), whereas others may forgo certain chapters or pages in the text or specific sets of learning activities.

Step Six: Provide Small-Group or Individualized Instruction for Students Who Have Not Mastered All the Objectives But Can Do So Quickly

Teachers can provide differentiated opportunities to instruct high-potential students who qualify for compacting, but have not yet mastered all the objectives. If this occurs, teachers can reduce the number of groups in their classrooms and provide help for students who have high potential but have not mastered all of the objectives as their more academically advanced chronological peers. This may enable teachers to have fewer groups in their classrooms.

Content compacting differs from skills compacting. As the name implies, it compresses overall course material that students have already mastered or are able to master in a fraction of the normal time. Skills compacting, on the other hand, eliminates specific skills that students have already acquired. Content compacting is also designed for general knowledge subjects—social studies, science, and literature—whereas skills compacting is intended for mathematics, spelling, grammar, and language mechanics.

Skills compacting is easier to accomplish. Pretesting is a simpler process, and mastery can be documented more efficiently. Content compacting, on the other hand, is more flexible, as students can absorb the material at their own speed. In content compacting, the means of evaluation are also less formal; teachers may require an essay, an interview, or an open-ended, short-answer test.

Step Seven: Offer Academic Alternatives for Students Whose Curriculum Has Been Compacted

Alternatives often exist to provide acceleration or enrichment for students whose curriculum has been compacted. This step proved to be the most challenging and the most creative for teachers who participated in our study. The possibilities for replacement activities include the following:

- Providing an accelerated curriculum based on advanced concepts
- Offering enhancements using technology such as Renzulli Learning
- Offering more challenging content (alternative texts, fiction or nonfiction works)
- Adapting classwork to individual curricular needs or learning styles
- Initiating individual or small-group projects using contracts or management plans
- Using interest or learning centers
- Providing opportunities for self-directed learning or decision making
- Offering minicourses on research topics or other high-interest areas
- Establishing small seminar groups for advanced studies
- Using mentors to guide in learning advanced content or pursuing independent studies
- Providing units or assignments that are self-directed, such as creative writing, game creation, and creative and critical-thinking training

Teachers will have to decide which replacement activities to use, and their decisions will be based on factors such as time, space, resources, school policy, and help from other faculty (such as a gifted program teacher or a library media specialist).

Although practical concerns should be considered, however, what should ultimately determine replacement activities are the degree of academic challenge *and* students' interests. If students understand that if they demonstrate proficiency, they will earn some time to pursue their own interests, they will often work to earn this opportunity. Our role as teachers is to escalate the challenge level of the material students are pursuing to be able to provide adequate academic challenges. Additional suggested alternatives for students are provided after Step Eight.

Step Eight: Keep Records of the Compacting Process and Instructional Options for Compacted Students

Any differentiated program requires added record keeping. Unlike a regular classroom where all students are on the same page or exercise at any given time, teachers who provide a compacted curriculum have students doing different assignments at different levels and different times. Keeping concise records, then, is essential and can be time consuming without proper planning. Teachers and administrators should collectively decide how the compacting process should be documented, and all written documentation should include these basics:

a. Student strength areas, as verified by test scores or performance
b. The pretests used to determine mastery and the learning objectives that were eliminated
c. Recommended enrichment and acceleration activities

The Compactor form was expressly designed to track the compacting process. Teachers employed in states with mandates for gifted education may be able to substitute the compactor form for the IEP, thus curbing the paperwork required for state-funded services. No matter what record-keeping vehicle they use, it is critical that teachers thoroughly chronicle the compacting process. The facts and figures they compile can be used in parent-teacher files. They can also be included in students' permanent academic files. The information can even help win support for compacting when the idea is being "sold," because people tend to react more favorably to issues presented in a written format.

EXAMINING CURRICULUM ALTERNATIVES

The most challenging part of compacting is deciding what students should do with time that they have earned. In deciding which curriculum alternatives to use, teachers should first list all the enrichment and acceleration activities available in their school districts. These can be organized around five major areas:

1. Classroom Activities—Independent or small-group study, escalated coverage of the regular curriculum, minicourses, special-interest groups, clubs, interest development centers, and special lessons for furthering cognitive and affective processes.

2. Resource Room and Special Class Programs—These include the same activities as the previous but are often held in locations outside of the classroom and may be taught by special teachers.

3. Accelerated Studies—Grade skipping, honors and Advanced Placement courses, college classes, summer or evening classes, early admission to kindergarten or first grade, cross-grade grouping, continuous progress curricula, and special seminars.

4. Out-of-School Experiences—Internships; mentorships; work-study programs; and community programs, such as theater and symphonic groups, artists' workshops, and museum programs.

5. District, School, or Departmental Programs—Encompasses the previous options, plus correspondence courses and programs for independent study, special counseling, career education, and library studies.

ENRICHMENT MATERIALS IN THE CLASSROOM

Gifted-education teachers or enrichment specialists are excellent sources for enrichment activities. The services they supply range from alternative teaching units or materials to mentoring student projects. For teachers who do not have access to these specialists, there are a host of commercially published materials on the market. These kits, books, and activity cards, which offer high quality at reasonable prices, can be adapted to individuals or small student groups of all ages.

ASSESSING STUDENTS' INTERESTS

Student interests are key in choosing enrichment or acceleration options, as explained in our discussion of Total Talent Portfolios. When asked what they enjoy most about compacting, children consistently cite the freedom to select their own topics of study; conversely, their biggest objection to regular curriculum is the limited opportunity to pursue their favorite subjects. We commonly assume that when a student excels in a given area, he or she has a special interest in it. This is not always true. Often, students perform well in a course because they have been directed and rewarded by parents and teachers. Students may also lean toward one academic area simply because they have had little exposure to others. Still, if a youngster is outstanding in math, for example, the teacher should try to promote further interest in the subject. A good way to do this is to suggest an accelerated math activity; if the student and parents agree to it, they should proceed. If, however, the student would rather work on a self-initiated project, then the teacher should try to accommodate those wishes while also considering how to provide an appropriate level of challenge.

The Interest-a-lyzer (Renzulli, 1977b) is a 13-item questionnaire devised to help students examine and focus their interests. Basically, the youngsters are asked to imagine themselves in a series of real and hypothetical situations and then relate how they would react. The primary purpose of this exercise is to stimulate thought and discussion. Students not only come to know themselves better but also get a chance to share their discoveries with both teachers and peers.

Teachers play a dual role in fostering student interests. Once they have identified general categories of interest, they must refine and focus them, then provide students with creative and productive outlets for expressing them. A child who enjoys rock music, for instance, may want to become a musician, but there are other avenues students can pursue as well, such as that of radio announcer or concert producer. Teachers must be sensitive to students' talents and inclinations in their fields of interest, and at the same time, encourage them to explore a range of options in those fields.

INTEREST CENTERS

Creating interest development centers is also an effective strategy. Unlike traditional learning centers that focus on basic skills, interest centers invite students to investigate topics in a general theme, such as bicycling or the education of people with hearing impairments. Shelves, therefore, must be stocked with manipulative, activity-oriented tools. Films, pamphlets, magazine articles, library books, slides, display items—all are standard fare. Resources that introduce children to research skills, not just reference skills, are valuable, too. An interest center on bicycling, for example, could feature texts on how to make a bike path, seek city council permission to erect public bike racks, or plan a bike safety rodeo.

Once teachers have set up the center, they should formally unveil it to their students. A 20-minute session revolving around a film, speaker, or discussion is generally all it takes to enthuse children about the new resource. Not all students will want to explore every interest center topic, but when several centers are established over the school year, most youngsters delve into at least one activity. Evaluating students' interest inventories should help teachers launch projects that appeal to the majority of students.

Perhaps the most critical success factor, however, are teachers' attitudes. If teachers insist that only students who finish their work can use the center, then some students will erroneously equate center activities with skill development. On the other hand, those teachers who allocate time for all students to enjoy center projects send the message that exploratory and creative pursuits are just as valuable as textbook and worksheet assignments. Encouraging children to be risk takers and information gatherers reinforces important behaviors—behaviors that lead to a love of independent learning.

RESEARCH ON CURRICULUM COMPACTING

A national study completed at the University of Connecticut's National Research Center on the Gifted and Talented (Reis et al., 1992) examined curriculum compacting for use with students from a wide diversity of school districts. A total of 465 second- through sixth-grade classroom teachers from 27 school districts throughout the country participated in this study. Classroom teachers were randomly assigned to participate in either the treatment (implemented compacting) or the control group (continued with normal teaching practices). Treatment and control-group teachers were asked to target one or two candidates in their classrooms for curriculum compacting, and all participating students in treatment and control groups were tested before and after treatment with above-level Iowa Tests of Basic Skills. Next-grade-level tests were used to compensate for the "topping out" ceiling effect that is frequently encountered when measuring the achievement of high-ability students.

The most important finding from this research might be described as the more-for-less phenomenon. Approximately 40% to 50% of traditional classroom material was compacted for targeted students in one or more content areas. When teachers eliminated as much as 50% of regular curricular activities and materials for targeted students, no differences were observed in posttest achievement scores between treatment and control groups in math concepts, math computation, social studies, and spelling. In science, the students who had 40% to 50% of their curriculum eliminated actually scored significantly higher on science achievement posttests than their peers in the control group. Students whose curriculum was specifically compacted in mathematics scored significantly higher than their peers in the control group on the math concepts posttest. These findings point out the benefits of compacting for increases on standard achievement assessments. Analyses of data related to replacement activities also indicated that students viewed these activities as much more challenging than standard material.

The vast majority of teachers were able to implement curriculum compacting for the students they selected, although many experienced some frustration over a lack of expertise in knowing what to substitute for high-ability students, the limited time they had to plan to meet individual differences, and the logistics of teaching different topics to different groups of students. Some also indicated the lack of support staff needed to implement replacement activities (reading and math specialists, gifted-and-talented-program staff) and other concerns relating to classroom management. Although curriculum compacting is a viable process for meeting the needs of high-ability students in the regular classroom, it does takes time, effort, and planning on the part of classroom teachers. With urban teachers, especially those who work with students placed at risk because of poverty, compacting requires different types of efforts, particularly in finding different materials to substitute in environments that often rely primarily on addressing deficits and remedial instruction. Many factors contribute to the creation of a supportive school environment for the use of curriculum compacting, such as administrative support, encouragement, availability of materials and resources for substitution of the regular curriculum, the availability of guided practice and coaching, and teachers' increased ease and reflections about how to fit compacting into their professional practices.

Our follow-up research study also indicated that a substantial number of teachers involved in the study indicated that they were able to extend curriculum compacting to other students, many of whom were not identified and involved in the gifted program (Reis et al., 1993). This finding may indicate the usefulness of extending the types of gifted-education pedagogy often reserved for high-ability students to a larger segment of the population, as has been previously suggested (Renzulli & Reis, 1991), and the need to extend differentiation services to a broader segment of the school population (Renzulli & Reis, 1997).

In another recent study, teachers were asked to use both curriculum compacting and self-selected Type III enrichment projects based on students' interests as a systematic intervention for a diverse group of underachieving talented students. In this study, underachievement was reversed in the majority of students. The use of compacting and replacement of high-interest projects (Renzulli, 1977a) specifically targets student strengths and interests to cause this reversal (Baum et al., 1995).

ADVICE FROM SUCCESSFUL TEACHERS WHO HAVE IMPLEMENTED COMPACTING

Research (Reis et al., 1993) showed that the most successful teachers to use compacting implemented the following strategies to successfully implement compacting. *First,* they worked with a colleague or colleagues with whom they shared a common bond. They wanted to improve their teaching practices and were not afraid to ask each other for help or support. *Second,* they started with a small group of students and not their entire class. The successful teachers understood that this process would take some time and organization and became committed to trying to work with a group who really needed the process first. By not trying this with all students, they reduced the stress and challenges they would have encountered if they tried to do too much in the beginning of the process. *Third,* they asked for help from their liaisons, the district content consultants, and each other. In each successful district, teachers asked each other how they were handling pretesting and assessment. They shared strategies for management and for replacement, and they visited each other's classrooms at their own suggestions or because a liaison suggested it. The modeling and sharing success stories made a difference. *Fourth,* they also understood that like a novice practicing piano scales, they would continue to improve by trying and reflecting on their work in this area. The teachers who did the best work consistently asked their colleagues and liaisons what had worked best and how current practices could extend and improve this practice. By reflecting on what had worked, they were able to modify and change their own attempts and consistently improve. In the most successful schools, teachers were provided with time to work with liaisons, small amounts of material funds for curricular replacement costs, and substitutes to enable them to visit and observe direct modeling in each other's classrooms.

SUMMARY

The many changes that are taking place in schools require all educators to examine a broad range of techniques for providing equitably for *all* students. Curriculum compacting is one such process. It is not tied to a specific content area or grade level, nor is it aligned with a particular approach to school or curricular reform. Rather, the process is adaptable to any school organizational plan or curricular framework, and it is flexible enough to be used in the context of rapidly changing approaches to general education. The research described in this chapter and the practical experiences gained through several years of field testing and refining the compacting process, particularly in urban areas and in schools that serve culturally diverse students, have demonstrated that many positive benefits can result from this process for both students and teachers, particularly talented students who may be at risk for underachieving in school.

Like any innovation, curriculum compacting requires time, energy, and acceptance from teachers. Yet educators we have studied who compact effectively indicate that it takes no longer than normal teaching practices. More important, they reported that the benefits to all students certainly make the effort worthwhile. One teacher's comment about the compacting process reflects the attitude of most teachers who have participated in research about compacting: "As soon as I saw how enthusiastic and receptive my students were about the compacting process, I began to become more committed to implementing this method in all my classes" (Reis et al., 1993, p. 87).

THE MULTIPLE MENU MODEL: A GUIDE TO IN-DEPTH LEARNING AND TEACHING

The second category of procedures covered in this chapter consists of three curriculum models that can be used to create instructional units. They differ from traditional approaches because they place greater emphasis on (a) content and process, (b) students as firsthand inquirers, and (c) the interconnectedness of knowledge. The Multiple Menu Model (Renzulli, 1988a) is a guide that teachers and curriculum writers can use to develop in-depth curriculum units for classroom use. It is based on the work of theorists in curriculum and instruction, including Ausubel (1963), Bandura (1986), Bruner (1960, 1966), Kaplan (1986), Passow (1982), Phenix (1964), and Ward (1961). It consists of a series of six interrelated components (see Figure 5.2) called menus because each contains a range of options from which curriculum developers can choose as they create units of study.

The six components include the Knowledge Menu, the Instructional Objectives and Student Activities Menu, the Instructional Strategies Menu, the Instructional Sequences Menu, the Artistic Modification Menu, and the Instructional Products Menu, which is composed of two interrelated menus, the Concrete Products and Abstract Products Menus. The first menu, the Knowledge Menu, is the most elaborate and concerns the field of selected study (e.g., mythology, astronomy, choreography, geometry). The second through the fifth menus deal with pedagogy or instructional techniques. The last menu, Instructional Products, is related to the types of products that may result from student interactions with knowledge about a domain or interdisciplinary concepts and how that knowledge is constructed by firsthand inquirers. Although it was originally developed as a way of differentiating curriculum for high-ability students, the guide can easily be used by teachers who want to encourage firsthand inquiry and creativity among all students.

The Knowledge Menu

This menu is underpinned by two particularly important assumptions: (a) the belief that it is futile, if not impossible, to teach everything important in a discipline, and (b) the necessity of inquiry.

Rather than focusing on the conclusions of a discipline, the Multiple Menu Model focuses on inquiry itself, asking curriculum developers to select the most important concepts to teach learners. Accordingly, the first menu, the Knowledge Menu, requires curriculum developers to examine a discipline from four perspectives: its purpose and placement in the larger context of knowledge, its underlying concepts and principles, its most representative topics and contributions to the universe of knowledge and wisdom, and its method. This first of these perspectives follows.

Locating the Discipline

Teachers using curriculum units based on the Multiple Menu Model must first locate for students the targeted discipline in the larger domain of knowledge (e.g., the novel is a field in the domain of literature). Teachers and students construct a knowledge tree to illustrate how the selected area of knowledge fits in the larger domain. Next, they examine the characteristics of the discipline and subdisciplines to

92

Figure 5.2 The Multiple Menu Model

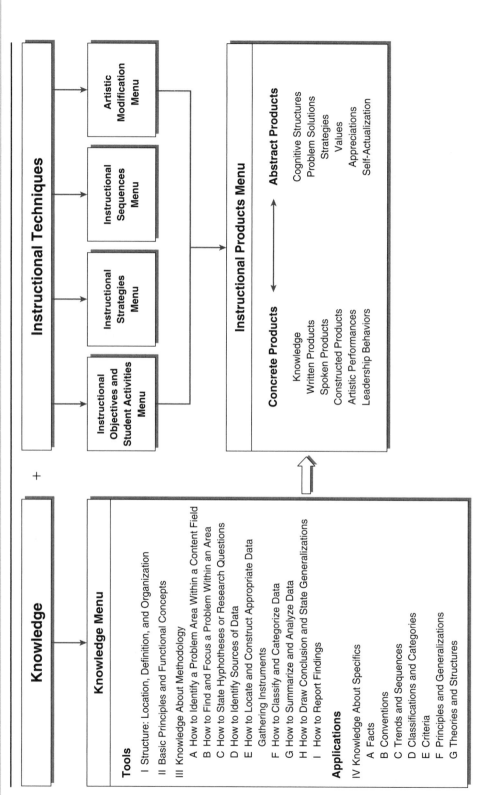

Curriculum = Knowledge + Instructional Techniques

learn the reasons people study a particular area of knowledge and what they hope to contribute to human understanding. This first dimension of the Knowledge Menu helps students examine, for example, What is sociology? What do sociologists study and why? How is sociology similar to and different from other disciplines (e.g., psychology and anthropology)? What, then, is social psychology or social anthropology, and how does each fit into the larger picture and purpose of the social sciences? These questions about the structure of disciplines help students understand not only where the discipline is located but also the discipline's connectedness with other disciplines.

Selecting Concepts and Ideas

Subsequently, the teacher identifies and selects basic principles and concepts to teach—the second perspective of the Knowledge Menu. Representative concepts and ideas consist of themes, patterns, main features, sequences or organizing principles, and structures that define an area of study. With respect to science, for example, organizing principles and structures include, not exclusively, change, stability, systems, interactions, energy, chemical composition, volume, light, and color. With respect to the novel, representative elements that cut across all literary contributions include plot, setting, character, and theme. Large concepts exist in each of these elements, as well. For example, the buffoon and tragic hero are archetypal characters who appear in literary contributions throughout time. It is precisely because these concepts and ideas exist across time that they can be used as the bases for interdisciplinary units. Accordingly, curriculum developers must select representative concepts that will most clearly define the discipline being taught.

Selecting Representative Topics

Third, teachers select curricular topics to illustrate the basic principles and representative concepts. In some ways, the selection process is similar to the process that teachers have used in the past; namely, the material must take into consideration the age, maturity, previous study, and experiential background of the students. Beyond age, grade, maturity level, and experience, however, the Multiple Menu Model selection process is different. Unlike traditional instruction, which asks teachers to cover an entire text by the end of the year or semester, the Multiple Menu Model asks teachers to winnow down all the possible pieces to those few that truly represent the field's principles and concepts. A three-phase approach to the selection of content is recommended. This approach takes into consideration the interaction between intensive coverage and extensive coverage as well as group learning and individual learning situations. The following example points out how the procedure has been used in a literature course.

Phase I (Intensive/Group). In Phase I, a representative concept in literature, such as the genera of tragic heroes, was dealt with through intensive examination of three prototypical examples (e.g., *The Merchant of Venice, Joan of Arc,* and *The Autobiography of Malcolm X).* Selections of more than a single exemplar of the concept allow for both in-depth analysis and opportunities to compare and contrast authors' styles; historical perspectives; ethnic, gender, and cultural differences; and a host of other comparative factors that single selections would prohibit. Preteaching and learning analysis dealt with an overview of the concept and why it was being studied.

Because one of the main purposes is to learn *how* to study tragic heroes, *who* should be studied (i.e., which tragic hero) is less important, as long as the hero is representative of the genera. An emphasis on how rather than who also legitimizes a role for students. The payoff as far as transfer is concerned is to follow the in-depth coverage with a postlearning analysis that focuses on factors that define the representative concept of tragic heroes (e.g., characteristic themes, patterns, etc.). The goal of the postlearning analysis is to help consolidate cognitive structures and patterns of analysis developed through in-depth study of a small number of literary selections so that they are readily available for use in future situations.

Phase II (Extensive/Group). Phase II consists of the perusal of large numbers of literary contributions dealing with tragic heroes to which similar cognitive structures and patterns of analysis can be applied. In our sample situation, students working in small interest groups compiled categorical lists and summaries of tragic heroes in their respective areas of special interest. For example, groups focused on tragic heroes in sports, politics, science, civil rights, religion, the women's movement, arts and entertainment, or other areas in which special interests were expressed. Identifying tragic heroes in categories and preparing brief summaries of them developed research and writing skills as well as communication skills for group discussions and oral presentations, which were a part of the planned activities. A key feature of this phase of the work was that students were not expected to read entire books about the people on their lists. Summaries of nonfictional people were prepared from descriptions found in textbooks or encyclopedias, and fictional tragic heroes were summarized from material found in *Master Plots* or *Cliffs Notes*. Although perusal of large numbers of texts is recommended, coverage should be purposefully superficial, *but geared toward stimulating follow-up on the parts of interested individuals or small groups.*

Phase III (Intensive/Individual or Small Group). Phase III consists of in-depth follow-up of selected readings based on the personal preferences of students who emerge from Phase II. Phase III in our example was pursued in a variety of ways. Activities included formal study modeled after the procedures used in the *Great Books* or *Junior Great Books* study groups, informal discussions about selected tragic heroes by interested groups of students, or simply the more sophisticated appreciation that could now be derived from reading for pleasure or viewing a play or film based on the life or exploits of a tragic heroine. Some of this follow-up took place immediately, and in other cases, it was deferred until a similar process was followed with other genera. Of course, it can take place on a personal level at any time in the future. Once students learned how to analyze particular genera, and after they explored categorical representatives of a genus, they were empowered to apply these skills to future assignments or reading for pleasure.

The three-phase process described here requires that teachers understand the pivotal ideas, representative topics, unifying themes, and internal structures that define a field of knowledge or that horizontally cut across a number of disciplines. This is not an easy task for teachers who traditionally have relied on textbooks for curricular decision making. There are, however, excellent resources available to assist in this process. Books such as the *Dictionary of the History of Ideas* (Wiener, 1973) contain essays that cover every major discipline, but the emphasis of the essays is on interdisciplinary, cross-cultural relations. The essays are cross-referenced to direct the reader to other articles in which the same or similar ideas occur in other domains. Similar resources for teachers can be found in books such as the *Syntopicon*, the index of topics edited by Mortimer J. Adler for *Great Books of the Western World* (Adler & Hutchins, 1952), which is an organizational structure for the great ideas of the Western world.

New curricular materials are also available to assist teachers in the development of in-depth learning units. The recent concern about excellence for all students has prompted the development of new content area standards, including mathematics, science, and social studies standards. The development of these standards has, in turn, prompted the assessment of curricular materials. Some of these curriculum review initiatives are using criteria aligned with the central concepts of the Multiple Menu Model. Unlike traditional review criteria, which focused on readability levels and the sheer amount of factual material included in the text, the criteria for this new review were concerned, for example, with the significance of the scientific concepts covered and the amount of practice provided in the processes of scientific inquiry.

A Final Consideration: Appeal to the Imagination

In the context of in-depth teaching and learning, there is still one additional consideration that should be addressed. Phenix (1964) termed this concept the "appeal to the imagination," and he argues very persuasively for the selection of topics that will lift students to new planes of experience and meaning. First, he points out that the means for stimulating the imagination differ according to the individual, his or her level of maturity, and the cultural context in which the individual is located. Second, the teacher must model the imaginative qualities of mind we are trying to develop in students and be able to enter sympathetically into the lives of students. Finally, imaginative teaching requires faith in the possibility of awakening imagination in any and every student, regardless of the kinds of constraints that may be placed on the learning process.

There are, undoubtedly, different perspectives about how to select content that will appeal to the imagination. Topics with such a focus could easily fall prey to material that deals with seductive details or esoteric and sensational topics. Seductive details are not inherently inappropriate as topics for in-depth study. Indeed, they often serve the important function of stimulating initial interests and creating what Whitehead (1929) called the romance stage with a topic or field of study. But if seductive details and sensational topics become ends rather than means for promoting advanced understanding, then we have traded appeal to the imagination for romanticism and showmanship.

How, then, should we go about selecting curriculum material that appeals to the imagination but that is not based purely on sensationalism? The answer rests, in part, on selecting topics that represent powerful and controversial manifestations of basic ideas and concepts. Thus, for example, the concepts of loyalty versus betrayal might be examined and compared from political, literary, military, or family perspectives, but always in ways that bring intensity, debate, and personal involvement to the concepts. An adversarial approach to ideas and concepts (e.g., loyalty versus betrayal) also guarantees that the essential element of *confrontations with knowledge* will be present in selected curricular topics. In a certain sense, it would be feasible to write the history of creative productivity is a chronicle of men and women who confronted existing ideas and concepts in an adversarial fashion, and who used existing information only as counterpoints to what eventually became their own unique contributions to the growth of knowledge. It was these confrontations that sparked their imaginations, and it is for this reason that an appeal to the imagination should be a major curricular focus for the coverage of in-depth topics.

Throughout a unit of study, teachers explain, illustrate, and involve students in the process of research as defined by the method dimension of the Knowledge Menu (e.g., identify a problem area in the study of tragic heroes, focus the problem, state a hypothesis, locate resources, classify and organize data, summarize data, draw conclusions, report findings). The cluster of diverse procedures that surround the acquisition of knowledge—that dimension of learning commonly referred to as process or thinking skills—should themselves be viewed as a form of content. It is these more-enduring skills that form the cognitive structures and problem-solving strategies that have the greatest transfer value. When we view process as content, we avoid the artificial dichotomy and the endless arguments about whether content or process should be the primary goal of learning. Combining content and process leads to a goal that is larger than the sum of the respective parts. Simply stated, this goal is the acquisition of a scheme for acquiring, managing, and producing information in an organized and systematic fashion.

Armed with the tools learned in the Knowledge Menu and a more mature understanding of the method of the field, students are no longer passive recipients of information and are able to begin the process of generating knowledge in the field. With respect to the tragic heroes unit that has been developed, students may want to interview contemporary authors regarding which characteristics they believe define the tragic heroes of today.

The Instructional Techniques Menus

The second, third, fourth, and fifth menus from the model concern pedagogy or instruction. Specifically, these menus provide curriculum developers with a range of options related to how they will present learning activities to students based on the principles and concepts they have selected. The Instructional Objectives and Student Activities Menu focuses on the thinking and feeling processes (e.g., application, analysis, synthesis) that are used by learners as they construct knowledge about a discipline. It is important that curriculum writers design learning activities that incorporate a balanced variety of these thinking and feeling processes. The balance provides learners with practice in the spectrum of encoding and recoding activities associated with learning new information, concepts, and principles. The next menu, the Instructional Strategies Menu, provides a range of specific teaching methods (e.g., discussion, dramatization, independent study) that teachers can use to present new material. A variety of carefully selected instructional strategies from this menu provides students with multiple ways to be engaged with knowledge and to employ the full range of their intellectual abilities and learning styles. Teachers and curriculum writers are provided with a relatively fixed order of events for teaching information through the next component, the Instructional Sequences Menu. For example, teachers open most lessons by gaining the attention of their students, linking the present lesson with previously covered material, and pointing out other applications for what has been introduced. Accordingly, the Instructional Sequences Menu is a rubric that can accommodate any instructional or pedagogical strategy. Finally, the Artistic Modification Menu invites teachers to personalize lessons by sharing an anecdote, observation, hobby, or personal belief about an event, topic, or concept. As such, it can be used with any instructional strategy and during any point in the instructional sequence. Personalizing lessons in this fashion generates interest and excitement among students.

The Instructional Products Menu

The Instructional Products Menu is concerned with the outcomes of learning experiences presented by the teacher through the curricular material and pedagogy; in this case, however, outcomes are viewed in much more complex learning behaviors than the lists of basic skills typically found in the literature on standards and outcomes. Two kinds of outcomes emerge: concrete products and abstract products. The concrete products are physical constructions that result from learner interaction with the knowledge, principles, and concepts. These physical constructions include, for example, speeches, essays, dramatizations, and experiments. Abstract products include behaviors (such as leadership activities related to an issue), increased self-confidence, and the acquisition of new methods (such as interviewing skills). Note that the two kinds of products are mutually reinforcing. As students produce new kinds of concrete products, they will also demonstrate new abstract products, such as methods skills and self-assurance. As self-confidence and leadership opportunities increase, it is likely that additional physical products will emerge as well.

What makes the Multiple Menu Model unique is its deep connections with the how-to of disciplines. Other models provide teachers with the skills to enrich curriculum by increasing the amount of material related to a subject, increasing the rate at which it is covered, or varying the products that emerge from learner interaction with the material in a discipline. *The Multiple Menu Model takes the teacher and student to the very heart of a discipline to examine its location in the domain of information and to understand the method employed by those who produce knowledge in the field.* Accordingly, this model enables learners to become firsthand inquirers and creators of information, a far more intensive, productive engagement in the school setting than what students experience as consumers of information.

What teachers teach is at the very heart of professional competence. The textbook analysis and surgical removal process offers teachers an opportunity to come together as a group of professionals around specific tasks in and across grade levels and subject areas. Effective group work using this process will undoubtedly contribute to individual teacher growth as far as content mastery is concerned, and this approach has the added benefit of promoting the types of consultation and sharing of knowledge and experience that characterize other professions. For this process to occur, however, school leaders need to make available the time and resources for this essential school improvement activity, and teachers must be willing to devote some of their nonteaching professional time to the process.

Interdisciplinary Models

Kaplan's Grid

Kaplan (1986) developed a model to guide the construction of curricular units called the Grid. Although it was written as a model to differentiate instruction for high-ability students, it can be used as a model to develop talent among all children. Specifically, the Grid helps curriculum writers make decisions about an overarching theme, the essential elements of curriculum, and the format for the creation of learning experiences.

Kaplan (1986) suggests that curriculum writers begin developing units by identifying themes or concepts, such as power, humor, extinction, the unexpected, or journeys. Like the concept of the tragic hero described earlier, these themes are principles that cut across time and disciplines. It is precisely for this reason that they can be the center of interdisciplinary units. Kaplan suggests that four questions guide the selection of concepts:

1. Is the theme related to a discipline?

2. Is it a significant area of study?

3. Is the theme neither age nor time dependent?

4. Does the theme allow for a variety of teacher and student options for study?

The theme becomes a way to organize and connect individual learning units, thereby providing meaningful connections among the disciplines studied in school.

Once curriculum writers have identified the theme with which they will work for a specified period of time, Kaplan (1986) suggests they focus on selecting the content, processes, and products for the unit. *Content* refers to the knowledge or subject matter that is to be taught, and Kaplan believes that the selection of content is the most difficult aspect of curriculum development. She provides specific rules for selecting content. Content should: (a) be related to the theme under consideration, (b) be multidisciplinary (allow for extensions to other disciplines), (c) be consonant with the needs of the learner, and (d) provide a time orientation, wherein past, present, and future are related. *Processes* refer to skills or competencies related to the subject matter (e.g., note taking, interpreting, analyzing) that students will be required to learn. Kaplan recommends that teachers refer to a variety of taxonomies during this phase of the curriculum-writing process and that targeted competencies be part of a larger scope and sequence of process skills that students are required to learn. *Products* refer to the forms of communication students need to learn to transmit the knowledge they have assimilated (e.g., essays, debates, dramatizations, computer software applications). The value of the product is twofold, according to Kaplan. First, it is verification that learning has taken place, and second, it is a tool that can be used again and again.

We can summarize this chapter, then, by reiterating that we want textbooks to improve, and we believe that the strategies for textbook use and modification described here can serve as a driving force for reconsideration on the parts of textbook publishers. The consumer-driven marketplace will become more responsive to the issue of textbook quality if educators become more sophisticated about the levels of present texts and if they take specific steps to augment or replace existing texts. If, on the other hand, we sit idly by and do nothing, textbooks will continue to be the dominant force in the school curriculum. Making changes in the ways we use texts, and in the substitution of in-depth material for mundane textbook content, will require three conditions on the parts of teachers and policy makers.

First, teachers will need to pursue the kinds of professional growth that will empower them to analyze textbook content and to gain deeper understandings of the material they are teaching. For example, teachers cannot prepare and teach an in-depth unit on the genera of tragic heroes unless they acquire an in-depth understanding of this topic. Second, school and departmental faculties will have to organize themselves into special purpose teams that focus on increased knowledge and know-how about both content and process, and about improved pedagogy, as well. Finally, policy makers and school leaders need to provide the time and staff development resources necessary for curricular modification and, perhaps most important, for the sincere endorsement of the process.

FREQUENTLY ASKED QUESTIONS ABOUT CURRICULUM COMPACTING

Q. What type of staff development is initially necessary to help teachers compact curriculum?

A. Teachers and staff should first get a general overview of compacting and differentiating through reading a book like this. After everyone has been oriented to compacting, they should meet to determine learning objectives, methods of pretesting, and other critical elements in the process. In addition, teachers should try to observe, in a classroom setting, other teachers who successfully compact curriculum.

Q. Can classroom teachers compact curriculum without the help of teachers who work with gifted children?

A. Yes! In fact, classroom teachers bear the primary responsibility for implementing the compacting process. If teachers of the gifted or enrichment specialists are available, however, they can ease the job by procuring enrichment resources or upgrading the challenge level of the regular curricular materials.

Q. What about administrative support—should I tell my administrator about my decision to compact?

A. Absolutely. We feel that most administrators will be supportive, but because compacting is such a major innovation, it is essential that they be consulted before you begin. Doing this may prompt your administrator to ask other teachers to participate.

Q. Should parents be informed if their child's curriculum has been compacted?

A. We want parents to be active partners in compacting and, therefore, strongly recommend that they be notified once it has been initiated. A good way to do this is through a brief letter that describes the process. Parents should understand, for example, that compacting may change the amount or type of paperwork their children bring home.

Q. What should I tell my class about compacting?

A. Compacting should be explained in simple terms to all students. Among the points you should touch on are pretests, the fact that some students may already know the material being tested, and that exciting learning activities exist for students who have already mastered the material.

You should also spell out, in advance, the rules regarding behavior while students are doing alternative work. Two such rules may include working as quietly as possible and not interrupting the teacher while he or she instructs the rest of the class.

Q. At what grade level should compacting be introduced?

A. The ideal time to start compacting is as soon as children enter school. We have found that when the process begins in kindergarten, youngsters learn to use their independent time more appropriately and choose more suitable enrichment activities.

Similarly, it is often easier to compact in an elementary classroom than it is in a secondary class. Elementary teachers generally see students perform for a larger block of time and in more than one subject area. Secondary teachers, on the other hand, may have them for only one 50-minute session a day. This gives them limited time to determine competence.

Q. What are the least difficult subject areas to compact?

A. Usually, skill areas with highly sequential curricular organization, such as spelling, mathematics, and grammar, are the least difficult to compact. Once you are familiar with the process, you may compact any subject area. Teachers have even reported wonderful results in art and music.

Q. Am I correct in assuming that if I teach process writing or use a "whole-language" approach, compacting is unnecessary?

A. No. With process writing, youngsters who master the writing objectives for their grade level should not just move up another difficulty notch, as is often the case. Instead, they should be allowed to pursue enrichment assignments or projects of their choice.

The same holds true for the whole-language approach. If students show mastery of the learning objectives, simply replacing time with grade-level trade books, for example, may not be the best option. The alternatives presented must be challenging and keyed to students' interests.

Q. Is it better to compact by time period (every marking period, for instance) or by instructional unit?

A. Compacting by instructional unit is best. A "unit" generally refers to an instructional period that revolves around a theme, chronological time period, or set of academic objectives. For example, to compact a sixth-grade unit on Johnny Tremaine, the teacher would modify the curriculum for students who have either read the novel or who could read and master the learning objectives more quickly than their classmates. At the elementary level, teachers frequently compact a basic skills unit of instruction, such as the teaching of long division.

Q. Do you recommend compacting an entire semester, leaving the last two months free for student self-selected projects, or compacting 2 1/2 days a week, leaving the rest of the time for alternative work?

A. Most teachers prefer to compact two or three days a week, and set aside one or two days or short blocks of time for enrichment assignments. When you compact a semester, it demands tremendous time and energy to plan a full two months of enrichment options.

Q. Will I be more successful if I initially compact one student's curriculum instead of a whole group's?

A. Teachers have effectively compacted curriculum for individual students, but the students often feel uncomfortable being singled out. It is better, then, to start with a small group. Working with several students does not demand much more time, or many more resources, than working with one student.

Q. If I compact my high-ability students' curriculum and eliminate instruction for them, will the quality of my classroom discussions suffer?

A. Many teachers have expressed this concern, which is merited to some degree. However, we must also remember that less-able students are sometimes intimidated by the presence of brighter students and, consequently, will not contribute to the discussions. To resolve the problem, teachers might try some classroom sessions with the gifted students and some without them; if the discussions succeed better with the advanced students, then it makes sense to include them.

Q. Do students who are not in the gifted program ever benefit from compacting?

A. Yes, most definitely. According to our field tests, many average students get great value from curriculum compacting in one or more content areas. We believe that the compacting process actually helps reverse the "dumbing down" of the curriculum, which benefits all students, as do the enrichment materials brought into the classroom for use during compacted time.

Q. What about lower ability students—can they take part in enrichment opportunities?

A. All students, regardless of ability, should be given time to enjoy enrichment opportunities. Everyone would agree that every student should, in fact, learn the problem solving, creative-thinking skills, and other facets of process training that alternative activities provide. Teachers could schedule a special time for these activities, such as Friday afternoons from 2 to 3 P.M.

Q. Should curriculum be compacted for underachievers?

A. Underachievers should be considered for compacting. Youngsters who underachieve are often bright students who are bored with the regular curriculum. In many instances, they have also discovered that finishing their lessons before their classmates only means that they are assigned more of the same work. Case studies show that compacting can break this unproductive cycle. By directing underachievers to more challenging work, rather than simply extra work, we give them an incentive to excel.

Q. How do I grade when I compact curriculum?

A. You should grade on the regular curriculum that has been compacted. In our opinion, grades should reflect mastery of content and not time spent in a subject area. When you do substitute independent study, we don't think it should be graded. Our preference is to provide some qualitative, holistic evaluation of the work done.

Note: If you find that students are not using their time for alternative study wisely, you should talk over the problem with them. You might reiterate the concept of compacting and explain what the next step would be if behavior doesn't change (such as a parent meeting). Compacting represents a radical educational departure for most students, and it takes time for them to adjust.

Q. Is there a way to physically reorganize my classroom space to make compacting easier?

A. Yes! You can set up "student stations" and interest centers consisting of a desk or table with two or three chairs for independent study or free reading. A small, comfortable library corner, or special learning or interest centers, can also be established.

Q. How expensive is compacting to implement?

A. To facilitate compacting, you will need additional resources. You may have to order pretests and other instruments to measure proficiency. If your students do not have access to a gifted-education specialist, you will have to arrange in-class activities for them instead. With some start-up funds, and an annual budget to supplement these funds, per building, a library of enrichment resources can readily be made available and stored in a central location for teachers to use when needed. These items can be loaned to classrooms as needed. Curriculum compacting and differentiation can be used to help ensure a better match between the achievement levels of individual learners and the curriculum. It can be used with traditional curriculum in any subject area and grade level, and it can also be used to make modifications in teacher-developed curricular activities.

6

Enrichment Learning and Teaching

The Enrichment Triad Model

nrichment learning and teaching are practices based on the ideas of a small number of philosophers, theorists, and researchers. The work of these theorists, coupled with our own research and program development activities, has given rise to the concept that we call "enrichment learning and teaching." The ultimate goal of enrichment learning is to replace dependence and passive learning with independence and engaged learning. Although all but the most conservative educators will agree with these principles, much controversy exists about how these (or similar) principles may be applied in everyday school situations. Developing a school program based on these principles is not an easy task. Over the years, however, we have achieved a fair amount of success by gaining faculty, administrative, and parental consensus on a small number of easy-to-understand concepts and related services, and by providing resources and training related to each concept and service delivery procedures related to implementing the Triad Model.

The Enrichment Triad Model (Renzulli, 1976) was developed in the mid-1970s and initially implemented by school districts in the United States. The model, which was originally field tested in several districts in New England, proved to be quite popular, and requests from all over the United States for visitations to schools using the model and for information about how to implement the model increased. A book about the Enrichment Triad Model (Renzulli, 1977a) was published, and more and more districts began asking for help in implementing this approach. Dozens and then hundreds of programs based on the Enrichment Triad were and continue to be

103

developed. In the sections that follow, we present each component of the Triad Model. As you review these sections, keep in mind the interactions between and among the three types of enrichment, and the ways in which this interaction can be heightened through debriefing and postlearning analysis. Remember also that the Triad Model is part of the service delivery component that is targeted at three school structures: the regular curriculum, the enrichment clusters, and the continuum of special services. In many ways, enrichment learning and teaching can be thought of as a transparent overlay that can be applied to these three school structures.

AN OVERVIEW OF THE ENRICHMENT TRIAD MODEL AND EXAMPLES OF TYPE III STUDENT CREATIVE PRODUCTIVITY

The Triad Model is designed to encourage creative productivity on the part of young people by exposing them to various topics, areas of interest, and fields of study and to further train them to apply advanced content, process-training skills, and methods training to self-selected areas of interest. Accordingly, three types of enrichment are included in the Enrichment Triad Model (refer to Figure 6.1). For enrichment learning and teaching to be applied systematically to the learning process of all

Figure 6.1   The Enrichment Triad Model

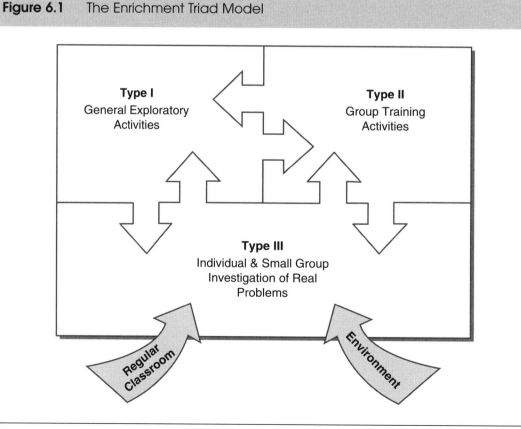

SOURCE: Courtesy of Creative Learning Press.

students, it must be organized in a way that makes sense to teachers and students. The Enrichment Triad Model (Renzulli, 1977) can be used for this purpose.

LEARNING IN A NATURAL WAY

The Enrichment Triad Model is based on the ways in which people learn in a natural environment, rather than the artificially structured environment that characterizes most classrooms. Just as scientists look to nature when they attempt to solve particular types of problems, the process of learning is examined as it unfolds in the nonschool world. This process is elegant in its simplicity. External stimulation, internal curiosity, necessity, or combinations of these three starting points cause people to develop an interest in a topic, problem, or area of study. Humans are by nature curious, problem-solving beings, but for them to act on a problem or interest with some degree of commitment and enthusiasm, the interest must be a sincere one and one in which they see a personal reason for taking action. Once the problem or interest is personalized, a need is created to gather information, resources, and strategies for acting on the problem.

Problem solving in nature almost always results in a product or service that has a functional, artistic, or humanitarian value. The learning that takes place in real-problem situations is *collateral learning*, which results from attacking the problem to produce a product or service. Consider a group of pioneers (or engineers or Boy or Girl Scouts) who want to build a bridge across a creek or river. They do not stand at the riverbank and say, "Let's learn about geometry." Rather, they examine the scope of the problem, what they already know, and what they need to know to build the bridge. In the process, they may learn about geometry, strength of materials, planning and sequencing, cooperation, structural design, spatial relationships, aesthetics, mechanics, and a host of other things necessary to get the job done.

It was precisely this kind of natural problem-solving situation that helped create the Enrichment Triad Model. The only difference between the natural learning that takes place in real-life situations and the use of the Triad Model in the more structured world of the school is that we view products as vehicles through which a wide variety of more enduring and transferable processes can be developed. The products are essential because they give reality, purpose, and satisfaction and enjoyment to the present endeavor. The processes developed in the context of real-problem learning are also essential because schools must be concerned with preparation for the future and with the continuity of development in young people over long periods of time. Learning that focuses on the interaction between product and process results in the kinds of learning experiences that enhance both the present and the future.

THE IMPORTANCE OF INTERACTION

A second general consideration about the Enrichment Triad Model is that the interaction among the three types of enrichment is as important as any type of enrichment or the collective sum of all three types. In other words, the arrows in Figure 6.1 are as important as the individual cells because they give the model dynamic properties that cannot be achieved if the three types of enrichment are pursued independently. A Type I experience, for example, may have value in and of itself, but it achieves maximum payoff if it leads to Type II or III experiences.

In this regard, it is a good idea to view Types I and II enrichment as identification situations that may lead to Type III experiences, which are the most advanced type of enrichment in the model. As Figure 6.1 indicates, the regular curriculum and the environment in general (i.e., nonschool experiences) can also serve as pathways of entry into Type III activities. An identification situation is simply an experience that allows students and teachers an opportunity to (a) participate in an activity, (b) analyze their interest in and reaction to the topic covered in the activity and the processes through which the activity was pursued, and (c) make a purposeful decision about their interest in the topic and the diverse ways further involvement may be carried out. Type I and Type II are general forms of enrichment that are usually pursued with larger groups of students, and they are often a prescribed part of enrichment offerings. Methods of presentation span the continuum from deductive to inductive methods of learning. Type III enrichment, on the other hand, is pursued only on a voluntary and self-selected basis, and the method is mainly inductive.

The interactive nature of the three types of enrichment also includes what are sometimes called the backward arrows in Figure 6.1 (e.g., the arrows leading back from Type III to Type I, etc.). In many cases, the advanced work (i.e., Type III) of students can be used as Type I and II experiences for other students. Thus, for example, a group of students who carried out a comprehensive study on lunchroom waste presented their work to other groups for both awareness and instructional purposes, and for the purposes of stimulating potential new interests on the parts of other students. In this regard, the model is designed to renew itself and to bring students inside the pedagogy of the school enterprise rather than have them view learning from a spectator's perspective.

The Enrichment Triad Model can be used as a model for a schoolwide enrichment, a model for classroom curriculum enrichment, or as a school magnet or charter theme. We have seen countless ways in which the Enrichment Triad Model has been adapted and adopted in diverse suburban and urban schools throughout the country.

TYPE I ENRICHMENT: GENERAL EXPLORATORY EXPERIENCES

Type I enrichment is designed to expose students to a wide variety of disciplines, topics, occupations, hobbies, people, places, and events that would not ordinarily be covered in the regular curriculum. In schools using this model, an enrichment team of parents, teachers, and students often organizes and plans Type I experiences by contacting speakers; arranging minicourses, demonstrations, or performances; or ordering and distributing films, slides, videotapes, or other print or nonprint media. We use Type I experiences to motivate students to such an extent that they will act on their interests in creative and productive ways. The major purpose of Type I enrichment is to include in the overall school program selected experiences that are purposefully developed to be motivational. This type of enrichment can also expose students to a wide variety of disciplines, topics, ideas, and concepts. Typical Type I methods of delivery include bringing in a guest speaker, creating an interest center, showing slides, or hosting a debate.

Type I enrichment experiences can be based on regular curricular topics or innovative outgrowths of prescribed topics, but to qualify as a bona fide Type I experience, any and all planned activities in this category must stimulate new or present interests that may lead to more intensive follow-up on the parts of individual students or small groups of students. An activity can be called a Type I experience only if it meets the following three conditions:

- Students are aware that the activity is an invitation to various kinds and levels of follow-up.
- There is a systematic debriefing of the experience to learn who might want to explore further involvement and the ways the follow-up might be pursued.
- There are various opportunities, resources, and encouragement for diverse kinds of follow-up.

An experience is clearly not a Type I if every student is required to follow up on an activity in the same or similar way. Required follow-up is a regular curricular practice, and although prescribed follow-up certainly has a genuine role in general education, it almost always fails to capitalize on differences in students' interest and learning styles. Three key descriptors relate to Type I experiences:

- They should be selected and planned so that there is a high probability that they will be exciting and appealing to students.
- A majority of Type I activities should be presented to all students in a classroom, grade level, or cross-grade group.
- Although Type I experiences are, by definition, planned and presented, they need to retain flexibility.

In this section, we briefly discuss each of these three key issues. First, to make Type I experiences exciting to students, visiting speakers, for example, should be selected for both their expertise in a particular area and their ability to energize and capture the imagination of students. People presenting Type I experiences should be provided enough orientation about the model to understand the objectives described previously and the need to help students explore the realms and ranges of opportunity for further involvement that are available in various age and grade considerations. Without such an orientation, these kinds of experiences may not be viewed as exciting experiences with potential for follow-up.

Second, it is important to incorporate Type I activities into the regular classroom because these activities need to be seen as rooted in classroom instruction. For example, it may be worthwhile to introduce all middle-grade students to a topic such as computer-assisted design (CAD) through a demonstration or presentation by a specialist on this topic. Following the activity and an assessment of the levels of interest of all students in the group, an advanced Type I might be planned for highly interested students that pursues the material in greater depth or that involves a field trip to a company or laboratory that uses CAD technology. In this case, there is an interest-based rationale for a special grouping or field trip that is different from offering field trips only to high-ability students. A general or introductory Type I should, of course, include all students at given grade levels.

In terms of the third key issue, the flexibility of Type I activities, teachers should remember that a good menu of Type I experiences should be diversified across many topics and curricular categories. Such diversification improves the probability of influencing broader ranges of student interest and, accordingly, increasing the number of students who will select an area in which they may like to pursue follow-up activities. In addition, even prescribed Type I topics should be planned in a way that encourages maximum student involvement in an activity. Enrichment learning and teaching are more than just presenting unusual topics. Problem-solving activities—and activities that require discussion, debate, and confrontations with topics and issues—prompt the kinds of affective reactions that help students personalize a topic and make a commitment to more intensive follow-up.

The Type I dimension of the Enrichment Triad Model can be an extremely exciting aspect of overall schooling because it creates a legitimate slot in the school for bringing the vast world of knowledge and ideas that are above and beyond the regular curriculum to students' attention. It is also an excellent vehicle for teams of teachers, students, and parents to plan and work together on a relatively easy-to-implement component of the model. Type I enrichment is an excellent vehicle for getting started in an enrichment cluster.

TYPE II ENRICHMENT: GROUP TRAINING ACTIVITIES

Most educators agree about the need to blend into the curriculum more training in the development of higher-order thinking skills. In this section, we discuss a systematic approach for organizing a process skills component related to Type II training. Type II enrichment includes materials and methods designed to promote the development of thinking and feeling processes. Some Type II enrichment is general, consisting of training in areas such as creative thinking and problem solving, learning-how-to-learn skills such as classifying and analyzing data, and advanced reference and communication skills. Type II training is usually carried out both in classrooms and in enrichment programs and includes the development of (a) creative thinking and problem solving, critical thinking, and affective processes; (b) affective and character development skills; (c) a wide variety of specific learning-how-to-learn skills; (d) skills in the appropriate use of advanced-level reference materials; and (e) written, oral, and visual communication skills. Other Type II enrichment is specific, as it cannot be planned in advance and usually involves advanced instruction in an interest area selected by the student. For example, students who became interested in botany after the Type I experience described previously would pursue advanced training in this area by doing advanced reading in botany and compiling, planning, and carrying out plant experiments and more advanced methods training for those who want to go further. When we refer to these strategies, we use the term *process skills* and include examples of specific skills in each of these five general categories (and related subcategories).

Type II enrichment also serves a motivational purpose similar to that discussed in connection with Type I activities. Next, we focus on two general considerations that should be taken into account in developing a schoolwide plan for Type II enrichment. These considerations are (a) levels and audiences for Type II activities and (b) the objectives and strategies for implementing this component of the Enrichment Triad Model. In each category of Type II enrichment, the targeted skills exist along a continuum ranging from very basic manifestations of a given skill to higher and more complex applications of any given process. Thus, for example, skills such as conditional reasoning or recording data from original sources can be taught to students at any grade, but the level and complexity of the specific activities will vary according to students' developmental levels. Primary-grade students, for instance, can learn observational and data-gathering skills by counting and recording the number of times that different kinds of birds come to a bird feeder during a given period of time. These data might be presented by using simple tallies or pictograms. Older students can develop the same skills at higher levels by, for example, observing and recording pulse and blood pressure measures while controlling for factors such as age, height and weight ratios, and specified periods of exercise. The advanced mathematics and computer skills of older students might enable them to engage in more sophisticated statistical analyses of their data.

Teachers' knowledge of students' developmental levels, together with students' previous experiences in using a particular thinking skill, are important considerations when selecting materials and activities for Type II training. One of the ongoing activities of teachers and curriculum specialists using the Schoolwide Enrichment Model (SEM) is to be continually searching for and examining enrichment materials that might enhance regular curriculum topics or that might serve as useful resources for enrichment clusters or special service situations. Professional journals, publishers' catalogs and Web sites, and displays of materials at conferences are good sources of new materials.

There are three different methods for presenting Type II enrichment. The first method consists of planned, systematic activities that can be organized in advance for any unit of instruction in the general curriculum. These are the kinds of Type II activities that are planned in advance and are part of an ongoing framework to develop a comprehensive scope and sequence of process-oriented activities that parallel regular curriculum topics. The main criterion for selecting Type II activities in this category is that the activity bears a direct or indirect relationship to the subject matter being taught. For example, an activity entitled *Gold Rush: A Simulation of Life and Adventure in a Frontier Mining Camp* (Flindt, 1978) can be used in connection with a social studies unit on westward expansion in U.S. history. This activity is designed to develop decision-making and creative-writing skills in the context of the historical period covered in the unit. Activities in this category are ordinarily used with all students in a particular classroom, although advanced-level follow-up or related Type II training should take student interests and learning styles into account.

The second method for presenting Type II enrichment consists of activities that cannot be planned in advance because they grow out of students' reactions to school or nonschool experiences. In other words, this dimension is characterized by responsiveness to student interests rather than preplanning. For example, a group of students who developed an interest in investigative reporting was provided with advanced training in questioning and interviewing techniques, verifying information sources, and other skills related to this area of specialization. The interest resulted from a Type I presentation by a local journalist; however, the interest could also have been an outcome of a unit on journalism in the language arts curriculum or a reaction to an important local or national news event. Enrichment in this dimension can also fulfill the motivational goal of the model by stimulating interests that may lead to more intensive follow-up in the form of Type III enrichment.

Type II enrichment in this category can also be used to provide direction for students in a particular enrichment cluster. Because a cluster is composed of students and teachers who have already declared interests in particular areas of study, Type II training that provides methods skills in the area will help the group generate problems to which the methods can be applied. For example, a group of students who expressed strong interests in environmental issues was provided with a minicourse that taught them how to analyze the chemical properties of soil and water. A brainstorming and problem-focusing session resulted in making contact with a state agency, meeting with water pollution specialists, and eventually conducting a very professional study on acid rain in their geographic area. This is a good example of how learning the method first provided the impetus for the extended work of the cluster that followed.

The third method for presenting Type II enrichment consists of activities that are used in the context of already-initiated Type III investigations. Activities used in this way represent the best application of inductive learning. Simply stated, an individual or group learns a process skill because they need the skill to solve a real and present problem.

Strategies for Type II training provide students with training opportunities to improve a wide variety of process skills not normally taught in the grade-level curriculum. Teachers or other adults who provide Type II training do so for diverse purposes, in multiple settings, with varied teaching strategies and resources, and for a wide range of students. Seven major objectives for students participating in Type II training are as follows:

- Improve student ability to use higher-order cognitive skills to organize, analyze, and synthesize new information.
- Improve student leadership and interpersonal skills.
- Improve student ability to gather, organize, and analyze raw data from appropriate primary and secondary sources.
- Improve student ability to use a wide range of sophisticated reference materials and techniques when searching for answers to their personal research questions.
- Demonstrate a more organized and systematic approach to research, experimentation, and investigation.
- Improve the quality and appropriateness of the products that students create in conjunction with real-world problem solving.
- Use the methods and techniques of various adult professionals to find problems, gather and organize data, and develop products.

In general, Type II training provides students with various learning opportunities designed to improve their independent learning skills as well as the quality of their personal assignments, projects, and research. Type II enrichment also includes a broad range of affective training activities designed to improve interpersonal and intrapersonal skills and to promote greater degrees of cooperation and mutual respect among students. By placing this instruction in the framework of the regular curriculum or the enrichment clusters, teachers can offer these valuable training activities without the risk of having the training viewed as an end in and of itself.

Because the need for Type II training with a specific skill varies from student to student, from grade to grade, and from one subject area to another, there is no finite list of skills that should be taught as part of the Type II component. A taxonomy such as the one presented in Chapter Two (see Figure 2.3) can be used by teachers to gain a holistic perspective on the Type II component and its comprehensive nature and as a menu to help teachers select the most appropriate Type II skills and materials for their students.

In some districts, a committee of faculty members has used this list to create a scope and sequence document that specifies which Type II skills will be taught through large-group instruction in the regular classroom or in enrichment clusters or other multiage groupings. The scope and sequence document also ensures that their SEM program is offering a comprehensive set of training opportunities in all grade levels and to all students in the school. The 17 skill categories in the Type II taxonomy have also been used to create databases of selected commercial materials for the teaching of process skills. Although many teachers may prefer to create their own Type II lessons and units, many of these commercial materials can be used for supplementary activities or as resources for teachers who are unfamiliar with Type II instructional techniques.

Type II training can be offered as a result of observed student need, as a follow-up to a Type I exploration, as a result of expressed student interest, or within the parameters of a student's individual Type III investigation. It is extremely important to ensure that a specific Type II skill is offered at the appropriate time, in the appropriate setting, with the appropriate teaching strategies, and for the appropriate students. Teachers or faculties should use their knowledge of students and curriculum to make the best decisions possible about which students will receive specific kinds of Type II training and which settings and teaching strategies will be most advantageous.

Some classroom teachers who have modified their textbook-based curriculum and are designing their own curriculum units (Renzulli, 1988a) may integrate or infuse Type II training in these units as a way of teaching related process skills (e.g., teaching students how to conduct oral history interviews during a unit on the Vietnam War). At other times, classroom teachers may prefer to develop a stand-alone unit that focuses exclusively on a single Type II skill to ensure that novice learners receive explicit instruction on how to acquire and use this skill process (e.g., teaching a unit on creative problem solving). Still other Type II skills can be embedded in students' investigations or research projects and taught only when they are needed for specific and immediate purposes (e.g., a student wants to learn how to recognize the trees in the woods behind the school because she is creating a nature trail).

In addition to varying the nature of the instructional strategy used to teach Type II skills, teachers should also vary the audience of students who will receive this training. Some Type II lessons can and should be taught to all students in a class or grade level, some skills can be taught in a small-group setting to only those students who have not already acquired the skill, and other skills might be taught to only those students interested in learning them. Teachers who sponsor or facilitate enrichment clusters may also find their students need or request Type II training as a result of their common interest in a subject area or local problem. A cluster of students interested in journalism might receive training in editing, proofreading, layout, or advertising techniques. An enrichment cluster concerned with environmental problems might receive Type II training in how to draft a petition, how to lobby effectively, how to write an editorial, or how to write a letter to key government officials.

The resources for teaching these Type II skills can also vary. Although many classroom teachers will assume responsibility for teaching specific Type II skills to all students or small groups of students in their class, enrichment specialists can also schedule a variety of minicourses for interested students. This approach facilitates multiclass and multiage groupings and allows teachers to progress to advanced levels because of heightened student interests. Community resources (doctors, gardeners, lawyers, dietitians, etc.) and content-area teachers or specialists from the faculty or among the student population can also be recruited to offer Type II training to interested groups of students. In addition, learning centers, computer software, pamphlets, videos, and how-to books can be used by individual students who prefer self-instruction for selected Type II skills. Care should be taken, however, to ensure that Type II training is offered on an as-needed basis as often as possible. Teachers must be aware that some students have already acquired many of the Type II skills through modeling or informal learning opportunities; other students require a great deal of time, explicit teaching, and coaching to master new skills; and still others will not be ready to learn a given Type II skill until they see the immediate relevance for the skill's use.

Whether Type II skills are infused in the content curriculum, taught explicitly, or embedded in a student's interest exploration or problem-solving endeavors, all students who participate in Type II training should have numerous extension opportunities to transfer and apply their learned skills to new academic content, to their own research questions, or to their product development efforts. Although process skill training has been a staple of gifted education programs for many years, our research has shown that this kind of training can be used with all students. Although it may be true that not all students will use their newly acquired skills for personal research, experimentation, or investigation, all students can apply these skills to new and challenging academic content. When successful, Type II training helps students improve their academic achievement by showing them how to acquire and assimilate new content more rapidly and effectively, and these skills also have important transfer value to subsequent learning and the world of work.

We have consistently maintained that Types I and II enrichment are good for all children, and as research on this model continued (Renzulli, 1994; Renzulli & Reis, 1985, 1997), it became clear that many schools were doing an excellent job at implementing this model for their gifted program, but that few programs were providing enrichment opportunities for students who were not already identified as gifted and talented, despite a concentration on this concept. Therefore, the Triad Model is the instructional or curriculum basis for the SEM, an expanded version focusing on providing clearer guidelines for the organization of enrichment opportunities for all students.

TYPE III ENRICHMENT: INDIVIDUAL AND SMALL-GROUP INVESTIGATIONS OF REAL PROBLEMS

Type III enrichment is investigative activities and the development of creative products in which students assume roles as firsthand investigators, writers, artists, or other types of practicing professionals. Although students pursue these kinds of involvement at a more junior level than adult professionals, the overriding purpose of Type III enrichment is to create situations in which young people are thinking, feeling, and doing what practicing professionals do in the delivery of products and services. Type III enrichment experiences should be viewed as vehicles in which students can apply their interests, knowledge, thinking skills, creative ideas, and task commitment to self-selected problems or areas of study. In Type III enrichment, students

- acquire advanced-level understanding of the knowledge and methods used in particular disciplines;
- develop authentic products or services directed toward bringing about a desired effect on one or more audiences;
- gain self-directed learning skills in the areas of planning, problem finding and focusing, organizational skills, resource utilization, and time management; and
- develop task commitment, self-confidence, feelings of creative accomplishment, and the ability to interact effectively with other students and adults who share common goals and interests.

Type III enrichment is the vehicle through which everything from basic skills to advanced content and processes blend in student-developed products and services. In much the same way that all of the separate but interrelated parts of an automobile come together at an assembly plant, this form of enrichment serves as the assembly plant of the mind. This kind of learning represents a synthesis and an application of content, process, and personal involvement. The student's role is transformed from one of lesson learner to firsthand inquirer, and the role of the teacher changes from an instructor and disseminator of knowledge to a combination of coach, resource procurer, mentor, and, sometimes, a partner or colleague. Although products play an important role in creating Type III enrichment situations, a major concern is the development and application of a wide range of cognitive, affective, and motivational processes.

Because this type of enrichment is defined in terms of the pursuit of real problems, it is necessary to define this term at the outset. The term *real problem*, like many other concepts in education, gets tossed around so freely that after a while it becomes little more than a cliché. Research on the meaning of a real problem (Renzulli, 1983) did not produce a neat and trim definition, but an examination of various connotations of the term yielded four characteristics that serve as the basis for our discussion. First, a real problem must have a personal frame of reference for the individual or group pursuing the problem. In other words, it must involve an emotional or internal commitment in addition to a cognitive or scholarly interest. Thus, for example, stating that global warming or urban crime are real problems does not make them real for an individual or group unless they decide to do something to address the problem. These concerns may affect all people, but until a commitment is made to act on them, they are more properly classified as "societal issues." Similarly, telling a person or group that "you have a problem" does not make it real unless the problem is internalized and acted on in some way.

A second characteristic of real problems is that they do not have existing or unique solutions for people addressing the problem. If there is an agreed-on, correct solution or set of strategies for solving the problem, then it is more appropriately classified as a training exercise. As indicated earlier, it is not our intent to diminish the value of training exercises. Indeed, many of the activities that make up the Type II dimension of the Triad Model are exercises designed to develop thinking skills and research methods. They fail, however, to qualify as real problems because they are externally assigned and there is a predetermined skill or problem-solving strategy that we hope learners will acquire. Even simulations that are based on approximations of real-world events are considered to be training exercises if their main purpose is to teach content or thinking skills.

The third characteristic of a real problem is best described in terms of why people pursue these kinds of problems. The main reason is that they want to bring about some form of change in actions, attitudes, or beliefs on the parts of a targeted audience, or they want to contribute something new to the sciences, arts, or humanities. The word *new* is used here in a local rather than global way; therefore, we do not necessarily expect young people to make contributions that are new "for all humankind." But even replications of studies that have been done many times before are new in a relative sense if they are based on data that have not been gathered previously. Thus, for example, if a group of young people gathered data about television-watching habits across grade levels in their school or community, these data and the resulting analysis would be new in the sense that they never existed before.

The final characteristic of real problems is that they are directed toward a real audience. Real audiences are defined as people who voluntarily attend to information, events, services, or objects. A good way to understand the difference between a real and contrived audience is to reflect for a moment on what students might do with the results of a local oral history project. Although they might want to practice presenting the material before their classmates, an authentic audience would more properly consist of members of a local historical society or people who choose to read about the study in a local newspaper, magazine, or shopping guide. The practicing professional, on whose work Type III enrichment is modeled, almost always begins his or her work with an audience in mind. Audiences may change as the work evolves, but they serve as targets that give purpose and direction to the work.

These characteristics of real problems, coupled with our earlier examination of inductive learning, can be used to guide teachers and students in the Type III process. The discussion that follows is organized around five essential elements of Type III enrichment.

Interest-Based Learning

The first essential element is that problems being pursued through this type of learning experience must be based on individual or group interests. Teachers and other adults can certainly provide guidance and some creative steering toward the formulation of a problem, but they must avoid at all costs crossing the line from suggestion to prescription. If a problem is forced on students, we endanger the personal frame of reference discussed earlier and the kind of affective commitments that result in a willingness to engage in creative and demanding work. In most cases, the division of labor that takes place in group Type III situations causes a broader range of talents to be developed and promotes the kinds of real-world cooperation and mutual respect that we are attempting to achieve in the SEM. In addition to allowing for various types of involvement, problems that require a diversity of specialties also create opportunities for more personalization on the parts of individuals in the group. When each person feels that he or she owns a part of the problem, the first characteristic of a real problem is met.

A Focus on Advanced-Level Knowledge

The second essential element of Type III enrichment is that it should draw on authentic, advanced-level knowledge. If we want students to approximate the roles of practicing professionals, then it is important to examine the characteristics of people who have displayed high levels of expertise in their respective domains of knowledge. During the past two decades, cognitive psychologists have devoted much research to the topic of experts and expertise and the role of knowledge in attaining expert performance. Studies ranging from the characteristics of chess masters to the acquisition of routine tasks in unskilled or semi-skilled jobs (e.g., taxi driving) have uncovered a number of generalizations across the various domains that have been studied.

Experts mainly excel in their own domain, and they spend much more time than novices analyzing information in their respective fields of study. Experts also perceive large, meaningful patterns in their domain, and they understand how knowledge is organized in their domain. They tend to represent problems at deeper levels by creating conceptual categories rather than categories based on surface or superficial features, they are goal oriented, and they access knowledge mainly for its applicability to present problems. Finally, experts develop self-regulatory skills such as judging problem difficulty, apportioning their time, asking questions, reviewing their knowledge, and predicting outcomes.

High levels of expertise in a topic or domain obviously emerge from extensive experience gained over long periods of time. If we contrast this characteristic of expert performance with the traditional 42-minute period allotted for instruction in most schools—combined with superficial coverage of topics—it is clear that we must extend the amount of time that students are allowed to work on problems that have a personal frame of reference. Time allocations for individual or small-group Type III investigations, whether in enrichment clusters, regular classes, or other organizational arrangements, should be unbounded and expandable, as long as motivation remains high and progress toward goals is clearly evident.

The amount and complexity of knowledge available to students pursuing advanced studies and investigations must also be expanded. Guidelines for identifying both advanced-level content and methods are available through content standards developed by various professional associations, such as the National Council of Teachers of Mathematics and the National Council of Teachers of English. Finally, there has been a significant movement in teacher education programs to emphasize subject area competence as well as pedagogy. The amount of advanced-level knowledge that teachers possess will be a major determinant of the level of the courses they teach.

A Focus on Method

The third essential element of Type III enrichment is the use of authentic methods. This characteristic is essential because one of the goals of Type III enrichment is to help students extend their work beyond the usual kinds of reporting that often result when teachers and students view research as merely looking up information. Some reporting of previous information is a necessary part of most investigations. Indeed, the pursuit of new knowledge should always begin with a review of what is already known about a given topic. The end result of a Type III investigation, however, should be a creative contribution that goes beyond the existing information typically found in encyclopedias and other "all about" books.

Every field of organized knowledge can be defined, in part, by its method, and the methods of most fields can be found in certain kinds of guidebooks or manuals.

These how-to books are the key to escalating studies beyond the traditional report-writing approach that often passes for research. Every field of knowledge can also be partly defined by the kinds of data that represent the raw material of the field. New contributions are made in a field when investigators apply well-defined methods to the process of making sense out of random bits and pieces of information. Although some investigations require levels of sophistication and equipment that are far beyond the reach of younger investigators, almost every field of knowledge has entry-level and junior-level data-gathering opportunities.

We have seen scientifically respectable questionnaire studies on food and television preferences carried out by primary-grade students. A group of middle-grade students gathered and analyzed water samples as part of a large regional study on the extent and effects of acid rain. This work was done with such care that the students' findings were requested for use by a state environmental agency. Another group of elementary students used professional techniques in every aspect of producing a weekly television show broadcast by a local cable television company. A fifth-grade student wrote a guidebook that was adopted by his city's government as the official historical walking tour of the city. The success and high level of product development reflected in these examples can be traced to the proper use of authentic methods and techniques, even if these techniques were carried out at a somewhat more junior level than those used by adult inquirers.

The teacher's role is to help students identify, locate, and obtain resource materials or people to provide assistance in the appropriate use of investigative techniques. In some cases, it may be necessary to consult with librarians or professionals in various fields for advice about where and how to find method resources. Professional assistance may also be needed in translating complex concepts into material students can understand. Although method assistance is a major part of the teacher's responsibility in Type III enrichment, it is neither necessary nor realistic to expect teachers to have mastered a large number of investigative techniques. The most important skill is the ability to know where and how to help students obtain the right kind of material and the willingness to reach out beyond the usual school resources for specialized kinds of materials and resource people.

A Sense of Audience

The fourth essential element of Type III enrichment is that products and services resulting from this kind of involvement are targeted to real audiences. The magic key that has unlocked the success of so many Type III projects is the sense of audience that students have developed in connection with their work. This sense of audience gives students a reason for wanting to improve the quality of their products and develop effective ways of communicating their results with interested others. A sense of audience is also a primary contributor to the creation of task commitment and the concern for excellence and quality that has characterized so many Type III investigations.

If the Type III dimension of our model is to have maximum value in the overall development of young people, major attention must be given to helping them find appropriate outlets and audiences for their most creative efforts. This concern is modeled after the modus operandi of creative and productive individuals. If we could sum up in a few words the force behind creative and productive people, it would certainly be *effect on audience*. Type III enrichment provides natural opportunities for the kinds of personal satisfaction and self-expression that result from bringing an important piece of work to fruition. Writers hope to influence thoughts and emotions, scientists do research to find better ways to contribute new knowledge to their fields, and artists create products to enrich the lives of those who view their works. Teachers can help young people acquire this orientation by encouraging them to develop a sense of audience from the earliest stages of a Type III investigation.

The teacher's role requires helping students take one small but often neglected first step in the overall process of product development. This important step is to consider what people in a particular field produce and how they typically communicate their results with other interested people. Once again, we can look to the activities of practicing professionals and the how-to books for guidance. In most cases, young artists and scholars will be restricted to local outlets and audiences, but there will be occasions when products of unusual excellence can be shared with larger audiences.

Although school and local audiences are obvious starting points in the search for outlet vehicles, teachers should help students gain a perspective for more comprehensive outlet vehicles and audiences beyond local opportunities. Many organizations, for example, prepare newsletters and journals at the state and national levels, and they are usually receptive to high-quality contributions by students. Similarly, state and national magazines and Web sites often carry outstanding work by young people. The search for more widespread audiences should only be encouraged when student work is high quality and when it has achieved local recognition. Exploring external audiences helps students develop standards of quality, and it also provides them with real-world experiences about the rigors and challenges of reaching out to wider audiences. Exploring external audiences involves an element of risk taking and the chance that work will not be accepted in the wider arenas of publications and dissemination, but by beginning a search for audiences at the local level, an element of success is likely to be achieved.

Authentic Evaluation

The fifth essential element of Type III enrichment is that work carried out using this approach to learning is evaluated in an authentic rather than artificial manner. The ultimate test of quality in the world outside the school is whether products or services achieve a desired effect on clients or selected audiences. For this reason, Type III products should *never* be graded or scored. This traditional school practice is antithetical to the ways in which work is evaluated in the real world. Students can be provided with categorical feedback using a guide such as the Student Product Assessment Form (Renzulli & Reis, 1982), but even this instrument should only be used to help students refine and improve their work. Teachers and other adults should view their role in the feedback process as that of a "resident escalator." Sensitive and specific recommendations about how particular aspects of the work can be improved will help students move slowly but surely toward higher and higher levels of product excellence. Every effort should be made to pinpoint specific areas in which suggested changes should be implemented. This approach helps avoid student discouragement and reconfirm a belief in the overall value of their endeavors.

Type III enrichment involves students who become interested in pursuing a self-selected area and are willing to commit the time necessary for advanced content acquisition and process training in which they assume the role of a firsthand inquirer. Two case study examples of Type III enrichment completed by students are provided in the following. The first Type III was completed independently, and the second was a group project. The first is a book written by a fifth-grade student named Gretchen who had two major interests: the literature of Louisa May Alcott and cooking. Gretchen read all of Louisa May Alcott's books and identified each time a specific food was mentioned. She researched the recipes of the time that would have been used to make the food (such as buckwheat cakes), field tested each recipe (including making substitutions for ingredients no longer available), and created an original cookbook entitled *The Louisa May Alcott Cookbook*, published by Little Brown. In this Type III, both the process and the final product involve high levels of creative engagement and clear evidence of creative work.

A second example of a Type III involved the creation of a bike path in a city in the northwestern United States. The local high school students included a group of avid bikers as well as some students who just believed that automobiles should not own the road. The creative process of having the town council agree to the expenditure took this group of young people through a labyrinth of politics, legal issues, financial machinations, and finally, a tough vote. The bike path was built, and the creative process of political and civil action was a peak experience for these young people.

The Louisa May Alcott Cookbook

by Gretchen Anderson, Grade 5
    Haynes School, Sudbury, Massachusetts
    Description of the Type III

Gretchen spent a year and a half working on a cookbook that combined vignettes of scenes from *Little Women* and *Little Men* with many authentic nineteenth-century recipes for making the foods described in the novels. Cooking was Gretchen's hobby, and she became fascinated with the foods mentioned in the novels and learned how to re-create them. Because Gretchen believed that other youngsters would also be interested in these foods, she sent her book to Little Brown Company. *The Louisa May Alcott Cookbook* was accepted and became the first book contracted by them with a child author. Gretchen's teacher, Elizabeth D. Beloff, reported that Gretchen's enthusiasm for reading the books and researching the recipes could not sustain her through the writing of each scene and the incredible attention to detail necessary in creating the recipes.

Therefore, Ms. Beloff needed to complete the following steps to help Gretchen complete her project.

1. Vary the assignments (e.g., text writing, research, and recipe writing).
2. Assign tasks that could be completed in one or two sessions.
3. Break large segments into small parts.
4. Use a system to record accomplishments (e.g., weekly or daily check sheet).

Gretchen's teacher also indicated that Gretchen was always able to envision the book but had a problem getting organized. She was able to help her by suggesting ways of organizing information. Particularly useful was a file box to keep recipes and note cards that recorded steps to be taken.

SOURCE: Courtesy of Creative Learning Press.

The Bike Path System

by Sean Sweeney, Brenda Roos, Kim VanDell, Brian Mohr, Gary Gibb, Kevin Hatch, Allison Duchow, Jill Havens, Chris Soberg (Grades 8 and 9), Fowler Junior High School, Tigard, Oregon

Description of the Type III

Because many of the city streets of Tigard, Oregon, were barely wide enough for two cars to pass, this group of students worked with their teachers Bill Dolbeer and Jay Leet to get a ballot measure passed that would provide bike paths for the city. The following chronology tells the story.

Bike Path Project—Time Line, October through the next July

October

— Arrival at project idea.
— Visits from Raeldon Barker, city administrator in Tigard, and Frank Curry, Tigard Public Works director.
— Wrote to Eugene, Oregon, for its master plan—studied.
— Wrote to Beaverton, Oregon, for its master plan—studied.
— Visit from Washington County bikeway planner.
— Visit from member of Tigard Park board.

November

— Discovered Tigard's earlier "Comprehensive Plan for Bicycle/Pedestrian Pathways."
— One part of group focused in on Tiedeman Road, an extremely dangerous street adjoining the school.
— The other part decided to revise Tigard's 1974 plan and check community opinion about bike path needs.

December

—Development of community survey.
—Measurement and photographing of Tiedeman Road.
—Testing and revising of survey.
—Distribution of surveys (about 2,500).

January

—Tallying and analysis of surveys.
—Preparation of presentation for Tigard Park Board.
—Presentation of findings to Tigard Park Board.

February

—Development of a three-phase plan for bike paths.
—First presentation to Tigard City Council (February 17).
—Presentation to Tigard Rotary.

March

—Revision of phased plan.
—Presentations to city council.

—Presentation to Tigard Lions Club.
—Discussion of plan with individual city council members.

April

— City council agrees to place $200,000 serial level on May 19th ballot.
— Writing of measure and filing with county elections department (we thought!).
— Presentations to parent groups at Fowler, Charles F. Tigard Elementary, and Tigard High School.
— Preparation of flyer.

May

— Bike-a-Rama at Fowler (May 16th) with prize giveaway and five-mile ride on proposed streets.
— Mapping, producing, and posting of lawn signs around Tigard.
— Printing and door-to-door distribution of flyer (about 6,000).
— May 19th—Election Day—Our measure is not on the ballot!
— The county conducts an investigation. Findings—No one is at fault; all should share blame for lack of communication.
— The state conducts an investigation. Their findings to come out in June.
— In an emergency session May 22nd, Tigard City Council approves placing our measure on the ballot June 30th.
— We file the measure again in Hillsboro, May 26th.
— Channel 2 News does a story on our project.
— Down come the lawn signs.

June

— The secretary of state's report comes out, placing blame on the Washington County Elections Department (June 4th).
— Letter-writing campaign to all the radio and TV stations in Portland to have public service announcements made.
— Redesigning of flyer.
— Printing, stuffing, and mailing of new flyer (about 6,000).
— County elections responsibilities shifted to county administrator (June 9th).
— Lawn signs repainted and up again.
— Uh-oh! The state says our re-filed ballot measure may be invalid because of the ballot's wording (June 18th).
— At another emergency city council meeting (June 19th), one sentence is added to our measure to satisfy state requirements.
— The county election coordinator is suspended for two weeks without pay.
— Channel 8 TV News (John) does a feature on our project.
— June 30th—Election day. Our measure is on the ballot.

July

—Voter turnout is light, but our measure passes by more than a 2/3 margin.
—Channel 8 TV does a follow-up story on our project.
—Down come the lawn signs. Summer vacation begins.

APPLYING THE ENRICHMENT TRIAD MODEL TO ENRICHMENT CLUSTERS

The Enrichment Triad Model also serves as the background for enrichment clusters, nongraded groups of students who share common interests and who come together during specially designated time blocks to pursue these interests. The main rationale for participation in one or more clusters is that students and teachers want to be there. All teachers (including music, art, physical education, etc.) are involved in facilitating clusters, and their involvement in any particular cluster should be based on the same type of interest assessment that is used for students in selecting clusters of choice. Community resource people are also invited to organize enrichment clusters. Enrichment clusters are excellent vehicles for promoting cooperation in the context of real-world problem solving, and they also provide superlative opportunities for promoting self-concept.

Enrichment clusters are organized around major disciplines, interdisciplinary themes, or cross-disciplinary topics (e.g., an electronic music group or a theatrical or television production group that includes actors, writers, technical specialists, costume designers, etc.). The clusters are modeled after the ways in which knowledge utilization, thinking skills, and interpersonal relations take place in the real world. Thus, all work is directed toward the production of a product or service.

Enrichment clusters are a major vehicle for stimulating interests and developing creative potential across the entire school population. They are also vehicles for staff development, in that they provide teachers an opportunity to participate in enrichment teaching and subsequently to analyze and compare this type of teaching with traditional methods of instruction. In this regard, the model promotes a spillover effect by encouraging teachers to become better talent scouts and talent developers and to apply enrichment techniques to regular classroom situations. Enrichment clusters are used by some schools on a one-half day per week basis, and in other schools they meet daily. At the Webster Elementary School in St. Paul, Minnesota, for example, a broad array of interdisciplinary clusters are offered daily. At the Southeast School in Mansfield, Connecticut, enrichment clusters are offered two afternoons a month and are taught jointly by teachers and parent volunteers. One cluster is called "Flight School," organized by the superintendent of schools, who is a licensed pilot.

Thus, students learn only relevant content and use only authentic processes in this context, and instead of lesson plans, adults and children focus on three key questions that guide learning in an enrichment cluster:

- What do people with an interest in this area do?
- What knowledge, materials, and other resources are needed to produce student-generated products or services in this area?
- In what ways can the products or services affect an intended audience?

Like extracurricular activities and programs such as sports, yearbook, and other clubs, the clusters meet at designated times and operate on the assumption that students and teachers (or community resource people) choose or want to be there. Common goals make real cooperation a necessity, and divisions of labor in the clusters allow for differentiated levels of expertise and involvement, varying levels of challenge, and opportunities for different types of leadership to emerge on the part of students. For example, a student in a newspaper cluster can explore positions such as editor, artist, reporter, feature writer, sports writer, advertising manager, cartoonist, and so forth. This type of learning environment is highly supportive of individual differences and therefore promotes the development of self-concept, self-efficacy, cooperation, and positive feelings that result from being a member of a goal-oriented team. In the spirit of the "schoolwide" part of the SEM, all students are involved in the cluster program.

All teachers are involved in organizing the clusters, and numerous schools have also involved parents and other community resource people. Many schools provide enrichment opportunities to all students through the implementation of enrichment clusters.

At most schools, the idea to implement enrichment clusters is introduced at a faculty meeting, and reactions of teachers usually range from enthusiastic and affirmative to skeptical and concerned. Some teachers raise immediate and valid concerns, usually having to do with scheduling, the biggest obstacle in managing the program, yet the simplest to resolve for future years. Because the clusters are often implemented after the year had started and pull-out programs such as art, physical education, and music are usually already scheduled, there may be no available common time slot in the school schedule. Teachers can be concerned that the same group of students would miss a given special class (such as physical education or art) for several weeks in a row or that some teachers might have to forgo their planning time. By choosing a day with the least number of conflicts and juggling special schedules, a temporary solution can be reached. Scheduling problems can easily be avoided by setting aside a time block for clusters before the school year begins.

Another concern might be the issue of teacher planning time in general, as enrichment clusters might be viewed as "one more thing" added to an already overloaded curriculum. When teachers asked, "When are we supposed to plan for all this?" several points were considered. First, the cluster activities were not supposed to model traditional lessons with preplanned activities, but rather, involve more student directed, hands-on explorations. Second, pairs of teachers or instructional assistants could work together and share planning responsibilities. Through collaboration with local experts, parents, and businesspeople, the clusters quickly became viewed as enjoyable and exciting experiences (for staff as well as students), rather than an added burden or "extra class."

A final concern that might be raised regards behavioral problems; however, few behavior problems are usually found during the implementation of the clusters. Clusters are organized around interests—student interests and staff interests, which minimize the typical behavioral problems often observed in classroom settings. In addition, the hands-on, exploratory nature of the clusters invites students to become active participants in directing the activities pursued in the cluster, and students quickly adjust to becoming responsible for their own learning. On the rare instances when behavior problems do arise, students are removed from the clusters and lose the privilege of attending the cluster for that day.

Beginning to Implement Enrichment Clusters

After discussion and problem solving during faculty meetings, most faculty will agree to participate in a series of enrichment clusters, usually one in the fall and one in the spring for a series of 6 to 12 weeks. Clusters usually meet for an hour and a half to two hours, one day per week. Most teachers volunteer to facilitate clusters. In our research sites, for example, one teacher, who lived on a dairy farm, organized a cluster on farming (students subsequently investigated modern farming technology and explored developing various uses for milk in that cluster). Most teachers organize their cluster around an interest, and their ideas varied, including quilting, ornithology, video production, and painting.

Using additional staff suggestions, parents and community people were contacted, and they became interested in facilitating clusters. In just a few weeks, a wide variety of clusters on a variety of topics were formed, and a brochure and registration form that described the clusters was sent home with students to discuss with their parents or guardians. A high percentage of the registration forms are consistently returned the day after they were sent home, others soon followed, and those students who didn't return their forms were registered at school. A sample brochure description of one cluster is provided in the following:

> Young Sculptors, Inc.
> Facilitated by a local artist who has exhibited with the National Sculpture Society in New York and has pieces in private collections throughout the United States. He has often shared his studio with students.
> How does a sculptor work? How is a piece of rock transformed into a work of art? What happens to the finished piece? Explore the process of creating your own 3-dimensional work of art using authentic tools and plaster. You may discover that creating your piece is as much fun as enjoying the finished product! View some works in marble, and learn about one artist's perspective. The instructor is a local sculptor who has been carving for more than 20 years.
> P.S. Wear old clothes or bring a smock.

The first day of clusters is usually very exciting for teachers as well as students but some cautions need to be addressed, as younger students may be unaccustomed to going to different classrooms, working with new groups of students in mixed grades, and being with a new adult. After the second week, however, we have found that students at every grade level seemed to enjoy their clusters, and the transition period in the halls was typically filled with eager anticipation and commotion. Many principals have commented during cluster day that "You can feel the excitement!" By creating a simple bulletin board of pictures of students in their clusters, interest was stimulated throughout the week. Many animated conversations could be overheard in front of this display: "What did you get for a cluster? Mine is great, we get to make a sculpture!"

In some schools, clusters are organized after a formal assessment of student interests has been conducted, and the tabulated surveys resulted in a list of the highest interest areas. Results confirmed the top interests that might be expected from elementary students—dinosaurs, animals, magic, cartooning. Other interests may be surprising to some teachers, such as high interests in languages, such as Spanish and French, and the sciences, such as math and oceanography. In general, the sciences and arts have been found to be consistently popular.

In our research sites, every effort has been made to match staff interests with student interests, or to bring in people with targeted interests from the community. The major goal was to provide as many authentic experiences as possible that matched the findings from the interest surveys. In our research, exciting clusters included Life Undersea, facilitated by students from a university marine biology center; Paleontologists, with personnel from a dinosaur state park; Young Artists, with artists from a local art guild; the NASA Exploratory Group, with a university's planetarium director; Young Firefighters, with a local fire lieutenant; Forest and Wildlife Biologists, with foresters from a state forest; Invention Convention, with a physicist from a university physics labs; Detectives, with a police officer; and other clusters facilitated by school staff members. Community volunteers were dedicated and enthusiastic. These community volunteers provided an aspect of authenticity well worth the effort involved in contacting and involving them. These cluster facilitators were practicing professionals and had access to authentic resources and equipment and, in some cases, sites not available to a public school. Questions posed by students received answers that provided insights into real professions. Several clusters went on field trips that were designed to expose the children to authentic settings and situations encountered by professionals in each field. The firefighters went to the local fire department, Life Undersea to an aquarium, Young Lawyers to a courtroom, and the Chimers Handbell Choir to a church with handbells.

In our research sites, faculty and staff also developed some excellent new clusters for the second series of the year, and we found that exciting events occurred in the spring clusters. The Puppeteers Workshop created different puppets each week, and students had an opportunity to act out short plays. The Ukrainian Artists Guild learned about the Ukrainian custom of sharing an egg with a special friend. Students designed and decorated their eggs using wax, dyes, and a stylus. Computer Connection explored advantages of working online and formed new friendships with pen pals using e-mail. The Windham Horticulture Alliance designed and planted a landscape for the front of Windham Center School under the guidance of two teachers and a landscape architect. A group of younger students in the Sign Language Guild learned how it feels in part to be deaf and learned to communicate with each other using American Sign Language. The Police Academy worked as detectives with a teacher and a detective from the Youth Division of the local police. They helped "solve" crimes using techniques used by real detectives. The Multicultural Society experienced different cultures through food, art, and communication. Young Artists explored the art of stained glass with an instructional assistant who also had her own stained glass business, and they created works of art on slate and glass.

After the first series of enrichment clusters, as parents are familiar with the cluster program, some schools have registration for the clusters completed by students at school. Students were asked to select three clusters that interested them, then they were placed into one of their choices. This method avoided ranking choices and subsequent disappointment of not receiving a first choice. Some clusters were more popular than others, with many students selecting Animal Trainers, Life Undersea, NASA, and Aviators. Initially, only four students selected the Chimers Handbell Choir, so the facilitator recruited some musically talented students. Due to lack of student interest, two clusters had to be canceled, and their would-be facilitators agreed to assist with other clusters.

Maintaining flexibility is key to a successful cluster program. In one site, for example, the NASA Exploratory Group began as a cluster for K–2, but it became clear after the first week that the facilitator and content would be better suited to older students. It was originally a 10-week cluster, so after the first 5 weeks it was changed to accommodate students in Grades 2 through 5. Many of the students who registered for it were doing a unit on space, so they were able to make some valuable connections with their classroom learning and bring what they explored in their cluster back to class. Their teacher was delighted too, explaining that several eager students even had the opportunity to correct her on an astronomy point she made in class. In one school, the NASA cluster was so successful that the facilitator was recognized by NASA and the White House with a national award, in part for her involvement with the enrichment clusters.

Sharing Products and Services

Opportunities to share cluster activities accomplished three goals: (a) providing authentic audiences for clusters, (b) organizing Type I experiences for students on a variety of topics, and (c) generating interest in future clusters. After a series of clusters has ended, students share their activities with peers on an informal basis, or a more formal celebration takes place in which students share their products and cluster experiences. In some schools, these celebrations take place during a product fair as part of "Family Night" at the end of the year, with students available to provide explanations. The care and pride in each and every student product is usually evident when students describe their accomplishments.

In addition, many clusters had other ways to share and celebrate their products and services. In one school, a Friday evening performance was scheduled for performances by the Drama Cluster and the Chimers Handbell Choir, which generated much interest in future sessions of this cluster. In another school, the Computer Cluster members became consultants when they offered the service of teaching their classmates and teachers about accessing the Internet and using e-mail. In another school, the Bluebird Builders constructed several birdhouses and installed these in a nature area that they developed behind the school for everyone to enjoy. The School Newspaper Cluster developed a newspaper and distributed copies to everyone in the school. Inside were interviews, news articles about events in the school, illustrations, jokes, and features about other clusters such as the Young Paleontologists. In that school, the students in Young Paleontologists conducted "research" on a specific fictitious dinosaur, named their dinosaur using meaningful Latin origins, went on a "dig," and reported findings to classmates in a mock symposium complete with sketches and models. In another school, the Horticulture Alliance developed and planted an original landscape design with flowers and shrubs for the front of the school—a daily reminder of the endeavors of this cluster. In another cluster program, a cluster called the Gamers developed original board games, played by their classmates and families. Schoolwide displays are often developed by the Young Artists, Street Artists, the Horticulture Guild, and Sweet Confections clusters. The varied methods of communicating results with audiences helped enhance the authentic communication skills of students.

Teacher Reactions to Clusters

The most positive reactions about facilitating clusters are usually from those teachers who pursue their own interests. They often select topics that had nothing to do with their regular classrooms. In one school, the art teacher assisted with a cluster on art in the fall, but in the spring facilitated a cluster on computers. She admitted that this cluster was definitely a more exciting experience for her. Our experience suggests that teachers become increasingly positive and more relaxed as the year continues.

Teachers also expressed surprise at what students accomplish in their clusters. For example, in the Chimers Handbell Choir cluster, both the teacher and the students became surprised with the progress and students' enjoyment in learning to play and perform. Teachers usually find that cluster activities carried over into regular curriculum: 3-D structures in a math class were named by students using Latin names they learned in their Paleontology cluster; students in the NASA cluster used what they were doing in their cluster as a basis for a science project in their regular classroom; sign language was observed in the halls and in the classrooms; e-mail was taught by the online cluster members to their classmates. In all, our research has found that the majority of teachers explained that the enrichment cluster program influenced the content and methods in their regular classrooms (Reis, Gentry, & Maxfield, 1998).

In one research study (Reis et al., 1998), evaluation data were collected from all cluster facilitators and used to modify the program. The vast majority of teachers recognized the overwhelming interest in and excitement about clusters by students and saw tremendous value in the program. All teachers agreed that enrichment clusters enhanced learning and students' enjoyment in school. Collectively, the teachers decided to continue the enrichment clusters as a regular part of the SEM program.

Parent and Student Reactions

In research on clusters (Reis et al., 1998), parents were overwhelmingly positive toward the cluster program and frequently commented that they were thrilled that their children were able to participate in something during the school day that is generally only available at considerable expense and at considerable distance. Many asked if the program was going to continue. Each parent who inquired was encouraged to become involved in the enrichment program in subsequent years, as this was a good way to provide the resources and energy needed to continue and ensure future success.

Students' enjoyment and interest were apparent in many ways. For example, many chose to pursue cluster activities during their own time. Several students from the Ukrainian Artists came in during recess to work on their eggs. Other students from the computer cluster spent their own time and enrichment time using e-mail. In the Invention Convention cluster, two of the students decided to continue work on their inventions after the cluster finished. We have consistently found that when the cluster series finished, students are anxious to continue, and they ask: "Are we going to have clusters today? When do clusters start again? Will we have clusters next year?" Formal evaluations (Reis et al., 1998) in each cluster showed that 92% of the students liked their clusters, 95% "learned new things," 92% found their cluster facilitator "interesting," and 95% wanted to be in a cluster again.

Enrichment clusters usually generate a great deal of interest from the community and several other school districts. Articles often appear in local newspapers on clusters, and requests are often received from teachers and administrators from other districts to visit the program. Those visiting have been extremely enthusiastic about the program and expressed an interest in implementing them in their schools. "How do we begin?" is usually a question posed, and invariably other educators leave schools that offer clusters with information.

Benefits of Clusters

An enrichment cluster program has several benefits to a school. First, this program extends gifted-education services to all students on a regular basis. Although it is not designed to replace existing gifted programs, nor should it be used to do so, an enrichment cluster program can build a bridge between gifted education and general-education programs. All students have interests and can benefit by having those interests addressed during school; enrichment clusters provide a time and framework for doing so. Second, an enrichment cluster program involves all students and staff in exciting, inductive learning centered on common interests and focused on developing authentic products and services. Finally, such a program provides schools with a reason to involve community, businesses, and parents in a productive manner, thereby helping to develop real partnerships in learning.

Some may wonder, with all that currently exists in schools today, how a school could possibly afford the time to implement such a program. Given the benefits, one might better ask, how a school could afford not to make the time to focus on student strengths, interests, and potentials—and to do so for all of a school's students, at least once in a while! The ultimate goal of learning that is guided by these principles and by the Enrichment Triad Model is to replace dependent and passive learning with independence, opportunities for creative productivity, and the pursuit of individual interest and engaged learning. We hope that as schools adopt this model, we can transform them into places for talent development through creative learning opportunities.

HOW CAN TEACHERS LEARN TO USE ENRICHMENT TEACHING?

This question is frequently asked, probably as a result of the ways in which we have prescribed and organized the work of teachers. Teaching in a natural way actually requires very little training. However, it does require that teachers understand the importance of serving as a facilitator rather than an instructor. This method also requires that teachers know what to do in a situation that purposefully avoids lesson plans, unit plans, and other types of prescribed instructional approaches. Space does not permit a full explanation of this method of teaching, but some questions will illustrate how a group gets started in an enrichment cluster. Six key questions include the following.

1. What do people with an interest in this area do?
2. What products do they create and/or what services do they provide?
3. What methods do they use to carry out their work?
4. What resources and materials are needed to produce high quality products and services?
5. How, and with whom, do they communicate the results of their work to other potentially interested persons?
6. What steps need to be taken to have an impact on intended audiences?

The teacher's role as a facilitator, for example, includes helping the poetry subgroup identify places where they might submit their work for publication. With the help of a librarian, one teacher located a book entitled *Directory of Poetry Publishers*. This book, which contains hundreds of outlets for poets' work, is the type of resource that makes the difference between a teacher who teaches poetry in a traditional fashion and a facilitator who develops talent in young poets. The most difficult part of being a good enrichment cluster facilitator is to stop teaching and to replace traditional instruction with the kinds of "guide-on-the-side" responsibilities used by mentors and coaches. People who fulfill these roles instruct only when there is a direct need to accomplish a task that is part of product development. Many teachers who have served as yearbook advisors, drama club directors, 4-H Club advisors, athletic coaches, and facilitators of other extracurricular activities already have the techniques necessary for facilitating a successful enrichment cluster. The teacher's role in an enrichment cluster is to assist in the procurement of methodic resources and to help students understand how to use the resources. The only times that direct instruction should take place is when the instruction is necessary to help produce and improve the product or service. Thus, for example, students doing a community survey in a social science cluster might receive direct instruction on procedures for developing an authentic questionnaire, rating scale, or survey instrument.

APPLYING THE TYPE III PROCESS TO ENRICHMENT CLUSTERS

The enrichment clusters are ideal places to implement Type III enrichment. By using information from the Total Talent Portfolio to form the clusters, we are assured of at least some commonality of interest on the parts of students in the various clusters. Mutual interests are a good starting point for accelerating motivation and promoting harmony, respect, and cooperation among group members. An orientation session should emphasize the objectives and essential elements of Type III enrichment and the characteristics of a real problem. Students grasp this approach to learning quickly if teachers are consistent in their transformed role as coach and mentor rather than conventional instructor.

The biggest single problem in implementing Type III studies is getting started. Type III enrichment represents qualitatively different learning experiences, and it is important for teachers to realize that they themselves must engage in some activities that differ from the traditional activities that define the traditional teacher's role. This point cannot be overemphasized. It is impossible to foster *differential* types of learning experiences through the use of ordinary teaching methods. If we want young people to think, feel, and act like practicing professionals (or firsthand inquirers), then teachers must also learn how to raise a few of the questions that professionals ask about the nature and function of their own work. In other words, teachers must go one step beyond the questions that are ordinarily raised in problem-solving situations. This step involves problem finding and problem focusing, which is how practicing professionals begin their work.

Almost everything that young people do in traditional classrooms casts them in the role of lesson learners. Even when working on so-called research reports, students nearly always perceive their main purpose as that of "finding out about..." One need only ask youngsters why they are working on a particular report. Invariably, they reply: to find out *about* the eating habits of the gray squirrel, *about* the exports of Brazil, or *about* the Battle of Gettysburg. There is nothing wrong with finding out about things—all student and adult inquirers do it—but practicing professionals do it for a purpose beyond merely finding out about something for its own sake. This purpose, which we might refer to as the application purpose, is what Type III enrichment is all about. Thus, the key to helping youngsters feel like firsthand inquirers rather than mere absorbers of knowledge is to explore with them some of the questions that professionals raise.

Exploration of these questions can be pursued in a variety of ways. Type I experiences in the form of visiting speakers, discussions of career education materials, displays of typical products from the fields around which a cluster is organized, or videos of professionals at work can provide a picture of the products, services, and activities that characterize various fields of study. A library trip organized around a scavenger hunt format is a good way to help students broaden their perspective about the products and communication vehicles associated with various areas of inquiry.

Type II activities that provide direct or simulated experiences of typical pursuits in a particular field are also useful in helping young people answer the questions. How-to books are an especially valuable source for locating such activities. Thus, for example, a social science cluster can experience data-gathering and analysis methods by using one of the sample activities on surveying, observing, or developing a research hypothesis that can be found in the book, *A Student's Guide to Conducting Social Science Research* (Bunker, Pearlson, & Schultz, 1999). This entire book can be used at the introductory stages of a cluster to provide know-how and to generate ideas that will help students identify their own research interests. It is important, however, for students to be informed in advance that planned, deductive activities are preparatory for the self-selected, inductive work that should be the primary focus of an enrichment cluster. *Research Comes Alive! A Guidebook for Conducting Original Research With Middle and High School Students* (Schack & Starko, 1998) and *Chi Squares, Pie Charts and Me* (Baum, Gable, & List, 1987) are two excellent resources for use with enrichment clusters.

The teacher's role in encouraging Type III learning is threefold:

1. Teachers should organize and guide, but not dominate, the exploration process.

2. Teachers should assist in the location of methodic resource materials such as a book on puppet making or presenting data in graphic or tabular forms.

3. Teachers need to open doors for connecting student products with appropriate audiences.

The Enrichment Triad Model was designed to help students gain personal knowledge about their own abilities, interests, and learning styles. If, as Socrates said, "The unexamined life is not worth living," then we should also consider a corollary to this axiom about life in school: "The unexamined lesson is not worth learning." Although it would be desirable to apply this corollary to all school experiences, the types of enrichment advocated in the Triad Model are excellent vehicles for examining preferences, tastes, and inclinations that will help students gain a greater understanding of themselves.

When teachers assume these different kinds of responsibilities, students develop an entirely new attitude toward both their work and their teachers. There is one overriding goal to developing learning opportunities based on the concept of Type III enrichment. This goal is larger than the products students prepare or the methods they learn in pursuing their work. The largest goal is that students begin to think, feel, and act like creative and productive individuals. The Type III component of the Enrichment Triad is designed to develop an attitude that has reinforced the work of effective people since the beginning of time: I can do . . . I can be . . . I can create.

7

Applying the Schoolwide Enrichment Model (SEM) to Content Areas

The SEM in Reading

During the last several years, in both urban and suburban schools across the country, an alternative approach to traditional reading instruction has occurred on a daily basis. The Schoolwide Enrichment Model in Reading (SEM-R; Reis et al., 2003) is an enrichment-based approach to reading that evolved from the SEM (Renzulli, 1977a; Renzulli & Reis, 1997) and has been used as an approach to providing enrichment and talent development in reading opportunities for all students. The SEM-R focuses on enrichment for all students through engagement in challenging, self-selected reading, accompanied by instruction in higher-order thinking and strategy skills. A second core focus of the SEM-R is differentiation of instruction and reading content, coupled with more challenging reading experiences and advanced opportunities for metacognition and self-regulated reading.

It is important to try alternative methods of teaching reading such as the SEM-R, as the scores continue to decline among culturally diverse students and those who live in poverty. For example, only 51% of last year's high school graduates who took the ACT examination had the reading skills they needed to succeed in college or job-training programs, the lowest proportion in more than a decade. The news is even more disappointing for culturally or linguistically diverse students, as 79% of Black students, 67% of Hispanic students, and 33% of students from families with annual incomes less than $30,000 were found not prepared for college-level reading (ACT, 2006).

Differentiation of instruction is also important, as a wide variation exists in the range of reading levels in most elementary and middle-school classrooms. In elementary and middle-school classrooms that use the SEM-R, we found that the range of reading instructional levels spans eight or nine grade levels. For example, we have routinely found that some third-grade students read on a first-grade level, whereas others in the same class read on an eighth-grade level.

The SEM-R has been implemented in more than a dozen schools under rigorous research conditions during the last four years with successful results in every study (Reis et al., 2005). Results in the initial years were so promising that additional federal funds enabled us to "gear up" with additional studies on the SEM-R in sites across the country.

Educators and researchers agree that reading and literacy contribute to academic success (S. M. Burns, Griffin, & Snow, 1999; National Reading Panel [NRP], 2000). Being able to read fluently and understand text is a critical skill, as strong reading comprehension predicts performance on achievement tests (Allington, 2002). When we can improve reading instruction for children who live in poverty, some of the inequities in school systems are lessened. Common sense tells educators that reading more can also make a difference. Ivey and Fisher (2005) describe the use of silent reading as opposed to direct instruction in two high schools with very different outcomes. In one high school, planned reading was replaced with a direct-instruction approach to reading. Scores declined and library use plummeted, whereas in the other high school, which maintained a sustained silent reading program, students' reading scores increased and state standards were met. The NRP (2000) called for research on the effectiveness of encouraging students to engage in independent reading and emphasized the need for rigorous experimental studies that measure reading fluency and comprehension. The work we are doing on SEM-R described in this chapter responded to this call.

The SEM-R (see Figure 7.1) has three general categories of reading instruction that are dynamic in nature and designed to enable flexibility of implementation and content in response to both teachers' and students' needs. This approach is based on Renzulli's Enrichment Triad Model (Renzulli, 1977a; Renzulli & Reis, 1997), with three levels of enrichment: broad exposure to areas in which students might have interests, higher-order thinking skills training and methods instruction, and opportunities to pursue self-selected topics of interest. The emphasis of the SEM-R is on enjoyment of the learning process with a focus on planned, systematic enrichment experiences based on the Enrichment Triad Model.

In some schools, the SEM-R is integrated into regular reading instruction; in others, as an additional literacy block; and in still others, as an afterschool literacy experience. With only one day of training and a manual that described all aspects of this approach, teachers learned to use the SEM-R and integrate higher-order thinking skills with students of all reading levels. They use a variety of higher-order thinking skills and questions to meet the needs of readers as they implement this enrichment approach to reading. The three phases of SEM-R help students be exposed to good literature, learn to be more self-directed in reading, apply higher-level thinking skills, and use independent reading to pursue interests.

Figure 7.1   Components of the SEM-R Framework

Phase 1 - Exposure	Phase 2 - Training & Self-Selected Reading	Phase 3 - Interest & Choice Components
• High-interest book hooks for read-aloud • Higher-order thinking probing questions • Bookmarks for teachers with questions focusing on advanced thinking skills and reading skill instruction that is relevant to a broad range of literature	• Training and discussions on Supported Independent Reading • One-on-one teacher conferences on higher-level reading strategy and instruction • Bookmarks for students posing higher-order questions regarding character, plot, setting, considering the story, and other useful topics *Increasing degree of student selection*	• Introducing creative thinking • Exploring the Internet • Genre studies • Literary exploration • Responding to books • Investigation centers • Focus on biographies • Buddy reading • Books on tape • Literature circles • Creative or expository writing • Type III investigations
Type I Activities	**Type II Activities**	**Type II & Type III Investigators**

Figure 7.2   Bookmarks From SEM-R

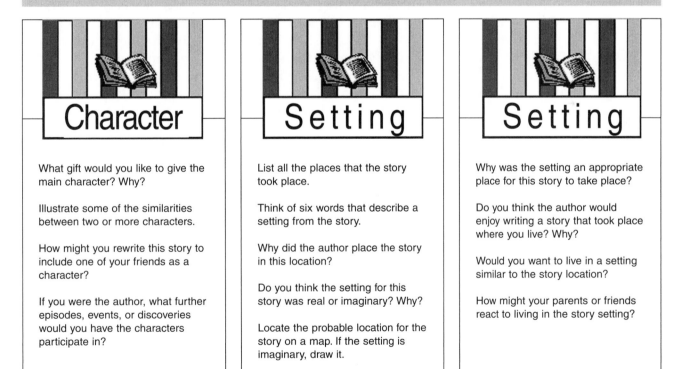

Character

What gift would you like to give the main character? Why?

Illustrate some of the similarities between two or more characters.

How might you rewrite this story to include one of your friends as a character?

If you were the author, what further episodes, events, or discoveries would you have the characters participate in?

Setting

List all the places that the story took place.

Think of six words that describe a setting from the story.

Why did the author place the story in this location?

Do you think the setting for this story was real or imaginary? Why?

Locate the probable location for the story on a map. If the setting is imaginary, draw it.

Setting

Why was the setting an appropriate place for this story to take place?

Do you think the author would enjoy writing a story that took place where you live? Why?

Would you want to live in a setting similar to the story location?

How might your parents or friends react to living in the story setting?

PHASE 1: HOOKING KIDS ON LITERATURE WITH TEACHER READ-ALOUDS

In Phase 1 of the SEM-R, teachers select diverse literature across a variety of genres to read aloud to students, interspersed with higher-order questioning and thinking skills instruction. These "book hook" sessions began with 10 to 20 minutes of high-interest, challenging books designed to "hook" children on reading. All teachers received a collection of approximately 125 books to augment their classroom collections. We identified books from different genres across various grade levels that are of high interest to students at different reading levels. Teachers were also provided with suggestions for engaging students' interests and exposing them to a variety of literary genres including mysteries, poetry, historical and science fiction, biographies, autobiographies, and other nonfiction. Teachers also received laminated bookmarks with higher-order questions to help teachers differentiate instruction and ask higher-order thinking skills questions with all students (available for download at www.gifted.uconn.edu/semr; see Figure 7.2). In our studies, teachers asked significantly more high-level questions in the SEM-R Phase 1 read-aloud instruction than they did in control classrooms (Fogarty, 2006).

PHASE 2: SUPPORTED INDEPENDENT READING AND DIFFERENTIATED CONFERENCES

Phase 2 of the SEM-R is designed to increase students' engagement and self-direction in supported independent reading of self-selected, high-interest books, supported by individualized, differentiated reading conferences with their teachers (Guthrie & Humenick, 2004). During Phase 2, Supported Independent Reading, teachers encouraged students to select books that are slightly more difficult than their current reading level. Teachers continually assessed whether books were an appropriate match through weekly or biweekly conferences with students. Our research demonstrates that initially, the majority of the students selected books that were quite easy for them. They were told to bring these easier books home to read because, during school, it was their job to select books that were more challenging to read, that is, books with some words they did not know and some ideas that were new to them. In other words, teachers urged students to engage in reading in an area of personal interest that was slightly more difficult than their current independent reading level.

In our work with SEM-R, we found that initially, most students could read these books for only 5 to 10 minutes a day without losing concentration or focus, and most displayed little self-regulation in reading. Teachers added a minute or two each day of reading time, eventually extending the time students read to 30 to 45 minutes daily. During this in-class reading time, teachers circulated around the room conducting 5- to 7-minute conferences to provide individualized support and differentiated instruction. The types and levels of reading strategies, as well as higher-order thinking skills instruction, helped increase students' skills and self-regulation in reading. A series of lessons on how to increase self-regulation in reading was provided to teachers in the SEM-R manual. With more advanced and self-regulated readers, teachers discussed higher-order themes and asked critical questions about reading focusing on synthesis, evaluation, and discussion.

The focus of this phase of SEM-R was the use of individualized reading strategies and students' application and use of these strategies to monitoring how they plan, test, and revise strategy use as they read more challenging books. Teachers discussed higher-order questioning with all students and asked critical-thinking questions focusing on synthesizing, making inferences, and determining importance. The questions gave open-ended opportunities for children of all reading levels to reflect on and discuss their books. The conferences also gave teachers time to scaffold their own strategies for critical analysis and higher-order thinking skills. Teachers also discussed literature that challenged and enriched children's experiences. During conferences, teachers were able to informally assess their students' comprehension and decide when and how to apply higher-level thinking skills. Teachers also used formative assessment, as students recorded the number of pages they read daily in a reading log to document the books they read as well as questions or strategies that worked for students.

In conferences, SEM-R teachers were able to use a wide range of strategy questions and used approximately equal numbers of higher-level questions with readers of high, average, and low reading achievement (Fogarty, 2006). During many of the conferences, students were encouraged to jot down ideas as they read to remember details and record their own questions or ideas. They used sticky notes that attached to pages in their book to remind them of ideas to discuss with their teacher during their next conference. Connecting writing to their reading in this way enabled students to understand that their own questioning was a strategy that strengthened their comprehension of their reading.

PHASE 3: INTEREST AND CHOICE ACTIVITIES

In Phase 3 of SEM-R, students are encouraged to participate in opportunities for self-choice activities. Teachers usually gave students five or six different options for 15 minutes each day, or some teachers used one period of language arts for this phase of SEM-R. The choice activities included opportunities to explore technology and read online (e.g., e-books, children's authors' Web pages), writing activities, creativity training in language arts, learning centers on topics in which students had an interest or interest-based projects (e.g., Type III, Renzulli Learning System: www .renzullilearning.com), continuation of self-selected reading, reading with a friend, and book chats in literature circles. The intent of these experiences was to provide time for developing and exploring student interest in reading. These experiences gave students time to develop and explore their interests, as well as to apply creative and critical-thinking skills to self-selected work. They also pursued advanced training in the use of the Internet to find information about literary genres such as biographies and autobiographies.

Teachers used interest centers with creativity training activities in language arts and critical-thinking activities. A focus of Phase 3 was to enable students to learn to read critically and to locate other enjoyable and challenging reading materials, especially high-quality, challenging literature. Options for independent study were also made available for students during this component to enable students to apply these skills to areas of interest. Each component of the SEM-R was developed to help students enjoy reading, increase their reading skills with individual differentiated reading strategies, and apply higher-order thinking and reading strategy instruction while reading books in an area of personal interest.

Teachers were given three ready-to-use interest centers with creativity training activities in language arts, critical-thinking activities, and activities about safe use of the Internet. Options for independent study were also made available for students during this component. Each component of the SEM-R was developed to help students increase their reading skills with practice and coaching of differentiated reading strategies, in conjunction with efforts to increase automaticity and self-regulation in reading.

RESEARCH ON THE SEM-R

We implemented the SEM-R in urban and suburban schools. In each study, students were randomly assigned to the SEM-R group or continued with normal reading instruction as a control group. Teachers were also randomly assigned to teach either the treatment or control-group classes. In our first year of study, the SEM-R was implemented in two urban schools with a population of more than 90% culturally diverse and free and reduced lunch students. Students in these schools participated in a direct instruction, 90-minute reading block in the morning, and SEM-R was implemented in an additional one-hour afternoon literacy block for 12 weeks during second semester. Students who participated in the SEM-R had significantly better attitudes toward reading and higher reading comprehension and oral reading fluency scores. During the second year of the study, the SEM-R was implemented in two other schools for 12 weeks as half of a regular, 2-hour basal language arts program. One of the schools had a majority population of culturally and linguistically diverse students who spoke Spanish as their first language. Students who were in the SEM-R group had significantly higher reading fluency and comprehension, and all readers, from talented to average and below-average readers, benefited from the program. In another study, an afterschool reading program was implemented in an urban school using SEM-R, and after only 6 weeks and 12 two-hour sessions, most students had significant increases on reading fluency when compared to a control group (Reis & Boeve, in press). Currently, we are studying the implementation of this approach to reading over an entire academic year in five urban schools, with high populations of students in poverty and lots of cultural diversity. In summary, our research on this alternative method for reading resulted in positive attitudes toward reading, increased reading fluency and comprehension scores, and increases in student confidence in answering higher-order thinking questions.

The positive changes that resulted from this study extend beyond the increases in test scores. We saw students who could not wait to begin reading time, students who groaned when it was time to put their books down at the end of the reading period, and students who rarely read prior to the intervention devour an entire book series. Teachers have consistently reported positive changes in their own teaching practices and a general excitement about reading and using higher-order thinking skills in reading instruction. They also found students were able to have more advanced conversations about what they were reading. As a teacher in Florida explained, "My Phase 2 SEM-R conferences with kids expanded from one-word answers at the beginning of the year to long, thoughtful conversations about literature and themes. I actually had to cut them off—I am completely convinced now that this was due to the SEM-R training in higher-order thinking skills." In that school, after a year of using this approach, the number of students who did not pass the state mastery test decreased by 66%.

8

A Dozen Assistants in Your Classroom

Implementing the Schoolwide Enrichment Model by Using a New Online Resource for Enrichment and Differentiation

The newest part of our work with the Schoolwide Enrichment Model (SEM) is the implementation of an online program called Renzulli Learning (RL; http://www.renzullilearning.com), which is the electronic version of SEM. The infinite resources now available through the Internet inspired the development of RL at the University of Connecticut's Neag School of Education. Sponsored by the University of Connecticut Research and Development Corporation and supported by income from subscriptions, further development of RL is anticipated during the next few years.

The use of instructional technology, and especially the Internet, has evolved rapidly over the past decade. First-generation use of technology consisted mainly of what might be called "worksheets online," with the added advantage of providing students with immediate feedback about correct responses and incorrect answers. This generation was not unlike the teaching machines of the 1950s. The next generation consisted mainly of courses online, and although this innovation enabled students to have access to teachers and professors with expertise beyond what might be available locally, it usually followed the same pedagogy as traditional courses (i.e., read the chapter, answer questions, take a test). The third generation was a great leap forward because of the advent of hypertext. Students could now click on highlighted items in online text to pursue additional, more-advanced information and the kinds of scaffolding that consume more time than most teachers can devote to individualized learning.

RL can be viewed as the next generation of applying instructional technology to the learning process and to enrichment learning and teaching. This program is not a variation of earlier generations of popular e-learning programs or Web-surfing devices being offered by numerous software companies. It is a totally unique use of the Internet that combines computer-based strength assessment with search engine technology, thus allowing true differentiation in the matching of thousands of carefully selected resources to individual strengths. RL is theoretically aligned with the Enrichment Triad Model and the SEM. With minimal skills in the use of the Internet, and only a small amount of the teacher's time, interested teachers can use RL to implement enrichment teaching in their classrooms and school, providing teachers, we believe, with the equivalent of a "dozen assistants" to help. RL is a four-step procedure based on our 30 years of SEM research and development dealing with advanced-level thinking skills, motivation, creativity, and engagement in learning.

A project management tool guides students and teachers to use specifically selected resources for assigned curricular activities, independent or small-group investigative projects, and a wide variety of challenging enrichment experiences. Another management tool enables teachers to form instructional groups and enrichment clusters based on interests and learning-style preferences. Teachers have instant access to student profiles, all of the sites students have visited in RL, and the amount of time spent on each activity. There is a teacher site that has multiple tools, including a search feature of all RL enrichment sites, a grouping function that enables teachers to create groups, differentiation tools for compacting and differentiation, and the ability to send different types and levels of enrichment activities to different groups and achievement levels of students. Parents may also view (but not change) their own child's profile and Web activities. To promote parent involvement, we suggest that students show and work on some of their favorite activities with their parents.

STEP ONE: STRENGTH ASSESSMENT USING THE ELECTRONIC LEARNING PROFILE (THE TOTAL TALENT PORTFOLIO ONLINE)

The first step consists of a computer-based diagnostic assessment that creates a profile of each student's academic strengths, interests, learning styles, and preferred modes of expression. The online assessment, which takes about 30 minutes, results in a personalized profile that highlights individual student strengths and sets the stage for Step Two of RL. The profile acts like a compass for the second step, which is a differentiation search engine that examines thousands of resources that relate specifically to each student's profile. A sample profile is reproduced in the following. Student profiles can also be used to form groups of students who share common interests, to help teachers to get to know students better, to address special interests and discipline problems, and to help locate projects for students.

Liza's Profile

Liza is a fifth-grade student who has special interests and abilities in school. She described her grades as average in math, average in science, above average in reading, and average in social studies. She seems to have several areas of interest. Her primary interest appears to be in athletics. She seems to like physical activity and may be interested in learning about sports, nutrition, physical therapy, or sports medicine.

Liza's second area of interest appears to be in history and social studies. She seems to have an interest in studying the past to learn about famous historical figures and events, antiques, old photographs, and oral histories (talking to people about their past experiences).

Liza's third area of interest appears to be in reading, as she seems to like reading novels, stories, poetry, and other types of literature.

Liza also has specific, preferred instructional styles. Learning or instructional styles are the ways students like to learn and the strategies parents and teachers use to help them learn. Liza has very clearly defined learning preferences. Her preferred instructional style is through simulations that help her to learn content and skills through role-playing people or events. Liza also likes acting or pretending to be a character, and she may like to study history by participating in simulations. For example, she may want to role-play Thomas Jefferson in the signing of the Declaration of Independence or Eleanor Roosevelt during World War II. Her second choice of learning style is programmed instruction that may occur when Liza reads a chapter and then answers questions, or when she is asked to complete workbook pages after a review of some material in class. Liza also enjoys learning games that enable her to learn content by playing games or participating in activities with cards, board games, or even electronic games. These activities can be completed individually, in small groups of students, or in a whole class of students.

Liza also has a preferred product style. That is, she has certain kinds of products that she likes to complete. Her first product choice is artistic as she likes to draw, paint, or sculpt, and she may also enjoy choosing colors and working with design or texture. Her second choice of product style is dramatic. She enjoys participating in theatrical performances, such as acting and role playing. Liza's third choice of product style is musical. She enjoys listening, playing, and thinking about various forms of music.

As Liza has a chance to consider some of her choices and think about what she really enjoys doing, it is our hope that these opportunities will enable her to fully develop her interests through the variety of exploratory activities in the Renzulli Learning System database. When she takes a virtual field trip to a museum, interviews a favorite author on the Web, or explores a historical site online, she will be learning to further explore her interests and learning styles. These kinds of exploratory activities can introduce Liza to new ideas and experiences and let her explore many possible interests.

SOURCE: www.renzullilearning.com.

STEP TWO: ENRICHMENT DIFFERENTIATION DATABASES

In Step Two, the differentiation search engine matches student strengths and interests to an enrichment database of 16,000 enrichment activities, materials, resources, and opportunities for further study that are grouped into the following categories:

Figure 8.1 Renzulli Learning

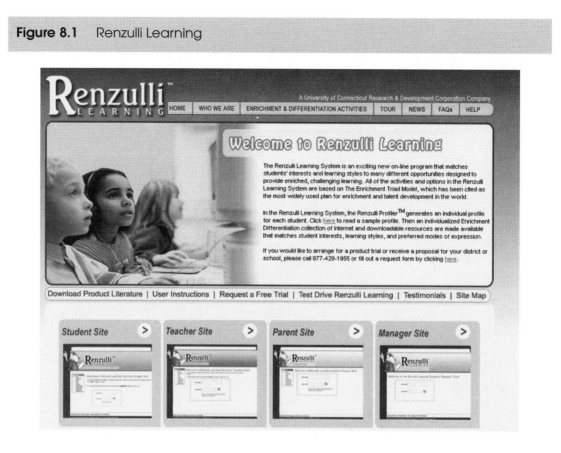

Virtual Field Trips

Real Field Trips

Creativity Training

Critical Thinking

Projects and Independent Study

Contests and Competitions

Web Sites

Fiction Books

Nonfiction Books

How-To Books

Summer Programs

Online Classes and Activities

Research Skills

Videos and DVDs

These resources in RL are not merely intended to inform students about new information or to occupy their time surfing around the Web. Rather, they are used as vehicles for helping students find an area of interest or focus on a problem or creative exploration of personal interest that they might like to pursue in greater depth. Many of the resources provide the methods of inquiry, advanced-level thinking and creative problem-solving skills, and investigative approaches characterized by Type III studies. Students are guided toward the application of knowledge and the development of original research studies, creative projects, and action-oriented undertakings that put knowledge to work in personally meaningful areas of interest. The resources also provide students with suggestions for outlets and audiences for their creative products. A set of learning maps for teachers is provided for each of the 14 enrichment resource databases and for the many other resources available for teachers. Teachers can also download numerous curricular activities for use in their classrooms, and management tools classify and cross-reference activities by subject area, thinking skill, and subject matter standards.

Our goal in this approach to learning is to promote high levels of engagement by providing a vehicle for enrichment and for Type III studies. Research on the role of student engagement is clear and unequivocal—high engagement results in higher achievement, improved self-concept and self-efficacy, and more favorable attitudes toward school and learning. A strong body of research points out the crucial difference between "time spent" and "time engaged" in school achievement. In the recently published international Program for International Student Assessment study (Organisation for Economic Co-operation and Development, 2006), the single criterion that distinguished between nations with the highest and lowest levels of student achievement was the degree to which students were engaged in their studies. This finding took into account demographic factors such as ethnicity and the socioeconomic differences among the groups studied. In a longitudinal study comparing time spent versus time engaged on the achievement of at-risk students,

Greenwood (1991) found that conventional instructional practices were responsible for the students' increased risk of academic delay. A study by Ainley (1993) reported that there were important differences in achievement outcomes favoring engaged over disengaged students of similar ability.

The resources available in students' enrichment activities also provide students with sites where they can pursue advanced-level training in their strength areas and areas of personal interest. Online courses and summer programs that focus on specific academic strengths and creative talents are ways that any school or parent can direct highly able and motivated students to resources that may not be available in the regular school program.

STEP THREE: THE WIZARD PROJECT MAKER

Another feature of RL is a project organization and management plan for students and teachers called the Wizard Project Maker. This interactive tool enables teachers to help students use their Web-based explorations for original research, investigative projects, and the development of a wide variety of creative undertakings. The sophisticated software used in this tool automatically locates potentially relevant Web-based resources that can be used in connection with the student's investigative activity. This management device is designed to fulfill the requirements of a Type III enrichment experience. Specifically, the project maker provides students with the metacognitive skills that help them define a project and set a goal, identify and evaluate both the resources to which they have access and the resources they need (e.g., time, Internet sites, teacher or mentor assistance), prioritize and refine goals, balance the resources needed to meet multiple goals, learn from past actions and project future outcomes, monitor progress, and make necessary adjustments as a project unfolds.

The Wizard Project Maker helps students make the best use of Web resources and focus their interests as they pursue advanced-level work, and it is a built-in safeguard against using RL for more exploratory surfing of the Web. It also establishes a creative and viable responsibility for teachers in their role as the guide on the side. By helping students pursue advanced levels of challenge and engagement through the use of the Wizard Project Maker, students see teachers as mentors rather than task masters or disseminators of knowledge. The Wizard Project Maker also has a metacognitive effect on students, that is, they have a better understanding about what investigative learning is all about. Teachers have consistently told us that using the Wizard Project Maker helps students understand the "why" of using the Internet. A Wizard Project Maker Super Starter Project is provided in Appendix B, and interested readers are encouraged to go online to view the Wizard Software built into RL to help students acquire resources for the various sections of this planning device.

STEP FOUR: THE TOTAL TALENT PORTFOLIO

The final step in the Renzulli Learning System is an automatic compilation and storage of all student activity from Steps One, Two, and Three into an ongoing student record called the Total Talent Portfolio. A management tool allows students to evaluate each site visited and resource used, students can complete a self-assessment of what they derived from the resource, and if they choose, they can store favorite activities and resources in their portfolio. This feature allows easy return access to ongoing work. The portfolio can be reviewed at any time by teachers and parents through the use of an access code, which allows teachers to give feedback and guidance to individual students and provides parents with information about students' work and opportunities for parental involvement. The portfolio can also be used for

Providing points of reference for future teachers

Making decisions about possible class project extra-credit options

Selecting subsequent enrichment preferences

Designing future projects and creative activities

Exploring online courses and competitions

Participating in extracurricular activities

Deciding on electives in middle and high school

Guiding college selection and career exploration alternatives

As noted earlier, a student's Total Talent Portfolio travels with students throughout their educational career. It can serve as a reminder of previous activities and creative accomplishments that they might want to include in college applications, and it is an ongoing record that can help students, teachers, guidance counselors, and parents make decisions about future educational and vocational plans.

RENZULLI LEARNING SYSTEM

The RL is based on a learning theory called the Enrichment Triad Model, which was developed in 1977 and implemented in thousands of schools in the United States and several overseas nations. A wide range of programs based on the Enrichment Triad Model have been developed by classroom teachers and enrichment specialists in different school districts across the country that serve diverse populations of students at all grade levels. Many examples of creative student work were completed as part of the enrichment opportunities built around the SEM. Teachers using the model worked very hard to access resources to provide enrichment for students, but the many responsibilities of classroom teachers and the amount of time required to track down resources made this a daunting task. In the Renzulli Learning System, thousands of resources and enrichment materials are provided for teachers and students with the click of a mouse. What makes this system unique is that these resources are individually tailored to students' abilities, interests, and learning styles. The resources can be accessed in school, during afterschool programs, or even at home when students want to pursue enriched learning opportunities on their own.

The Enrichment Triad Model was designed to encourage advanced-level learning and creative productivity by (a) exposing students to various topics, areas of interest, and fields of study in which they have an interest or might develop an interest; (b) providing students with the skills and resources necessary to acquire advanced-level content and thinking skills; and (c) creating opportunities for students to apply their skills to self-selected areas of interest and problems that they want to pursue.

Type I enrichment is designed to expose students to a wide variety of disciplines, topics, occupations, hobbies, people, places, and events in RL. Type I enrichment includes virtual field trips; online activities that challenge student thinking; exciting Web sites; books, videos, and DVDs related to areas of special interest; and other exposure activities that are associated with independent projects and other components of the system. These Type I experiences might be viewed as the motivational hook that causes individual students to become turned on to particular topic or area of study that they will subsequently pursue in greater depth.

Type II enrichment consists of materials and activities designed to develop a broad range of higher-level thinking processes and advanced inquiry skills. In RL, Type II enrichment is embedded across many of the enrichment activities, including critical and creative thinking, research skills, online activities, and how-to books. A quick tour of the various categories will help you become familiar with the vast array of resources that can be used for all three types of enrichment in the Triad Model.

Our experience in using the Enrichment Triad Model over the years has shown that Types I and II enrichment or interests gained in the regular curriculum or out-of-school activities will motivate many students to pursue self-selected topics in greater depth. In RL, the Type III component can emerge from almost any of the options that students choose to pursue. They can, for example, get an idea for what they might like to learn more about by becoming involved in a virtual field trip or a real field trip. They might find an idea from a creativity training exercise or critical-thinking activity. The most logical way for students to become involved in a Type III project is by pursuing an independent study or by becoming involved in a contest or a competition. We have also found that students may become interested in doing in-depth research by using any of the other components of RL such as special topic Web sites; fiction, nonfiction, and how-to books; summer programs; online activities; and research skills. There are also numerous options in RL for students to pursue Type III studies in specialized content areas. An easy way to start students on a Type III study is to have them become involved with starting a Superstarter Project using the Wizard Project Maker.

To help students understand the difference between an authentic Type III and the more traditional kinds of reports that they typically do in school, we have developed the Wizard Project Maker, a completed sample of which is presented in Appendix B. This form also highlights the specific ways in which teachers can provide guidance in helping students find and focus on a problem, examine potential outlets and audiences, and obtain the necessary resources to carry out their investigative activities. Blank copies of this form can be downloaded at the RL Web site. The teacher's role in this type of enrichment becomes more like a coach and guide on the side rather than a disseminator of knowledge. The teacher's role is an active one, but it requires minimal time because it does not require large amounts of face-to-face instruction. Teachers can learn more about the role that teachers play in facilitating Type III enrichment by reviewing the short article on this topic in the Teacher Resource section of RL.

One of the questions that teachers frequently ask is, "Where will students find the time to do Type III projects?" All students can use RL, but we have found that some above-average ability students—those who can master the regular curriculum at a faster pace than others—can buy some time for enrichment activities through curriculum compacting.

THE VALUE-ADDED BENEFITS OF LEARNING WITH TECHNOLOGY

The conditions of learning have changed dramatically for young people going to school today. Don Leu and his team of New Literacies researchers (Leu, Leu, & Coiro, 2004) at the University of Connecticut have pointed out that the Internet is this generation's defining technology for literacy and learning and that profound changes have already taken place in higher education, adult learning, and the workplace, all situations for which we are preparing the young students who are in our classrooms today. There was a time when teachers and textbooks were the gatekeepers of knowledge, but today, virtually all of the world's knowledge is accessible to any student who can turn on a computer and log onto the Internet. One of the dangers of a content-abundant resource such as the Internet, however, is that we might be tempted to simply use it to cram more information into students' heads! By applying a learner-centered pedagogy rather than a traditional drill-and-practice approach, however, we can harness the power of the Internet in a way that respects more authentic learning practices. A crucial question, therefore, is will we use this information wisely? Or will we simply turn the powerful resources available through the Internet into electronic worksheets, test-preparation tutorials, and online courses that adhere to the same prescriptive model for learning that almost all reform initiatives have followed thus far—a model that has indeed left so many young people bored, disengaged, and behind? Or will the new technologies be the workhorse that can finally allow teachers to truly differentiate learning experiences for all students? These technologies now make it possible to apply to all students the pedagogy typically used with high-achieving students.

With almost unlimited access to the world's knowledge, a critical issue for educators is selecting the software and providing the training that will help young people use this access safely, efficiently, effectively, and wisely. Leu et al. (2004), as well as Leu and Kinzer (2002), define the five major skill sets of the new literacies as follows:

1. Identifying important questions

2. Locating relevant information

3. Critically evaluating information

4. Synthesizing information

5. Communicating effectively

In addition to improved academic achievement and opportunities for creative productivity, which are the major goals of the Renzulli Learning System, there are a series of metacognitive tools that result from computer-based learning environments. Metacognition is generally defined as the monitoring and control of one's own thinking processes. Metacognitive tools are skills that help students organize and self-regulate their learning so that they can make the most efficient use of time, resources, and the cognitive skills that contribute to higher levels of thinking. Metacognition involves problem-solving skills such as exploring alternative options and strategies in open-ended problem situations and applying critical-thinking skills such as examining the sources of evidence, the logic of arguments, and how to find and use reliable information. Training and experiences in metacognitive skills may be the single biggest difference between the education provided in high- and low-achieving schools!

Several researchers studying constructivist models of learning and metacognition have developed or modified traditional theories of learning to explain the role of computer environments in mediating the interactions between and among the cognitive, metacognitive, affective, and social processes that are involved in learning complex material (Bandura, 1986; Corno & Mandinach, 1983; Pintrich, 2000; Schunk, 2001). Promising results have emerged from these new developments in theory and research on the ways in which computer learning environments facilitate metacognitive skill development.

The Internet can also be a good educational tool for hard-to-reach populations. Researchers from Michigan State University examined the positive effects of home Internet access on the academic performance of low-income, mostly African American children and teenagers involved in a home Internet project. In this research, 140 children aged 10 to 18 years (83% African American and 58% male) living in single-parent households (75%) with a $15,000 or less median income were followed for a 2-year period to see whether home Internet use would influence academic achievement.

The children who participated in the project were online for an average of 30 minutes a day. Findings indicate that children who used the Internet more had higher standardized test scores in reading and higher grade point averages (GPAs) at one year and at 16 months after the project began compared with children who used the Internet less, said lead author Linda Jackson and colleagues (2006). Internet use had no effect on standardized test scores in math.

"Improvements in reading achievement may be attributable to the fact that spending more time online typically means spending more time reading," said Dr. Jackson. "GPAs may improve because GPAs are heavily dependent on reading skills," she added (Jackson et al., 2006, p. 147).

An even more promising trend is emerging as computer use evolves from traditional e-learning (i.e., taking an online course or developing basic skills through computer-assisted instruction) to inquiry-based software that focuses on the application of knowledge to creative productivity and investigative research projects that promote high levels of student engagement. Students learn the basic difference between to-be-presented information that characterizes traditional instruction and just-in-time information, which is the hallmark of problem-based learning. Skills such as problem finding and focusing; stating research questions; task understanding and planning; identifying appropriate investigative methods; searching for, skimming, selecting, and interpreting appropriate resource material; identifying appropriate outlets, products, and audiences; and preparing effective communication vehicles are all value-added benefits when the learning theory that underlies the Enrichment Triad Model is combined with the vastness of resources available through the Internet.

RL CONCLUSIONS

RL is designed to be an aid to busy teachers who seek tools for effective enrichment and differentiation as they go about the process of dealing with a broad range of individual differences, diverse student needs, and increased pressures to improve student achievement. Through the use of technology and an approach to learning that is the opposite of highly prescriptive instruction, RL provides teachers with the dozen teaching assistants that every teacher would like to have in his or her classroom. The main goal of RL is to simultaneously increase achievement and enjoyment of learning by making available an inexpensive, easy-to-use, research-based system that promotes student engagement. Although student engagement has been defined in many ways, we view it as the infectious enthusiasm that students display when working on something that is of personal interest and that challenges them to stretch for the use of materials and resources that are above their current comfort level of learning. Research on the role of student engagement is clear and unequivocal—high engagement results in higher achievement, improved self-concept and self-efficacy, and more favorable attitudes toward school and learning. Numerous students involved in using RL over the last few years summed it up with one word—"Awesome!"

Appendix A

Research Summary of Studies Related to the Schoolwide Enrichment Model and Renzulli Learning

Author and Date	Description of Study	Sample	Results or Findings
Student Creative Productivity			
Baum, 1988	An enrichment program for gifted, learning-disabled students.	E $n = 7$	The Type III study, used as an intervention with high-ability, learning-disabled students, improved students' behavior, specifically the ability to self-regulate time on task; improved self-esteem; and developed specific instructional strategies to enhance the potential of high-potential, learning-disabled students.
D. E. Burns, 1987	The effects of group training activities on students' creative productivity.	E $n = 515$	Students receiving process skill training were 64% more likely to initiate self-selected projects (Type IIIs) than students who did not receive the training.
Delcourt, 1993	Creative productivity among secondary school students combining energy, interest, and imagination.	S $n = 18$ (longitudinal)	Students participating in Type III projects, both in and out of school, maintained interests and career aspirations in college. Supports the concept that adolescents and young adults can be producers of information, as well as consumers. Student giftedness, as manifested in performances and product development, may be predicted by high levels of creative and productive behaviors at an early age.
Hébert, 1993	Reflections at graduation: the long-term effect of elementary school experiences in creative productivity.	S $n = 9$ (longitudinal)	Five major findings: Type III interests of students affect postsecondary plans; creative outlets are needed in high school; a decrease in creative, Type III productivity occurs during the junior high experience; the Type III process serves as important training for later productivity; and nonintellectual characteristics with students remain consistent over time.
Newman, 1991	The effects of the Talents Unlimited Model on students' creative productivity.	E $n = 147$	Students with training in the Talents Unlimited Model were more likely to complete independent investigations (Type IIIs) than the students who did not receive the training.

Author and Date	Description of Study	Sample	Results or Findings
Reis & Renzulli, 1982	An analysis of the productivity of gifted students participating in programs using the Revolving Door Identification Model.	E $n = 1,280$	Students in the expanded talent pool (5%–20%) produced products of equal quality compared with students in the top 3% to 5% of the population.
Schack, 1986	Creative productivity and self-efficacy in children.	E, M $n = 294$	Self-efficacy was a significant predictor of initiation of an independent investigation, and self-efficacy at the end of treatment was higher in students who participated in Type III projects.
Starko, 1986b	The effects of the Revolving Door Identification Model on creative productivity and self-efficacy.	E $n = 103$	Students who became involved in self-selected, independent studies in Schoolwide Enrichment Model (SEM) programs initiated their own creative products both inside and outside school more often than students who qualified for the program but did not receive services. Students in the enrichment group reported more than twice as many creative projects per student (3.37) as the comparison group (0.50) and showed greater diversity and sophistication in projects. The number of creative products completed in school (Type IIIs) was a highly significant predictor of self-efficacy.
Westberg, 1999	A longitudinal study of students who participated in a program based on the Enrichment Triad Model from 1981 to 1984.	E, S $N = 15$ (longitudinal)	Students maintained interests over time and were still involved in creative productive work.
Special Populations and Affective Issues			
Baum, 1985	Learning-disabled students with superior cognitive abilities: a validation study of descriptive behaviors.	E $n = 112$	SEM recommended as one vehicle to meet the unique needs of gifted students with learning disabilities because of the emphasis on strengths, interests, and learning styles.

(Continued)

(Continued)

Author and Date	Description of Study	Sample	Results or Findings
Baum, Renzulli, & Hébert, 1995	Students who underachieve.	E, M N = 17	Reversal of underachievement through the use of SEM Type III projects.
Emerick, 1988	Academic underachievement among the gifted: students' perceptions of factors relating to the reversal of academic underachievement patterns.	H+ n = 10	Reversal of academic underachievement through use of various components of the SEM, including curriculum compacting, exposure to Type I experiences, opportunities to be involved in Type III studies, and an appropriate assessment of learning styles to provide a match between students and teachers. To reverse the academic underachievement in gifted students the following factors must be considered: out-of-school interests, parents, goals associated with academic performance, classroom instruction and curriculum, the teacher, and changes in the self.
Heal, 1989	Student perceptions of labeling the gifted: A comparative case study analysis.	E n = 149	The SEM was associated with a reduction in the negative effects of labeling.
Olenchak, 1991	Assessing program effects for gifted and learning-disabled students.	P, E n = 108	Supported use of the SEM as a means of meeting educational needs of a wide variety of high-ability students. SEM, when used as an intervention, was associated with improved attitudes toward learning among elementary high-ability students with learning disabilities. Furthermore, the same students, who completed a high percentage of Type III projects, made positive gains with respect to self-concept.

Author and Date	Description of Study	Sample	Results or Findings
Reis, Schader, Milne, & Stephens, 2003	Music and minds: Using a talent development approach for young adults with Williams syndrome.	S $n = 16$	One third of the participants had high levels of musical talent, and the use of participants' interests and advanced training in music was found to both enhance all participants' understanding of mathematics and to provide opportunities for the further development of their interests and abilities, especially their potential in music. The use of a talent-development approach focusing on strengths, interests, and style preferences was found to be successful for this group of young people with Williams syndrome.
Taylor, 1992	The effects of the Secondary Enrichment Triad Model on the career development of vocational-technical school students.	S $N = 60$	Involvement in Type III studies substantially increased postsecondary education plans of students (from attending 2.6 years to attending 4.0 years).
SEM as Applied to School Change			
Cooper, 1983	Administrators' attitudes toward gifted programs based on the Enrichment Triad/Revolving Door Identification Model: case studies in decision making.	Eight districts $n = 32$	Administrator perceptions regarding the model included greater staff participation in education of high-ability students, more positive staff attitudes toward the program, fewer concerns about identification, positive changes in how the guidance department worked with students, and more incentives for students to work toward higher goals. Administrators found SEM affected all students.
Olenchak, 1988	SEM in elementary schools: a study of implementation stages and effects on educational excellence.	P, E $n = 236$, teacher $n = 1,698$, student	The SEM contributed to improved teachers', parents', and administrators' attitudes toward education for high-ability students.
Olenchak, 1990	School change through gifted education: Effects on elementary students' attitudes toward learning.	P, E $n = 1,935$	Positive changes in student attitudes toward learning as well as toward gifted education and school in general.

(Continued)

(Continued)

Author and Date	Description of Study	Sample	Results or Findings
Reis, Gentry, & Maxfield, 1998	The application of enrichment clusters to teachers' classroom practices.	E Two schools $n = 120$, teacher	Teachers trained to use enrichment clusters as part of the enrichment program were able to transfer and implement the use of advanced content and methods in their regular classrooms. Methods used by teachers included advanced content and methods, advanced vocabulary, authentic tools of the disciplines, and advanced references and problem solving.
Curriculum Modification and Learning and Product Styles			
Imbeau, 1991	Teachers' attitudes toward curriculum compacting with regard to the implementation of the procedure.	P, E, M, S $n = 166$	Group membership (peer coaching) was a significant predictor of posttest teachers' attitudes. Comparisons of teachers' attitudes toward curriculum compacting indicate a need for additional research on variables that enhance and inhibit the use of curriculum compacting as a classroom strategy.
Kettle, Renzulli, & Rizza, 1998	Products of mind: Exploring student preferences for product development using My Way, an expression style instrument.	E, M $n = 3,532$	Students' preferences for creating potential products were explored through the use of an expression-style inventory. Factor analytic procedures yielded the following 11 factors: computer, service, dramatization, artistic, audio/visual, written, commercial, oral, manipulative, musical, and vocal.
Reis, Westberg, Kulikowich, & Purcell, 1998	Curriculum compacting and achievement test scores: What does the research say?	K, E, M $n = 336$	Using curriculum compacting to eliminate 40% to 50% of curricula for students with demonstrated advanced content knowledge and superior ability resulted in no decline in achievement test scores.
Application of SEM to Curriculum and Content Areas			
Eleck, 2005	Implementing Renzulli Learning in enrichment programs and classrooms.	E, M $N = 200$	Students in enrichment and regular classrooms used Renzulli Learning with minimal training. Almost 50% of students had ideas for completing products using Renzulli Learning, and 80% enjoyed using Renzulli Learning completely or very much. Each of the pilot teachers using the system assigned projects to students online.

Author and Date	Description of Study	Sample	Results or Findings
Karafelis, 1986	The effects of the tri-art drama curriculum on the reading comprehension of students with varying levels of cognitive ability.	E, M $n = 80$	Students receiving experimental treatment did equally well on achievement tests as the control group.
Reis et al., 2005	The Schoolwide Enrichment Model in Reading.	E, M $N = 1,500$	Students who participated in an enriched reading program based on the SEM had significantly higher scores in reading fluency and reading comprehension than students in the control group. Students who participated in an enriched reading program based on SEM had significantly better attitudes toward reading than students in the control group.
Reis, Westberg, Kulikowich, & Purcell, 1998	Curriculum compacting and achievement test scores: What does the research say?	K, E, M $n = 336$	Using curriculum compacting to eliminate 40% to 50% of curricula for students with demonstrated advanced content knowledge and superior ability resulted in either higher test scores or no significant difference in achievement test scores.

NOTE: E = Elementary Grades 3–5; S = Secondary Grades 9–12; M = Middle Grades 6–8; H+ = post–high school; P = Primary Grades K–2; K = Kindergarten.

Appendix B

The Wizard Project Maker

The Renzulli Learning Wizard Project Maker.

The answer to the question, "What next?"

Once the Renzulli Profiler has been created for each student and the students have begun to explore the enrichment activities selected for them, teachers and students may ask, "What do I do next?" Teachers and students have different roles. To understand these roles, it is helpful to understand what we mean by enrichment learning.

Enrichment learning includes investigative activities and the development of creative products in which students assume roles as first-hand investigators, writers, artists, or other types of practicing professionals. Although students pursue this kind of involvement at a more junior level than adult professionals, the overriding purpose is to create situations in which young people are thinking, feeling, and doing what practicing professionals do in the delivery of products and services.

To facilitate enrichment learning, the teacher's role changes from the traditional model where the teacher plans and prescribes all learning, to a more supportive, reactive position. The teacher acts as the "guide-on-the-side," approaching the teaching/learning interaction from the perspective of a coach or mentor, providing instruction based on a specific, direct need a student has expressed in order to be able to accomplish a task.

The basic characteristics of this type of learning environment include the following:

- The student and teacher select a topic that may be an off-shoot of the regular curriculum or an independent topic based on the student's interest.
- The student produces a product and/or service that is intended to have an impact on a particular audience.
- The student uses authentic methods, technological resources, and advanced level content to produce his or her product or service.

The role of the teacher is to guide the student as he or she pursues an area of interest. The student's role is to choose a topic, area of interest, or problem during consultation with the teacher, and then to independently search for resources. This can be done using Renzulli Learning and other local, national or international resources available. The Wizard Project Maker helps students create their plans for learning with teacher input. The Wizard Project Maker walks students through the research process and provides an online organizational system where students can work and store the information they have gathered. Everything is in one place and is easily accessible.

Here is an example:

A group of students was interested in establishing a debate club at their school. Under their teacher's guidance, they examined several how-to books at this section of the Renzulli Learning Web site. They located a how-to book entitled *A Student's Guide to Social Action*. A detailed set of guidelines for writing a proposal gave these students the skills necessary to do a professional job in the proposal they were preparing. In order to determine student interest in having a debate club, they decided to survey students. The group used a Web site found by Renzulli Learning that allowed them to develop a questionnaire, input the data, and tabulate the results of their survey. This information was included in a PowerPoint presentation that they created and showed to the principal and student council, along with their written proposal for the club. The high student interest and the persuasive presentation by this group of students resulted in the creation of a debate club at their school.

 **R**enzulli™
learning

The Wizard Project Maker ™
for Individual and Small Group Work

Name(s): Liza Renzulli	Start Date: January 15, 2006 / Completion Date: June 15, 2006
Teacher: Ms. Latino	**Dates for Progress Meetings With My Teacher:**
School: Southeast School	2/21/06 3/11/06 4/2/06 5/13/06

Project Description: Write a brief description of the project, problem, topic, or interest area that you want to learn about and study. What do you hope to find out or learn?

I love theater and want to try to direct and produce a play starring some of my friends.
I will have to find some of the following kinds of information.

1. What is a good play for elementary students to perform?

2. What types of tasks will I have to do to successfully direct a play for kids?

3. What type of play will I select? Will I have to pay for it? What other tasks are involved in directing and producing a play?

Interest Areas for This Project

-------------- Check All That Apply----------------

O Architecture   ● Arts (drawing and painting)

O Athletics/Sports/Fitness

O Business/Management   O Building Things
(robots, models)

O Creative Writing

● Computers/Technology/Gaming

● Drama/Performing   ● Graphic
Design/Animation

O Foreign Languages

O Geography   O Helping in the Community

● History   ● Journalism   O Mathematics

O Music

● Photography/Video   O Reading/Literature

O Science

O Social Action   O Other:

Intended Project(s): What form or format will the final project take? How, when, and where will you share and communicate the results of your project with other people? In what ways will you share your work (competition, online magazine, art show, performance, science fair, etc.)?

1. Direct and produce a play for my class and, if it goes well, the school and even the community.

2. Design and build a set for the play; learn about lighting!

3. Design and produce a program for the play.

What Format Will Your Project Take?

----------------Check All That Apply----------------

● Artistic   O Audio/Video/DVD   O Display

● Drama/Performance   O Musical

● Photographic

● Written   O Service/Leadership

● Technology/Computer

O Oral/Discussion (speech, teach, presentation)

O Using My Hands to Make or Build Something

O Other:

(Continued)

(Continued)

Getting Started: What are the first steps you should take to begin your work? What types of information do you need to find to do your work? Where will you get the information you need? What questions do you have that you need answered to start your work? What help do you need from your teacher or parents? List that information here.

1. Learn how to direct a play and how to produce one.

2. Conduct research about children's plays and drama, and find specific information about which plays might be good for my class and for me.

3. Locate information on how to create sets and produce a play.

Project Skills, Resources, and Materials I Will Need: List the Renzulli Learning™ resources here along with other resources (people, organizations, businesses, etc.) you have located that will help you with your work. Include Web sites, contact names, addresses and phone numbers, lists of the materials you will need, etc.

Web sites:

Drama Map

This site helps you to organize your search for plays and other dramatic material. You can choose to organize your knowledge by character, setting, conflict, or resolution. This will help you keep information neat and organized.

http://www.readwritethink.org/materials/dramamap/

The American Century Theater

The American Century Theater
P.O. Box 6313
Arlington, VA 22206
703-553-8782
Dedicated to Great, Important & Neglected American Plays and Playwrights of the Twentieth Century! Ten years ago, a group of us started the American Century Theater because we felt that great Twentieth Century American plays and playwrights were getting short shrift in this area. Thanks to the indispensable assistance and support of Arlington County, we were provided with the opportunity to discover if enough other theater-lovers felt the same way.

http://americancentury.org/index.htm

At the following site, I will be able to consider directing and producing "Snow White" with my friends and classmates. I will need to also find out how I might earn the money to be able to buy the rights to stage this show. Maybe I can charge a minimum amount for tickets? I can also do some more searching for plays in the school library.

http://www.childrenstheatreplays.com/sw.htm

Try Out These Theater Games

If you are interested in drama, this is the activity for you. Practice your acting skills by playing these games in a group. Learn the art of being a mime or act out roles that you draw from a pile.

http://library.thinkquest.org/5291/games.html

How-to books:

Acting and Theatre
Author: Cheryl Evans and Lucy Smith
Copyright 1992
64 pages
ISBN: 0-7460-0699-3
Grade Level: 4–12

Introduce students to every aspect of the theatrical world! This book illustrates and explains some of the ways actors train and rehearse, as well as the practical arts of set, prop, and costume design and the technical basics of lighting and sound.

Break a Leg! The Kid's Guide to Acting and Stagecraft
Author: Lise Friedman and Mary Dowdle
Workman Publishing Company, 2002
ISBN: 0761122087

A complete drama course for kids in a book. *BREAK A LEG!* teaches budding thespians everything they need to know about stagecraft and the production of performances, in home or out. There are sections on body preparation, including warm-ups, stretches, and breathing exercises. Theater games, improv, miming, and other fun ways to develop technique. Important acting skills, such as voice projection, crying on command, learning accents, and staging falls and fights without getting hurt. The performance: analyzing scripts, building a character, what to expect from rehearsals, and overcoming stagefright. A backstage look at blocking, lighting, and other technical aspects of theater production. And for the fun of costumes and make-up, a 16-page color insert. In addition, it covers legends and lore (Why is Macbeth cursed? Why do we say "break a leg"?) and offers dozens of must-see movie recommendations. Plus, for the ambitious, talented, and just plain curious, there's advice on how to make a career of it all, with tips on agents and auditions and getting jobs in theater, film, TV, and radio.

Intended Audience(s): Who would be most interested in your work or project? Consider organized groups (clubs, organizations, societies, teams) at the local, state, regional, and national levels, and list them here. Also consider contests, places where your work might be displayed or published, and Web sites that include work done in your area of study. Include contact names, phone numbers, addresses, and e-mail addresses, along with meeting times and locations.

1. Class project
2. School play
3. Town play (open to public)
4. If I decide to write my own play, I can submit it to the following using Renzulli Learning:

http://www.edta.org/rehearsal_hall/thespian_playworks.asp

Create a Play for Thespian Playworks
Thespian Playworks
2343 Auburn Avenue
Cincinnati, OH   45219

Activity Type: Writing a play

Bring out the writer and director inside of you by entering this contest. Write a short (thirty minutes or less) play and send it in for review. If the judges select your work for the Thespian Festival, you will join them during the workshops that bring your play to life. In order to be eligible you must be enrolled in a high school and a member of the Thespian Society.

(Continued)

(Continued)

For Completion by Teacher *(Optional)*

List of state standards addressed with this project:

References

ACT. (2006). *Reading between the lines.* Retrieved from http://www.act.org/news/releases/2006/03–01–06

Adler, M., & Hutchins, R. (1952). *Great books of the western world.* New York: Encyclopedia Britannica.

Ainley, M. D. (1993). Styles of engagement with learning: Multidimensional assessment of their relationship with strategy use and school achievement. *Journal of Educational Psychology, 85,* 395–405.

Albert, R. S., & Runco, M. A. (1986). The achievement of eminence: A model based on a longitudinal study of exceptionally gifted boys and their families. In R. J. Sternberg & J. E. Davidson (Eds.), *Conceptions of giftedness* (pp. 332–357). Cambridge, MA: Cambridge University Press.

Allington, R. L. (Ed.). (2002). *Big brother and the national reading curriculum: How ideology trumped evidence.* Portsmouth, NH: Heinemann.

Amabile, T. (1983). *The social psychology of creativity.* New York: Springer-Verlag.

American Psychological Association Work Group of the Board of Educational Affairs. (1997). *Learner-centered psychological principles: A framework for school reform and redesign.* Washington, DC: American Psychological Association.

Archambault, F. X., Jr., Westberg, K. L., Brown, S., Hallmark, B. W., Emmons, C., & Zhang, W. (1992). *Regular classroom practices with gifted students: Results of a national survey of classroom teachers.* Storrs, CT: National Research Center on the Gifted and Talented.

Ausubel, D. (1963). *The psychology of meaningful verbal learning.* New York: Grune & Stratton.

Bandura, A. (1986). *Social foundations of thought and action.* Englewood Cliffs, NJ: Prentice-Hall.

Baum, S. (1985). *Learning disabled students with superior cognitive abilities: A validation study of descriptive behaviors.* Unpublished doctoral dissertation, University of Connecticut, Storrs.

Baum, S. (1988). An enrichment program for the gifted learning disabled students. *Gifted Child Quarterly, 32,* 226–230.

Baum, S., Gable, R., & List, K. (1987). *Chi squares, pie charts and me.* New York: Trillium.

Baum, S. M., Renzulli, J. S., & Hébert, T. P. (1995). Reversing underachievement: Creative productivity as a systematic intervention. *Gifted Child Quarterly, 39,* 224–235.

Berger, J. (1994). *The young scientist: America's future and the winning of the Westinghouse.* Reading, MA: Addison-Wesley.

Bloom, B. S., Engelhart, M. D., Furst, E. J., Hill, W. H., & Krathwohl, D. R. (Eds.). (1956). *Taxonomy of educational objectives, Handbook 1: Cognitive domain.* New York: David McKay.

Bollag, B. (2004). Foreign enrollments at American universities drop for the first time in 32 years. *Chronicle of Higher Education.* Retrieved May 5, 2007, from IEENetwork.org

Brophy, J., & Good, T. L. (1974). *Teacher-student relationships: Causes and consequences.* New York: Holt, Rinehart, & Winston.

Bruner, J. S. (1960). *The process of education.* Cambridge, MA: Harvard University Press.

Bruner, J. S. (1966). *Toward a theory of instruction.* Cambridge, MA: Harvard University Press.

Bunker, B. B., Pearlson, H. B., & Schultz, J. W. (1999). *A student's guide to conducting social science research.* Mansfield Center, CT: Creative Learning Press.

Burek, D. M. (1990). *Encyclopedia of associations: A guide to over 30,000 national and international organizations.* Detroit, MI: Gale Research.

Burns, D. E. (1987). *The effects of group training activities on students' creative productivity.* Storrs, CT: Unpublished doctoral dissertation.

Burns, S. M., Griffin, P., & Snow, C. E. (Eds.). (1999). *Starting out right: A guide to promoting children's reading success.* Washington, DC: National Academy Press.

Colangelo, N., Assouline, S. G., & Gross, M. U. M. (2004). *A nation deceived: How schools hold back America's brightest students.* Retrieved May 29, 2007, from http://nationdeceived.org

Cooper, C. (1983). *Administrators' attitudes toward gifted programs based on the enrichment triad/revolving door identification model: Case studies in decision making.* Unpublished doctoral dissertation, University of Connecticut, Storrs.

Corno, L., & Mandinach, E. (1983). The role of cognitive engagement in classroom learning and motivation. *Educational Psychologist, 18,* 88–109.

Council of Graduate Schools. (2006, March). *Findings from 2006 CGS international graduate admissions survey, phase 1: Applications.* Retrieved May 5, 2007, from http://www.cgsnet.org/portals/0/pdf/R_intlapps06_1.pdf

Delcourt, M. A. B. (1988). *Characteristics related to high levels of creative/productive behavior in secondary school students: A multicase study.* Unpublished doctoral dissertation, University of Connecticut, Storrs.

Delcourt, M. A. B. (1993). Creative productivity among secondary school students: Combining energy, interest, and imagination. *Gifted Child Quarterly, 37,* 23–31.

Dewey, J. (1913). *Interest and effort in education.* New York: Houghton Mifflin.

Dewey, J. (1916). *Democracy and education.* New York: Macmillan.

Dunn, R., & Dunn, K. J. (1992). *Teaching students through their individual learning styles: Practical approaches for grades 3–6.* Boston: Allyn & Bacon.

Dunn, R., & Dunn, K. J. (1993). *Teaching students through their individual learning styles: Practical approaches for grades 7–12.* Boston: Allyn & Bacon.

Dunn, R., Dunn, K., & Price, G. E. (1975). *Learning Style Inventory.* Lawrence, KS: Price Systems.

Dunn, R., Dunn, K., & Price, G. E. (1978). *Learning Style Inventory.* Lawrence, KS: Price Systems.

Dunn, R., Dunn, K., & Price, G. E. (1979). *Learning Style Inventory.* Lawrence, KS: Price Systems.

Eleck, S. (2005). *An investigation of Renzulli learning.* Storrs, CT: University of Connecticut, Neag School of Education.

Emerick, L. (1988). *Academic underachievement among the gifted: Students' perceptions of factors relating to the reversal of the academic underachievement pattern.* Unpublished doctoral dissertation, University of Connecticut, Storrs.

Evan, D. L., Bodman, S. W., Cooper, K. B., & Kincannon, C. L. (2002). *Measuring America: The decennial censuses from 1790 to 2000.* Washington, DC: U.S. Department of Commerce, Economics and Statistics Administration.

Flindt, M. (1978). *Gold rush: A simulation of life and adventure in a frontier mining camp.* Lakeside, CA: INTERACT.

Fogarty, E. A. (2006). *Teachers' use of differentiated reading strategy instruction for talented, average, and struggling readers in regular and SEM-R classrooms* (Technical report). Storrs, CT: National Research Center on the Gifted and Talented.

Gardner, H. (1983). *Frames of mind.* New York: Basic Books.

Gentry, M. L. (1999). *Promoting student achievement and exemplary classroom practices through cluster grouping: A research-based alternative to heterogeneous elementary classrooms* (RM99138). Storrs, CT: National Research Center on the Gifted and Talented, University of Connecticut. Retrieved May 29, 2007, from http://www.gifted.uconn.edu/nrcgt/gentry.html

Greenwood, C. R. (1991). Longitudinal analysis of time, engagement, and achievement in at-risk versus non-risk students. *Exceptional Children, 57,* 521–536.

Gruber, H. E. (1986). The self-construction of the extraordinary. In R. J. Sternberg and J. E. Davidson (Eds.), *Conceptions of giftedness* (pp. 247–263). Cambridge, MA: Cambridge University Press.

Gubbins, E. J. (1982). *Revolving Door Identification Model: Characteristics of talent pool students.* Unpublished doctoral dissertation, University of Connecticut, Storrs.

Guthrie, J. T., & Humenick, N. M. (2004). Motivating students to read. In P. McCardle & V. Chhabra (Eds.), *The voice of evidence in reading research* (pp. 329–354). Baltimore: Brookes.

Gutiérrez, R., & Slavin, R. E. (1992). *Achievement effects of the nongraded schools: A retrospective review.* Baltimore: Center for Research on Effective Schooling for Disadvantaged Students, Johns Hopkins University.

Heal, M. M. (1989). *Student perceptions of labeling the gifted: A comparative case study analysis.* Unpublished doctoral dissertation, University of Connecticut, Storrs.

Hébert, T. P. (1993). Reflections at graduation: The long-term impact of elementary school experiences in creative productivity. *Roeper Review, 16,* 22–28.

Hébert, T. P., Sorenson, M. F., & Renzulli, J. S. (1997). *Secondary Interest-a-lyzer.* Mansfield Center, CT: Creative Learning Press.

Henderson, H., & Conrath, J. M. (1991). *CAPSOL style of learning assessment.* Mansfield, OH: Process Associates.

Hoover, S. M., Sayler, M., & Feldhusen, J. (1993). Cluster grouping of gifted students at the elementary level. *Roeper Review, 16,* 13–15.

Hunt, D. E. (1971). *Matching models in education: The coordination of teaching methods with student characteristics.* Ontario, Canada: Ontario Institute for Studies in Education.

Imbeau, M. B. (1991). *Teachers' attitudes toward curriculum compacting: A comparison of different inservice strategies.* Unpublished doctoral dissertation, University of Connecticut, Storrs.

Iowa Test of Basic Skills, Form J. (1990). Chicago: Riverside.

Ivey, G., & Fisher, D. (2005). Learning from what does not work. *Educational Leadership, 63*(2), 8–15.

Jackson, L. A., von Eye, A., Biocca, F. A., Barbatsis, G., Zhao, Y., & Fitzgerald, H. E. (2006). Children's home Internet use: Predictors and psychological, social and academic consequences. In R. Kraut, M. Brynin, & S. Kiesler (Eds.), *Computers, phones and the Internet: Domesticating information technology* (pp. 145–167). New York: Oxford University Press.

James, W. (1885). On the functions of cognition. *Mind, 10,* 27–44.

Kagan, J. (1966). Reflection-impulsivity: The generality and dynamics of conceptual tempo. *Journal of Abnormal Psychology, 71*(1), 17–24.

Kaplan, S. N. (1986). The grid: A model to construct differentiated curriculum for the gifted. In J. S. Renzulli (Ed.), *Systems and models for developing programs for the gifted and talented* (pp. 180–193). Mansfield, CT: Creative Learning Press.

Karafelis, P. (1986). *The effects of the tri-art drama curriculum on the reading comprehension of students with varying levels of cognitive ability.* Unpublished doctoral dissertation, University of Connecticut, Storrs.

Kettle, K., Renzulli, J. S., & Rizza, M. G. (1998). Products of mind: Exploring student preferences for product development using My Way, an expression style instrument. *Gifted Child Quarterly, 42*(1), 49–60.

Kirschenbaum, R. J. (1983). Let's cut out the cut-off score in the identification of the gifted. *Roeper Review, 5,* 6–10.

Kirschenbaum, R. J., & Siegle, D. (1993). *Predicting creative performance in an enrichment program.* Paper presented at the Association for the Education of Gifted Underachieving Students 6th Annual Conference, Portland, OR.

Krapp, A. (1989). The importance of the concept of interest in education research. *Empirische Paedogogik, 3,* 233–255.

Kulik, J. A. (1992). *An analysis of the research on ability grouping: Historical and contemporary perspectives.* (Research Monograph No. 9204). Storrs, CT: National Research Center on the Gifted and Talented, University of Connecticut. Retrieved from http://www.gifted.uconn.edu/nrcgt/kulik.html

Kulik, J. A., & Kulick, C. L. (1987). Effects of ability grouping on student achievement. *Equity and Excellence, 23*(1–2), 22–30.

Larson, O. N. (1992). *Milestones and millstones: Social science at the National Science Foundation, 1945–1991.* New Brunswick, CT: Transaction.

Leu, D. J., Jr., & Kinzer, C. K. (2002). *Effective literacy instruction* (5th ed.). Upper Saddle River, NJ: Prentice Hall.

Leu, D. J., Jr., Leu, D. D., & Coiro, J. (2004). *Teaching with the Internet: New literacies for new times* (4th ed.). Norwood, MA: Christopher-Gordon.

McGreevy, A. (1982). *My book of things and stuff: An interest questionnaire for young children.* Mansfield Center, CT: Creative Learning Press.

National excellence: A case for developing America's talent. (1993). Retrieved May 29, 2007, from http://www.ed.gov/pubs/DevTalent/toc.html

National Reading Panel. (2000). *Teaching children to read: An evidenced-based assessment of the scientific research literature on reading and its implications for reading instruction.* Washington, DC: Author.

National Science Board. (2003). *The science and engineering workforce: Realizing America's potential.* Arlington, VA: National Science Foundation.

Newman, J. L. (1991). *The effects of the talents unlimited model on students' creative productivity.* Unpublished doctoral dissertation, University of Alabama, Tuscaloosa.

Oakes, J. (1985). *Keeping track: How schools structure inequality.* New Haven, CT: Yale University Press.

Ohio Department of Education. (2006). *Model student acceleration policy for advanced learners.* Retrieved May 29, 2007, from http://www.oagc.com/files/AccelerationPolicy4_12_06.pdf

Olenchak, F. R. (1988). The schoolwide enrichment model in the elementary schools: A study of implementation stages and effects on educational excellence. In J. S. Renzulli (Ed.), *Technical report on research studies relating to the Revolving Door Identification Model* (2nd ed., pp. 201–247). Storrs, CT: University of Connecticut, Bureau of Educational Research.

Olenchak, F. R. (1990). School change through gifted education: Effects on elementary students' attitudes toward learning. *Journal for the Education of the Gifted, 14*(1), 66–78.

Olenchak, F. R. (1991). Assessing program effects for gifted/learning disabled students. In R. Swassing & A. Robinson (Eds.), *NAGC 1991 Research Briefs.* Washington, DC: National Association for Gifted Children.

Olenchak, F. R., & Renzulli, J. S. (1989). The effectiveness of the Schoolwide Enrichment Model on selected aspects of elementary school change. *Gifted Child Quarterly, 32,* 44–57.

Organisation for Economic Co-operation and Development. (2006). *Assessing scientific, reading and mathematical literacy: A framework for PISA 2006.* Paris: Author.

Passow, A. H. (1982). *Differentiated curricula for the gifted/talented.* Ventura, CA: Leadership Training Institute on the Gifted and Talented.

Phenix, P. H. (1964). *Realms of meaning.* New York: McGraw-Hill.

Piaget, J. (1975). *The development of thought: Equilibration on of cognitive structures.* New York: Viking.

Pintrich, P. R. (2000). Multiple goals, multiple pathways: The role of goal orientation in learning and achievement. *Journal of Educational Psychology, 92,* 544–555.

Programme for International Student Assessment. (2003). *First results from PISA 2003: Executive summary.* Paris: Organisation for Economic Co-operation and Development. Retrieved May 5, 2007, from http://www.pisa.oecd.org

Reis, S. M., & Boeve, H. (in press). Using SEM-R to increase reading fluency in an after school program. *Gifted Child Quarterly.*

Reis, S. M., Burns, D. E., & Renzulli, J. S. (1992). *Curriculum compacting: The complete guide to modifying the regular curriculum for high ability students.* Mansfield Center, CT: Creative Learning Press.

Reis, S. M., Eckert, R. D., Jacobs, J. K., Coyne, M. K., Richards, S., & Briggs, C. (2003). *The Schoolwide Enrichment Reading Model framework.* Storrs, CT: National Research Center on the Gifted and Talented.

Reis, S. M., Eckert, R. D., Schreiber, F. J., Jacobs, J. K., Coyne, M. K., Richards, S., et al. (2005). *The Schoolwide Enrichment Reading Model: Technical report.* Storrs, CT: National Research Center on the Gifted and Talented.

Reis, S. M., & Fogarty, E. (2006, October). Savoring reading, schoolwide. *Educational Leadership,* 32–36.

Reis, S. M., Gentry, M., & Maxfield, L. R. (1998). The application of enrichment clusters to teachers' classroom practices. *Journal for Education of the Gifted, 21,* 310–324.

Reis, S. M., Gentry, M., & Park, S. (1995). *Extending the pedagogy of gifted education to all students.* [Research Monograph]. Storrs, CT: The National Research Center on the Gifted and Talented.

Reis, S. M., & Renzulli, J. S. (1982). A research approach on the Revolving Door Identification Model: A case for the broadened conception of giftedness. *Phi Delta Kappan, 63,* 619–620.

Reis, S. M., Schader, R., Milne, H., & Stephens, R. (2003). Music & minds: Using a talent development approach for young adults with Williams syndrome. *Exceptional Children 69,* 293–314.

Reis, S. M., Westberg, K. L., Kulikowich, J., Caillard, F., Hébert, T. P., Plucker, J. A., et al. (1993). *Why not let high ability students start school in January? The curriculum compacting study* (Research Monograph 93106). Storrs, CT: University of Connecticut, National Research Center on the Gifted and Talented.

Reis, S. M., Westberg, K. L., Kulikowich, J. M., & Purcell, J. H. (1998). Curriculum compacting and achievement test scores: What does the research say? *Gifted Child Quarterly, 42,* 123–129.

Renninger, K. A. (1989). Individual patterns in children's play interests. In L. T. Winegar (Ed.), *Social interaction and the development of children's understanding* (pp. 147–172). Norwood, NJ: Ablex.

Renninger, K. A. (1990). Children's play interests, representations and activity. In R. Fivush & J. Hudson (Eds.), *Knowing and remembering in young children* (pp. 127–165, Vol. 3). Cambridge, MA: Cambridge University Press.

Renzulli, J. S. (1976). The Enrichment Triad Model: A guide for developing defensible programs for the gifted and talented. *Gifted Child Quarterly, 20,* 303–326.

Renzulli, J. S. (1977a). *The Enrichment Triad Model: A guide for developing defensible programs for the gifted and talented.* Mansfield Center, CT: Creative Learning Press.

Renzulli, J. S. (1977b). *The Interest-a-lyzer.* Mansfield Center, CT: Creative Learning Press.

Renzulli, J. S. (1978). What makes giftedness? Re-examining a definition. *Phi Delta Kappan, 60,* 180–184, 261.

Renzulli, J. S. (1982). What makes a problem real: Stalking the illusive meaning of qualitative differences in gifted education. *Gifted Child Quarterly, 26,* 147–156.

Renzulli, J. S. (1983). Guiding the gifted in pursuit of real problems: The transformed role of the teacher. *Journal of Creative Behavior, 17,* 49–59.

Renzulli, J. S. (1986). The three-ring conception of giftedness: A developmental model for creative productivity. In R. J. Sternberg & J. E. Davidson (Eds.), *Conceptions of giftedness* (pp. 53–92). New York: Cambridge University Press.

Renzulli, J. S. (1988a). The multiple menu model for developing differentiated curriculum for the gifted and talented. *Gifted Child Quarterly, 32,* 298–309.

Renzulli, J. S. (Ed.). (1988b). *Technical report of research studies related to the enrichment triad/revolving door model* (3rd ed.). Storrs, CT: University of Connecticut, Teaching the Talented Program.

Renzulli, J. S. (1994). *Schools for talent development: A practical plan for total school improvement.* Mansfield Center, CT: Creative Learning Press.

Renzulli, J. S. (2005). The three-ring conception of giftedness: A developmental model for promoting creative productivity. In R. J. Sternberg & J. Davidson (Eds.), *Conceptions of giftedness* (2nd ed., pp. 217–245). Boston: Cambridge University Press.

Renzulli, J. S., & Reis, S. M. (1985). *The Schoolwide Enrichment Model: A comprehensive plan for educational excellence.* Mansfield Center, CT: Creative Learning Press.

Renzulli, J. S., & Reis, S. M. (1991). The reform movement and the quiet crisis in gifted education. *Gifted Child Quarterly, 35,* 26–35.

Renzulli, J. S., & Reis, S. M. (1994). Research related to the Schoolwide Enrichment Model. *Gifted Child Quarterly, 38,* 2–14.

Renzulli, J. S., & Reis, S. M. (1997). *The Schoolwide Enrichment Model: A comprehensive plan for educational excellence.* Mansfield Center, CT: Creative Learning Press.

Renzulli, J. S., & Reis, S. M. (2006). Curriculum compacting: A research-based differentiation strategy for culturally diverse talented students. In Wallace, B & Eriksson, G. (Eds.), *Diversity In Gifted Education* (pp. 73–85). London: Routledge.

Renzulli, J. S., Reis, S. M., & Smith, L. H. (1981). *The Revolving Door Identification Model.* Mansfield Center, CT: Creative Learning Press.

Renzulli, J. S., & Smith, L. H. (1978). *The compactor.* Mansfield Center, CT: Creative Learning Press.

Renzulli, J. S., Smith, L. H., & Reis, S. M. (1982). Curriculum compacting: An essential strategy for working with gifted students. *Elementary School Journal, 82,* 185–194.

Renzulli, J. S., Smith, L. H., White, A. J., Callahan, C. M., & Hartman, R. K. (1976). *Scales for rating the behavioral characteristics of superior students.* Mansfield Center, CT: Creative Learning Press.

Renzulli, J. S., Smith, L. H., White, A. J., Callahan, C. M., Hartman, R. K., & Westberg, K. L. (2002). *Scales for rating the behavior characteristics of superior students* (Rev. ed.). Mansfield Center, CT: Creative Learning Press.

Rogers, K. B. (1991). *The relationship of grouping practices to the education of the gifted and talented learner* (RBDMS9102). Storrs, CT: National Research Center on the Gifted and Talented, University of Connecticut.

Schack, G. D. (1986). *Creative productivity and self-efficacy in children.* Unpublished doctoral dissertation, University of Connecticut, Storrs.

Schack, G. D., & Starko, A. J. (1998). *Research comes alive! A guidebook for conducting original research with middle and high school students.* Mansfield Center, CT: Creative Learning Press.

Schack, G. D., Starko, A. J., & Burns, D. E. (1991). Self-efficacy and creative productivity: Three studies of above average ability children. *Journal of Research in Education, 1*(1), 44–52.

Schiefele, U. (1989). Motivated conditions of text comprehension. *Zietschrift Paeodgogik, 34,* 687–708.

Schunk, D. (2001). Social cognitive theory of self-regulated learning. In B. Zimmerman & D. Schunk (Eds.), *Self-regulated learning and academic achievement: Theoretical perspectives* (pp. 125–152). Mahwah, NJ: Lawrence Erlbaum.

Skaught, B. J. (1987). *The social acceptability of talent pool students in an elementary school using the Schoolwide Enrichment Model.* Unpublished doctoral dissertation, University of Connecticut, Storrs.

Slavin, R. E. (1987). *Cooperative learning: Student teams.* Washington, DC: National Education Association Professional Library, National Education Association.

Slavin, R. E. (1990). *Success for all: Effects of variations in duration and resources of a schoolwide elementary restructuring program.* Baltimore: Center for Research on Effective Schooling for Disadvantaged Students, Johns Hopkins University.

Smith, L. H. (1976). *Learning styles: Their measurement and educational significance.* Unpublished doctoral dissertation, University of Connecticut, Storrs.

Southern, T. W., & Jones, E. D. (1992). The real problems with academic acceleration. *Gifted Child Today, 15,* 34–38.

Stanley, J. C. (1989). A look back at educational non-acceleration: An international tragedy. *Gifted Child Today, 12,* 60–61.

Starko, A. (1986a). *It's about time: Inservice strategies for curriculum compacting.* Mansfield Center, CT: Creative Learning Press.

Starko, A. J. (1986b). *The effects of the Revolving Door Identification Model on creative productivity and self-efficacy.* Unpublished doctoral dissertation, University of Connecticut, Storrs.

Stednitz, U. (1985). *The influence of educational enrichment on the self-efficacy in young children.* Unpublished doctoral dissertation, University of Connecticut, Storrs.

Sternberg, R. J. (1984). Toward a triarchic theory of human intelligence. *Behavioral and Brain Sciences, 7,* 269–287.

Stewart, E. D. (1979). *Learning styles among gifted/talented students: Preferences for instructional techniques.* Unpublished doctoral dissertation, University of Connecticut, Storrs.

Stigler, J. W., & Stevenson, H. W. (1991). How Asian teachers polish each lesson to perfection. *American Educator, 15*(1), 12–21, 43–44.

Taylor, L. A. (1992). *The effects of the secondary Enrichment Triad Model and a career counseling component on the career development of vocational-technical school students.* Unpublished doctoral dissertation, University of Connecticut, Storrs.

Thorndike, E. L. (1921). Intelligence and its measurement. *Journal of Educational Psychology, 12,* 124–127.

Tomlinson, C. A. (1995). *How to differentiate instruction in mixed-ability classrooms.* Alexandria, VA: Association for Supervision and Curriculum Development.

Tomlinson, C. A. (2000). *Differentiation of instruction in the elementary grades* (Report No. ED 443572). Champaign, IL: ERIC Clearinghouse on Elementary and Early Childhood Education.

Torrance, E. P. (1962). *Guiding creative talent.* Englewood Cliffs, NJ: Prentice Hall.

Torrance, E. P. (1965). *Rewarding creative behavior.* Englewood Cliffs, NJ: Prentice Hall.

Torrance, E. P. (1974). *Norms—Technical manual: Torrance tests of creative thinking.* Bensenville, IL: Scholastic Testing Service.

Walberg, H. W. (1984). Improving the productivity of America's schools. *Educational Leadership, 41*(8), 19–27.

Ward, V. S. (1960). Systematic intensification and extensification of the school curriculum. *Exceptional Children, 28,* 67–71, 77.

Ward, V. S. (1961). *Educating the gifted: An axiomatic approach.* Columbus, OH: Merrill.

Westberg, K. L. (1999, Summer). What happens to young, creative producers? *NAGC: Creativity and Curriculum Divisions' Newsletter, 3,* 13–16.

Westberg, K. L., Archambault, F. X., Dobyns, S. M., & Salvin, T. J. (1992). *Technical report: An observational study of instructional and curricular practices used with gifted and talented students in regular classrooms.* Storrs, CT: National Research Center on the Gifted and Talented.

Whitehead, A. N. (1929). The rhythm of education. In A. N. Whitehead (Ed.), *The aims of education* (pp. 46–59). New York: Macmillan.

Wiener, P. P. (Ed.). (1973). *Dictionary of the history of ideas* (Vol. 1). New York: Charles Scribner.

Index